Cycling in Scotland
& North-East England

50 Great Traffic-free Routes!

Philip Routledge

Published by Sigma Leisure – an imprint of
Sigma Press, 1 South Oak Lane, Wilmslow, Cheshire SK9 6AR, England.

British Library Cataloguing in Publication Data
A CIP record for this book is available from the British Library.

ISBN: 1-85058-464-8

Typesetting and Design by: Sigma Press, Wilmslow, Cheshire.

Cover photograph: by Alex Gillespie – Scotland: a cyclist's delight

Maps and photographs: the author except where stated

Printed by: MFP Design & Print

Disclaimer: the information in this book is given in good faith and is believed to be correct at the time of publication. No responsibility is accepted by either the author or publisher for errors or omissions, or for any loss or injury howsoever caused. Only you can judge your own fitness, competence and experience.

Contents

Introduction

The Rides

Note for short-distance riders:

The distances quoted are for guidance only. You do not have to complete the full ride to enjoy it – just try a few miles and see how you feel!

Appendices

Scotland and North-East England: approximate locations of rides

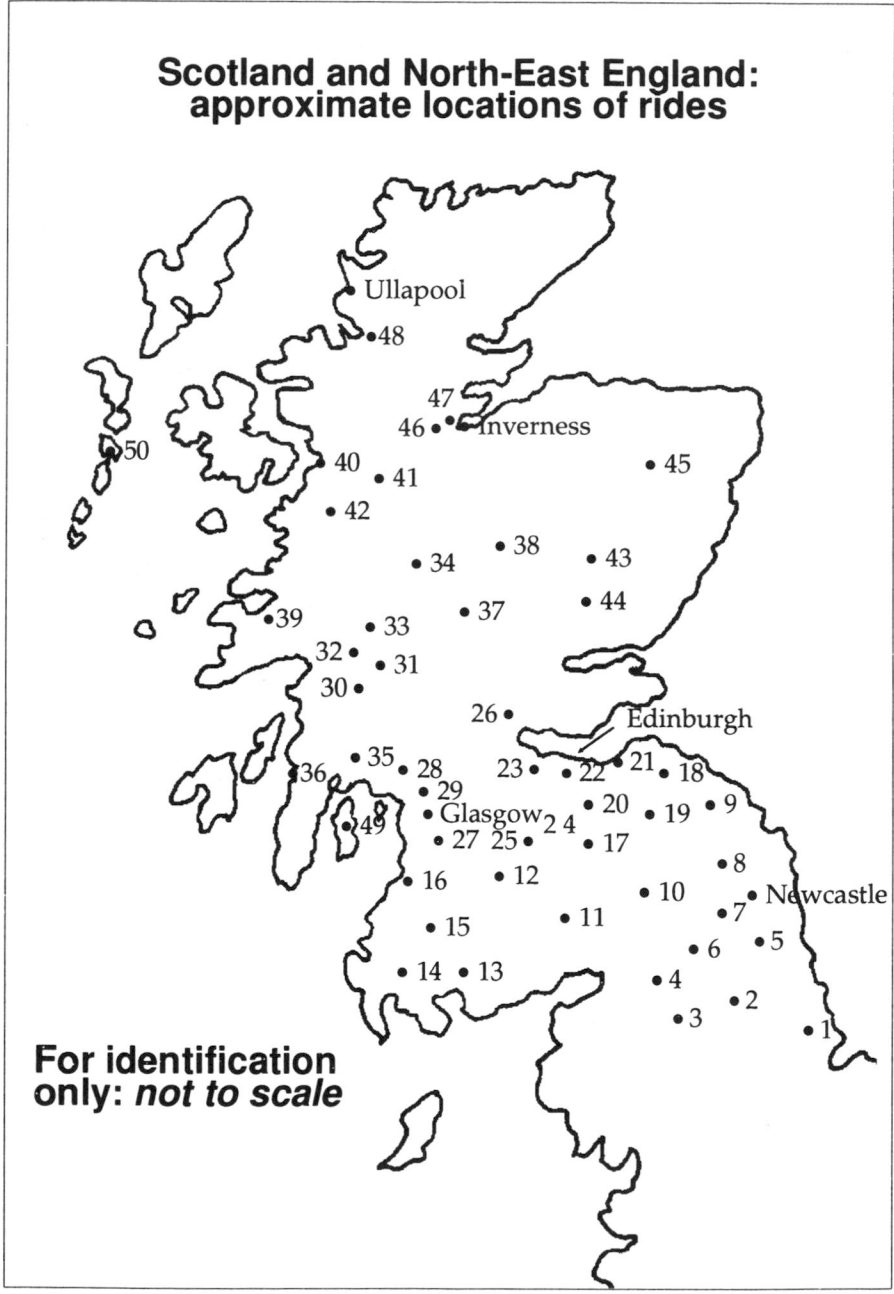

For identification only: *not to scale*

Introduction

He who is outside the door
has already a good part of the journey behind him.
– Dutch Proverb.

Cycling is one of the most pleasurable forms of transport and recreation yet devised by mankind. It is surely no coincidence that the particular member of mankind who made it all possible, in about 1840, was a Scotsman and a blacksmith named Kirkpatrick Macmillan. He lived near Drumlanrig Castle, just north of Dumfries, and he obviously realised that Scotland and the NE of England were a cyclist's paradise, so he did something about it. He invented the bicycle.

His breakthrough was through the modification of a hobby-horse. This was a device which was little more than a rich man's toy and was propelled by pushing one's feet along the ground in an undignified striding movement. Kirkpatrick Macmillan used his system of cranks to convert a hobby horse into a device that could be propelled without the feet having to contact the ground. His gearing converted the pumping motion of the feet and legs into a rotary motion of the back wheel, thus creating the first proper bicycle.

Kirk's bicycle was good, so good that he rode it on at least one round trip of over 200 miles. This claim is proven by the fact that he managed to get himself arrested for the world's first recorded cycling offence, when he knocked over a child in Glasgow. He appeared before the Gorbals South Side Police Court and was duly fined, convicted and told to handle his bicycle with greater care.

Apart from the law, other problems encountered by Kirk and the early cyclists were wind, hills and rough road surfaces. Technology has done little to counter wind resistance of touring and mountain bikes. On the contrary, modern bicycles and their well-dressed riders probably present a larger wind profile than the simple machines of Kirk's day, wind cheating technology only really finding a place in serious racing circles. The hills are still there but modern developments, in deference to motor vehicles and railway trains, have led to there being many more well-surfaced routes hugging a single contour or pushing the land aside to create new contours. This is particularly true in the forests where the forestry road systems have been designed and built to allow large trucks and plant to pass. Combined with the immense development of our multi-geared machines, the bicycle can now easily get to the parts that other forms of transport fail to reach.

It is ironic that in 1840, while Kirk was quietly inventing his bicycle, the railway engineers were at their peak of production. They thought that they were building railways but in a lot of cases they were not; they were building cycle paths. To keep the shareholders happy, it was agreed that trains would be allowed to use the railways for a hundred years or so until bicycles were properly developed and bright pigment paint jobs had been invented.

In truth, the great railway builders did a lot of the hard work for us in the 19th century. They moved the hills out of our way or bored through them.

Loch Achray

Their mighty embankments and viaducts now take us high over the valleys, so that we may enjoy magnificent vistas. Their gentle curves allow the landscapes to reveal themselves graciously in an orderly and uncluttered way and they even had the foresight to provide road bridges to allow bicycles a totally traffic-free passage.

We live in a 90mph world and the gentle pace of the bicycle provides an unusually fortifying tonic. With our eyeline on a par with a walker and our progress at the speed of a top class runner, we can see over hedges to enjoy the landscape and wildlife whilst making headway and covering real distances in a reasonable span of time and all for little effort. Whilst we are doing this, we are benefiting from the form of gentle exercise that is very much the dish of the day in modern medical research.

All of the rides in this book are family, friendly, fun routes, which can offer as much pleasure to the hardened, weather-worn touring or sports cyclist as to the complete beginner. Particular emphasis has been placed on the avoidance of traffic, wherever practical, and steep hills or rough ground have been studiously omitted. Scotland and North-East England offer some of the finest cycling on the face of this earth, so please enjoy these rides as much as I have enjoyed describing them. Do not forget to stop, relax and look around occasionally. That is half the fun.

Equipment

Remember additional equipment translates to additional weight and additional weight translates to additional effort, especially up hills. Assuming that your bicycle has pedals, wheels and security equipment, there are just a few simple accessories that are worth considering.

- [ ] Bell
- [ ] Frame Corner Pack
- [ ] Puncture Repair Kit
- [ ] Basic Tool Pack
- [ ] Pump
- [ ] Back (or front) Rack
- [ ] Single or Double Lightweight Pannier
- [ ] Front Mud or Spray Deflector

The **bell** might well be fitted to your bicycle anyway. If it is not do not worry; you can always sing, cough or loudly clear your throat, but a bell is easier. It is associated with cycling and is inoffensive.

The **frame corner pack** is useful because it is dedicated to carrying your **puncture kit, basic tool kit** and **first aid equipment**. Once it is packed, you can forget about it but it will be there when needed. Keep the tools to a minimum. On most bicycles, two Allen keys, a multi spanner and a Philip's head screw driver are sufficient. Your puncture repair kit is not much use without a **pump**.

A **rack** is so useful, I don't know how people manage without. **Panniers** in either single or double form enable you to carry spare clothing, sandwiches, cool drinks, your granny's spare teeth and anything else that takes your fancy.

You'll know why you need a **front spray deflector** the first time you ride on a wet or muddy surface.

¯ Security

A SAD STORY: Lock It or Lose It. (And don't leave it outside at night)

If you are leaving your bicycle out of sight, particularly in towns and cities, **do** lock it or you **will** lose it. It is a sad state of affairs but, according to crime prevention statistics, the chances of an unguarded and unlocked bicycle being stolen in the busy central area of a town the size of Swindon would be greater than 50% over a 48 hour period. The chances of a **locked** but unguarded bicycle being vandalised or having pieces taken off it (like wheels!) during periods of darkness are greater than 30% over the same period.

In other words, you are more likely to lose your bicycle than you are not to lose it, so here are a few simple tips:

1. Use a "D" lock around the frame, through the rear wheel and onto the most solid object you can find. A lot of towns and cities have "Sheffield Stands." These are strong "n" shaped metal stands which are specially designed for bicycle locking. If possible secure your front wheel, even if it means carrying another locking device.

2. Make sure that you have a photograph of your bicycle and a note of any serial numbers or distinctive markings and carry this with you. Use special invisible ultra violet markers and write your name or post code on the bicycle. By doing this and having the descriptive information readily available, at least you can give the police a chance.

3. Always make sure you are carrying your bus fare to get home. A long walk after the indignity of losing your bicycle will dim even the brightest spirit.

Safety

You could argue all day about which single factor is of most importance in leisure cycling safety, but really it depends on what type of accident you are having at that instant.

If you are about to fall on your head, your last thoughts, before unconsciousness sets in, may be of helmets. If you are about to plough into a four-year-old toddler who has not seen you coming, you will probably be wishing that you had used your bell a few moments previously. If you are about to be run over by a 36 tonne truck, you may be wishing that you had not ventured onto the road or that you had worn the correct bright clothing and bought some new batteries for your lights. If you have just ridden over a cliff, your thoughts may be of parachutes or maps. I could go on but basic safety depends on the simple applications forethought and common sense.

1. Keep off the roads whenever possible.

2. Be Safe Be Seen. Lights at night. Fluorescents by day.

3. Ring Your Bell when approaching pedestrians.

4. Helmets for rough, off-road riding.

5. Make sure that your bicycle is properly maintained.

6. Always wear a parachute when riding over cliffs.

Basic Service Maintenance

Get your bicycle serviced every winter, or do it yourself. Replace fraying cables, carry out the following basic service check regularly and you should be OK. Your bicycle can last indefinitely on this basis. In fact it will quite likely outlast your legs.

I can carry out this basic schedule and if I can do it, so can you! Try to remember this checklist every time you set off on a ride and you will go a long way to improving the basic safety and enjoyment of your riding as well as the life of your bicycle.

1. Oil the chain, the gears and the crank.

2. Pump up the tyres. The pressures are normally stamped on the tyre wall but 40 PSI is about normal for a typical mountain bike. That is a lot more than you will achieve with a normal hand pump, so try a foot pump or a stirrup pump. It is inadvisable to use garage forecourt compressors, as these can be too strong and cause the tyre to explode.

3. Check the saddle stem for security and make sure that it is set to your ideal height. A saddle that is wrongly set (especially too low) can cause you to use very much more energy than one that is correctly set.

4. Check the headstock. If it is loose, obviously tighten it up but if this happens often get it fixed or your bicycle's front forks may become unsafe.

5. Have a general look at the cables. If a cable is frayed it will break quite soon and it will break at the most inconvenient time possible. Front

brake cables usually break on steep hills, just before road junctions or bends, and gear cables break at the bottom of hills, when you are in the highest ratio. Ensure that the offending item is replaced before it breaks.

Tips for Northern Riders

Those Damned Scottish Midges

If you are at all susceptible to midges and mosquitos, get some insect repellent and use it. There are a lot of midges in Scotland. They like women more than men because, as we all know, women are sweet. Mosquitos are described as having long legs, elongated mouth parts and long slender abdomens. Surely the application of some insect repellent is better than being bitten by anything that looks like that.

Wind and its effect

A Dutch comedian was recently elected onto the Dutch Parliament on the strength of a crazy manifesto. One of his major pledges was to push for legislation for the compulsory introduction of tailwinds on all cycle paths. The Dutch are a nation of cyclists and they know the value of a good tailwind. You can travel for miles on flat surfaces without expending anything like the effort that you would in still wind conditions. Conversely, a headwind can cause as much extra work and exertion as a substantial up hill section.

If you have a choice, on a one-way trip, take the tailwind every time.

Hiring: The Pleasures and The Pitfalls

If you have not ridden a bicycle for a while, or if you have not ridden a bicycle at all, try hiring one and see how you get on. The hire centres normally have a range of bicycles to chose from, but do not get fobbed off with some old hack that has not seen the light of day since The Beatles ruled the pop charts.

Bicycle hirers have a generally good reputation but there is a clear potential for the development of a few bad eggs. The hit and miss way that hirers demand deposits, driving licences, credit cards, car keys and valuables is creating a situation that in some, more established, service industries, would be described as a potential shark's paradise.

The wide availability of cycle hire centres has happily created a situation whereby you do not need to own a bicycle to enjoy the routes in this book. The hirers that I have had dealings with, over the years, have all supplied good bicycles at reasonable charges and offered courteous advice. If they are the industry standard, this is an excellent way to go cycling.

Charges

It is up to you to decide if the charges are fair or not, but do be sure that you know exactly what you are expected to pay. Some hirers quote by the hour, some by the day and some by the week, so take care. Make absolutely certain that you and the hirer are in agreement and on the same wavelength. Are you paying the correct tariff for the particular bicycle that you have been given? Most hirers have different prices for different models. Shop around if you can.

Deposits

Do not leave your car keys. Effectively, your car is held as a deposit and this is disproportionate. Asking for car keys as a deposit smacks of a heavy handed attitude and unreasonableness. If there is an argument with the bicycle hirer at the end of your ride, at least you can drive home and sort it out later. If they have your car keys, you are completely over a barrel. In cases where car keys are demanded and no other form of deposit is acceptable, such as cash or credit card slip, walk away and find another hirer. Be sure to agree the terms of the deposit and agree any defects before you set out. Go through the bicycle with the hirer and write down any faults.

All hirers will, quite reasonably, insist on some form of identification. A driving licence, a credit card or a passport are usually acceptable either solely or in combination. A list of known bicycle hirers is included in the appendices.

Carrying your bicycle by car

These routes are described on the assumption that you have either obtained a hired bicycle or transported your own bicycle to the start of the ride, presumably by car. I am firmly of the opinion that cycling can only be enjoyed properly away from the busy roads and by taking your bicycle to the routes you will make the very best of this guide. Unless you are using a trailer, there are three basic methods of carrying your bicycle by car.

1. Roof rack clamp fittings.
2. Back Rack.
3. Tow Bar Rack.

The choice between roof and back rack is very much a matter of personal preference; the cost of the equipment is very similar either way and if you already own a roof rack there may be a saving by adopting this system. There is a plethora of different styles, and accessories in a multitude of qualities, prices and a dazzling range of coloured packaging. Remember that you will not be able to carry anything else on the roof rack once you have put one or more bicycles up there and you will not be able to open your boot lid or hatchback once your bicycle rack is installed. Both systems are easy to set up.

The third system is the tow bar rack. I am of the opinion that this is the best system for three good reasons. Firstly, it is very easy to take on and off the car. Secondly, it allows you access to your boot or hatch, even when the bicycles are loaded. Lastly, and without any doubt most importantly, your bicycle or bicycles can be locked onto the rack and the rack itself can be locked onto the car. As much security as you are likely to be able to get, not perfect but a lot better than the other systems in this respect. These racks are usually of more solid construction than the clip-on types and therefore should last longer. The disadvantage of this system is the requirement for a tow bar.

At the top of Duke's Pass

Arguably it is easier to lift bicycles onto a back rack or tow bar rack and you are less likely to scratch your car.

With the exception of the towbar rack, your bicycle is no more secure on a car carrying system, than it would be if it were hanging from a tree. I have seen a solution to this by the extreme method of drilling into the car body to fit clamps so that bicycle "D" clamps can be used. This method may be acceptable on an older car but is not a practical solution for a car of any real value.

Most systems recommend that you use bungee straps for holding the bicycles in place during transit and this seems a most effective method. By routing the straps through the spokes, you will stop the wheels windmilling in the wind as you drive along.

Bicycle racks: a few words of warning.

1. If you have any fast-fix, clip-on equipment such as pumps, drinking bottles, mudguards, pannier sets or anything else that is not welded or screwed to the bicycle, take it off or it will certainly fall off as soon as you drive over a bump.

2. If you are carrying your bicycles by the roof rack method, beware of car park barriers. Sadly, I have seen the result of some unfortunate soul who "Forgot about the bikes." Two terminally damaged bicycles, a bent roof and a broken back window. That is without mention of the damage to the car park barrier for which the local council will certainly wish to send you a repair bill.

3. Bicycles carried transversely on racks, on the backs of the cars, are generally wider than the car itself. If you are travelling along narrow lanes or through tight town streets, allow for that extra bit of width or you may end up with a "U" shaped bicycle.

4. On a lighter note, before you load the bicycles onto your back rack, make sure that everything you need out of the car boot is out and everything you need in the car boot is in. It may be that this is just a personal flaw - it does sound rather obvious - but I have been caught out by this trap on more occasions than I can recall, usually with the help of a drop of rain and the children's coats.

5. If you are transporting your bicycle on a back rack, make certain that your bicycle tyres are well clear of the car's exhaust. The hot exhaust gases can melt the tyre. I write from personal experience.

Your Good Health

There is some really good news for cyclists on this subject: we are all going to live longer and we are going to less stressed. This is partly a result of the exercise and its effect on our heart, lungs and circulation and partly a result of the quality of the leisure and relaxation levels that we will enjoy. There are one or two factors that could turn this statistic on its head and we should consider these when we are celebrating this good news.

If you mix your cycling with road traffic, your chances of a longer life are slimmed down considerably, especially if you get run over by a bus. Worse, if you mix your cycling with road traffic whilst pedalling down to the pub for drinks and cigarettes before picking up the fish and chips to take home, you have defeated the potential gains of the good exercise.

Popular medical opinion is very much in favour of quality relaxation and gentle exercise and there is no shadow of doubt that cycling can offer these to you in bucketfuls. If you are overweight, cycling is a more comfortable form of exercise than most other activities.

There is a very strong argument that cycling is good for the environment, but as I am encouraging my readers to transport their bicycles by car, I think I may be skating on thin ice here.

Rights of Way

Scottish and English laws concerning rights of way are quite different. In England, one is forbidden access to land unless granted rights waiving the landowner's rights. This waiver may come in the form of a public footpath, a bridle way, a highway or a permissive route. Canal towpaths and most railway paths are good examples of permissive routes.

In Scotland there is no common land and few access agreements but in broad terms, the individual may wander at will, unless special rights are granted to the land owner. The best application of this free policy is to be found in the Highlands where vast tracts of land are open to anyone and everyone.

Although there may appear to be a vast difference between England and Scotland, in real terms the difference is very small. The laws of each country have been applied over long periods of time and their application has brought about very similar end results. Historically, there have been so many rights granted in both England and Scotland that the effect on the public is minimal.

Generally, common sense will guide you if you lose your way. If in doubt, keep to well-used and established paths, look out for evidence of cycle tracks and follow your front wheel.

Cycling in the Forest and along Canal Tow Paths

It is easy to overlook the fact that the Forest is a working environment so do remember to obey all warnings. Keep well clear of tree felling or heavy machinery and guard against all risk of fire, especially after a dry spell.

Do not rely on finding a shop or a pub around the next corner, as you may have a long ride to find food or drink. Take some sandwiches and drinks and you will have no trouble finding a pretty spot to stop and enjoy a picnic.

Cycling on the canal towpath requires special care, patience and discipline. Most canals have their fair share of narrow and slippery sections of towpath and there are also invariably walkers, anglers, ropes and mooring stakes to look out for.

Canals are often widely used by cyclists and with care and patience present magnificent cycling opportunities.

Permits for British Waterways Board (BWB) Canals

Permits for riding on the BWB system can be obtained from any of their offices. Contact them at this address:

British Waterways Board, Countryside Ranger Union Canal, Canal House, Applecross Street, Glasgow G4 9SP; Tel: 0141 332 6936

The permits are free of charge and cover the whole BWB system. They are usually accompanied by a friendly warning about the etiquette and safety requirements of canal towpath cycling and a copy of the official BWB leaflet 'The Waterways Code' (Cycling on the Towpath)

Railways and Buses

Two of the pleasure cyclist's greatest allies are the tailwind and the downward gradient. Unfortunately, the basic laws of mathematics and geometry dictate that whatever goes up must come down and whatever blows you one way does not blow back the other way half an hour later when you happen to want to return. The answer to your dilemma may well lie in a bit of pre-planning and a railway station or a bus stop.

There is no point in me trying to list all of the many facilities offered by the bus and train operators because they tend to change in terms of detail and availability. There are, however, a multitude of facilities available to cyclists and their machines. The costs are not particularly high and some operators actually offer free passage for cycles. In most if not all cases, it is advisable to book in advance. For further details refer to the addresses in the appendices.

Ferries

There are more ferries in Scotland than in the rest of the UK collectively. With lochs slashing up the mainland regions and a large number of scattered islands, ferries form an essential part of the infrastructure. Most Scottish ferries will carry bicycles free of charge, as long as the rider pays the pedestrian fare. Refer to the appendices for addresses.

Waymarks and Notices

There is considerable information available to cyclists in the form of waymarks and notices. These can be rings or signs fixed to the street furniture, they can be bits of painted wood nailed to walls or wired to trees. There are waymarks carved in stone, painted on the tarmac, stencilled onto wood, routed into posts and set in concrete and there are all combinations of styles and materials.

It would be nice to believe that waymarking of any particular route is consistent in its format and presentation but be warned, it is not. Just because you have seen a run of twelve wooden posts with yellow tops and a routed message saying "Cycle Path" does not mean that the next post is not blue concrete with the message "Cycle Way" and buried in the back of the hedge. Beware of practical jokers who take delight in turning pointers to send you the wrong way and verify the route, especially in or near urban areas where petty vandalism may occur.

Keep a constant lookout for waymarks and try to find a pattern; it will greatly enhance your enjoyment of the ride. If you do come across any vandalism, report it to the responsible authority so that they may include the problem in their work schedules.

Ride 1

The Whitby to Scarborough Trailway (1885-1985): North East Coast

An enjoyable coastal ride along a sheltered railway path

Maps: Landranger 1:50,000, Sheet numbers 94 and 101.

Distance: Total return ride, 40 Miles (64km).

Waymarked: Yes. Generally marked as 'Railway Walk' or 'Rail Path'.

Gradients: Negligible.

Surface: Well drained, ash and stone. The odd muddy patch here and there.

Future proposals: Constant maintenance and improvement.

Other cycle routes linking: N/A.

Bicycle hire: Scarborough.

Shops and Refreshments: Plenty of opportunities on or near the route.

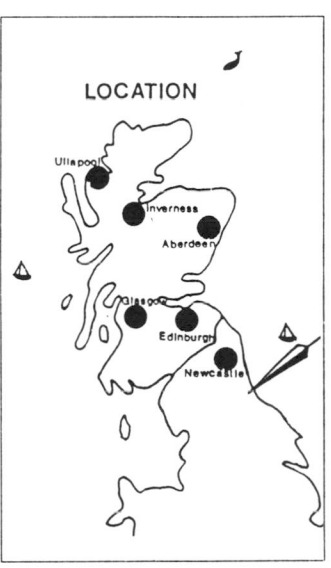

LOCATION

Introduction

The Whitby to Scarborough Trailway runs for twenty miles, mainly along the old trackbed of the Scarborough and District Railway which originally joined with the York to Scarborough branch of the York and North Midland Railway just outside Scarborough. It is a very scenic route enjoying extensive sea views. The route is virtually all rural and rich with wild plants and flowers. It is well away from the hustle and bustle of the road system and therefore untroubled by the noises and fumes of modern life.

Construction of the Scarborough and District Railway line commenced in

1872 but due to a general lack of enthusiasm from nervous investors it did not open for business until thirteen years later in 1885. As it transpired, the investors were right to be nervous - the line was a financial disaster. Although the total building cost was £650,000, the whole company was sold for a paltry £260,000 only shortly after the grand opening. Because the line had so many undulations and tight curves, the average speed of trains in those early days was restricted to little more than about 20 mph. In order to pull any form of economic load, enormous engines had to be employed where small tank engines were used on other comparable lines. The resultant capital and running costs proved to be uneconomic.

The line struggled on throughout its life and became quite popular with tourists. Despite this, the line was axed in 1965 under the Beeching cuts. The last train, a double headed steam excursion, was an emotional sight as it ran through the railway's eight stations on the 6th March 1965. It is said that on some hot, still summer days, the faint but distinct sound of the steam locomotives can still be heard from Robin Hood's Bay.

Look out for the signs

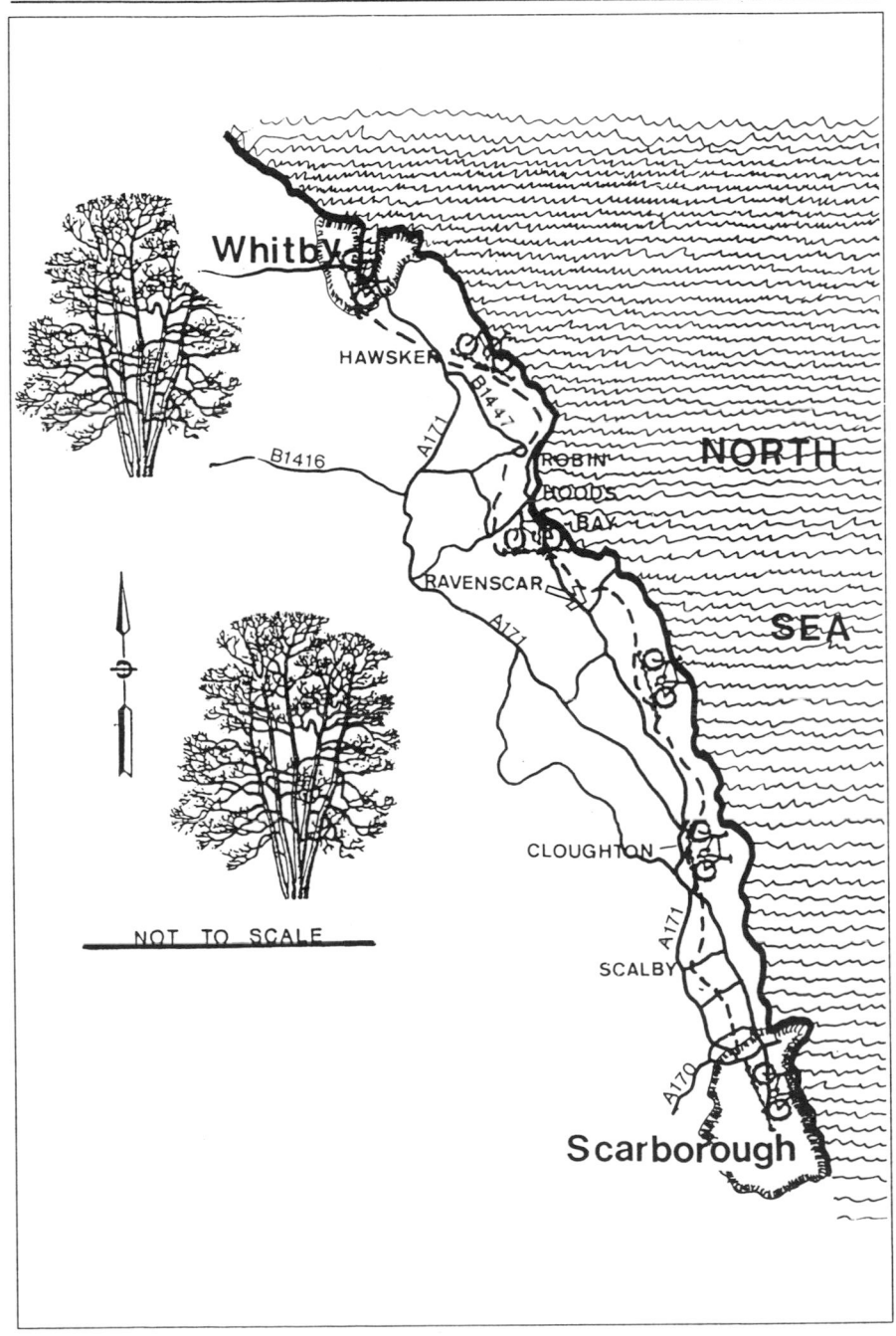

Main Access Points

The Trailway can be accessed at numerous points along the route. At Scarborough, the Trailway is joined at the Manor Road end of Woodland Ravine. At Whitby, the Trailway is joined at the Esk viaduct which can be approached from Larpool Lane.

Route

At Scarborough, the Trailway starts at the Manor Road end of Woodland Ravine. At Whitby, the Trailway begins at the Esk viaduct which can be approached from Larpool Lane. From these starting points or from any of the access points along the route, the Trailway's route is waymarked as a 'Rail Path' or is self explanatory.

At Scalby, the route passes through a modern housing estate, built where the station once stood. At Cloughton, the Trailway leaves the original trackbed and proceeds through the old goods yards that were once busy with constant shunting and clanging of couplings for the wagons. A typical load would have been the local output of coal and pit props. At Ravenscar, the tunnel is blocked off for safety reasons and the route continues via Station Road; the views here over Robin Hood's Bay are well worth stopping for.

Nearby

Call into the National Trust information centre and learn about Robin Hood's Bay. Robin Hood's Bay itself is well worth a visit. Legend has it that Robin Hood came here to help the local Abbot repel the Danes! Stories about smugglers, lovely little russet tiled cottages, steep twisting narrow streets, hidden alleyways and lots of cobbles all help to make an evocative scene.

Scarborough needs more explanation than can be provided here but do look at the Grand Hotel. It has 365 bedrooms, 52 chimneys, 12 floors and 4 (seasonal) turrets. Who needs a calendar here? Whitby is in two parts linked by a swing bridge which was built in 1909 and has a seventy foot span. A common 'stone' found on the foreshore at Whitby is not stone at all but is the black 'Whitby Jet' which is actually fossilised wood. In skilled hands, this can be used to make quite exquisite pieces of jewellery.

Ride 2

Hamsterley Forest: South West Durham

A fine ride in one of the great forests of South Durham

Maps: Landranger 1:50,000, Sheet numbers 92 and 93.

Distance: More than 20 miles (38½km).

Waymarked: Yes.

Gradients: Some routes are steep, others are fairly flat. The "Forest Drive" is an easy and very pleasant ride on solid well-drained surfaces and mild gradients.

Surface: Stone reinforced forestry roads and muddy tracks.

Future proposals: Constant basic maintenance of roads and tracks.

Other cycle routes linking: N/A.

Bicycle hire: Forest Enterprises. Enquire at Bedburn.

Refreshments: There are shops and a pub in Hamsterley village; take a snack and a drink with you if you go into the forest.

Shops: Hamsterley village.

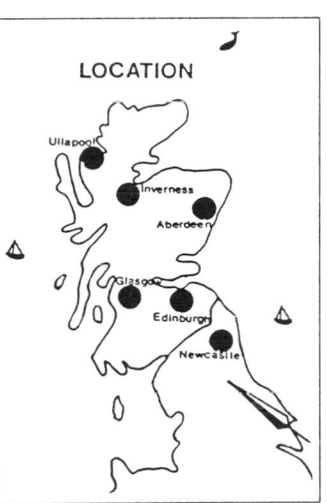

LOCATION

Introduction

Originally a sporting estate, owned by the wealthy Surtees family, Hamsterley forest was bought by the Forestry Commission in 1927. Set in the backwater splendour of the area known as Upper Weardale, south of the busy A689 and nine miles to the west of Bishop Auckland, the 2500 hectare forest is now well into its second rotation and boasts a great variety of tree species including large areas of mature broad leaved woodland.

The dominant trees within Hamsterley are tall Scots Pine, which can reach

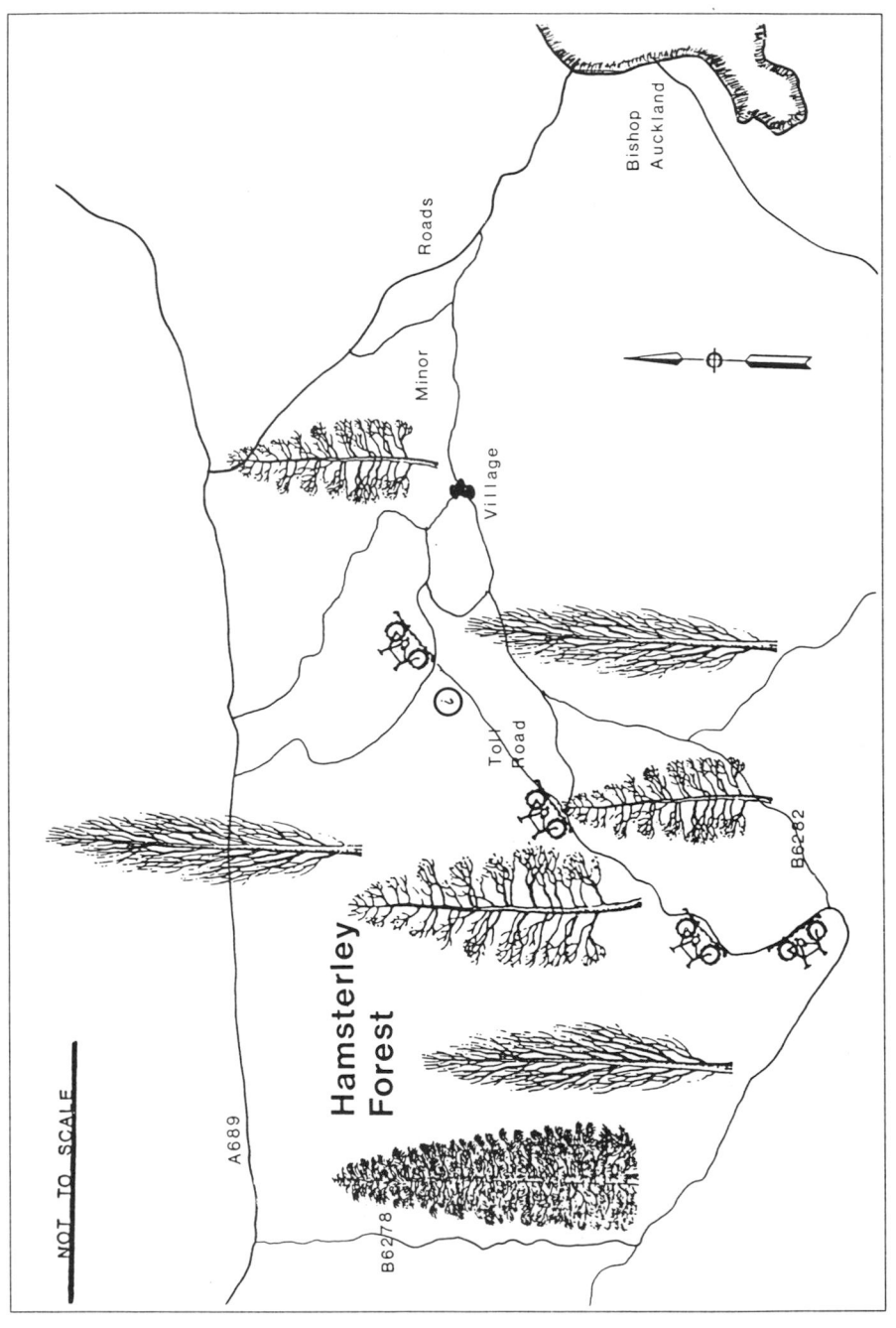

heights of 130 feet (39½ metres), hardy European larch, elegant western hemlock and Norway spruce (real Christmas trees, but most are far too big for your hallway). Other species include ash and cypress while some self sown examples of birch and oak are making ground in the clearings. Around parts of the perimeter are mature oak, ash and hawthorn which generally pre-date the managed forest.

The shy wildlife include roe deer and red squirrel, smaller than the more common grey squirrel and an older species in the British Isles. Red Squirrels are always attracted to conifer plantations because they love eating pine cones. If you want to find one, look in the forks of trees; their nests are built with twigs and bark. If you are lucky, you might see them feeding on a tree-stump. Amazingly, they use them as feeding tables.

Main Access Points

Bedburn Camp is a good place to base your rides. Access to the forest is by the Forest Drive toll road which is sign posted from the B6282 in the south and from Hamsterley village in the east.

The Route

From Bedburn Camp, there are trails leading through the forest in various directions. A very pleasant and easy route is marked as "The Forest Drive" and you should not be put off by the fact that this is shared with the occasional car. Whichever way you decide to go, you will never be far from Bedburn Beck, a little tributary of the River Wear. It forms a narrow vale through the heart of the forest and it is a delight to see the crystal clear water flowing confidently across the rock strewn stream bed. Have a rest on one of the lovely mossy shaded banks and look up through the tree canopy whilst you listen to the constant babbling of the water.

Along your chosen route, look out for industrial relics from the ancient lead mines which started their production in Roman times and carried on until the end of the nineteenth century. In the valley bottom, the rich soils have been left for pasture and hay meadows. Follow the waymarks and you will come back to where you started. See how you feel and perhaps try another route.

Nearby

Silver, as well as lead, was mined until the end of the nineteenth century in this area and an interesting feature for industrial archeologists will be the remains of the "chimney" from the smelting mill at Rookhope, north of the A689. It was built in 1802 and incredibly was 1½ miles (2½km) long, formed by a tunnel cut into the surface of the escarpment and reaching a height of 1829 feet (560 metres) at its top on Redburn Common. Manholes were cut, scattered along the route, and these allowed sweepers to recover minute quantities of lead and silver.

Ride 3

The Lanchester Way Railway Path: Consett to Durham

An historic route along a fine railway path.

Map: Landranger 1:50,000, Sheet number 88.

Distance: 23½ miles (38km) (total return).

Waymarked: Yes, at access points. The route is a railway track bed therefore it is self explanatory.

Gradients: Very mild.

Surface: Well-drained hard surfaces. Some ash sections and some Tarmac sections.

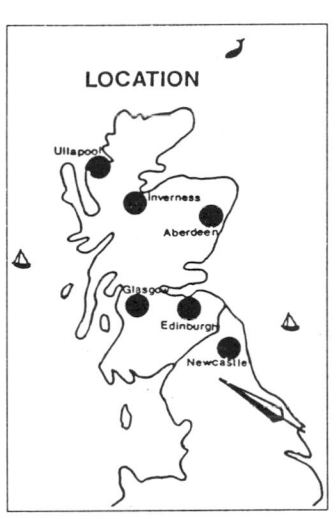

Future proposals: The Lanchester Valley Walk will eventually be joined to the cross country cycle route from west to east coasts.

Other cycle routes linking: The Lanchester Valley Way Railway Path forms part of the proposed route linking the North Sea and the Irish Sea. It also offers easy direct access to the following:

1. The Derwent Walk Railway Path.

2. The Waskerley Way.

3. The Consett to Sunderland Railway Path.

Plus easy indirect access to:

4. South Tyne Cycleway.

5. North Tyne Country Park Cycle Way.

6. The Bowes Railway Path and The Tanfield Railway.

7. The Deerness Valley Walk.

Bicycle hire: Rowland's Gill. Sunderland.

Shops and Refreshments: Plenty of opportunities near the route.

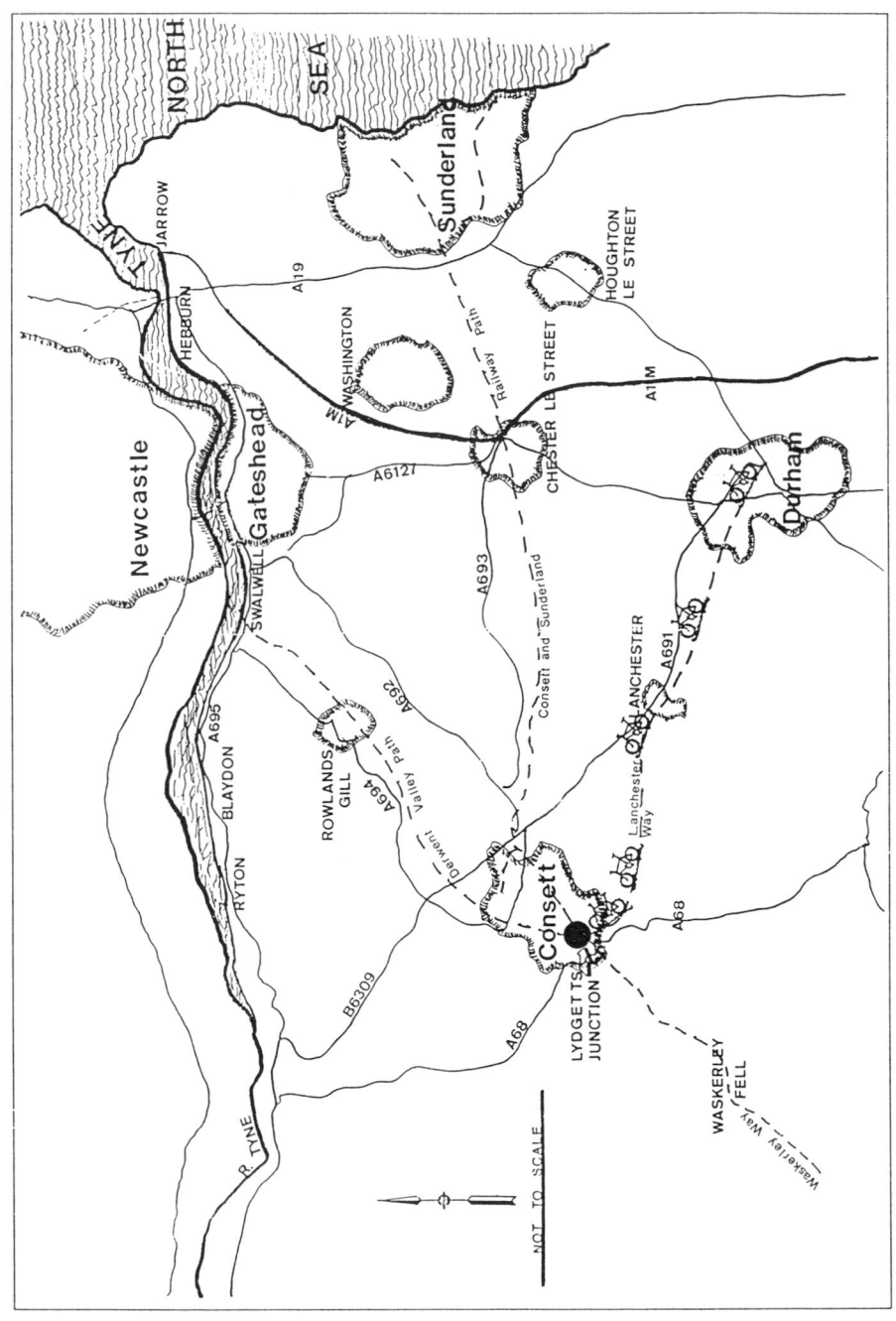

Introduction

The Lanchester Valley Railway Path closely follows the old route of the Lanchester Valley Railway and utilises some of the track bed along the route. The Railway was built in the mid-nineteenth century to serve the industrial steel town of Consett with the rich fuel from the coal fields of Durham.

The route has been revitalised as a recreational path and although some sections are incomplete, the linking road sectors are not renowned for heavy traffic and are generally safe to use.

The route links up with three other major off-road cycle routes at Consett which between them offer a fascinating insight into the industrial past of the region.

Malton Picnic Spot

Main Access Points

There are numerous access points along the route. At Lydgett's Junction Car Park and picnic area, just outside Consett, there is the unique junction of no fewer than four rail paths: the Waskerley Way, (12 miles, 19½km), the Lanchester Valley Way, (10 miles, 16km), the Derwent Valley Walk Rail Path, (11 miles, 17½km), and the Consett and Sunderland Rail Path, (22 miles, 35½km). To find the car park, imagine you are approaching Consett on the A692 after leaving the A68 and look out for the unmarked turn on the right forming part of the staggered cross roads. The car park is a little haven at the end of this road. Even if you do not intend to go down the Waskerley Way, ride the half mile (approx 1km) or so to Howns Gill Viaduct just to enjoy the view. (Only open your eyes if you have a head for heights.)

The Route
From Lydgett's Junction Car Park and picnic area, just outside Consett, the route, clearly marked, heads off to the south. The way forward is well waymarked and although some sections are not yet complete the route is quite useable by accompanied family groups.

Nearby
Durham is a beautiful medieval city full of fascination and offering a new treasure at every corner. Sited on the River Wear as it winds its way onto the east coast, the double centre pieces of this magical old city are the magnificent Cathedral which boasts a history as far back as the the 11th century and the equally majestic Castle which, of similar age, has been dated back as far as 1070.

The original founder Bishop of the Cathedral was William of Calais who dedicated a shrine to St Cuthbert. The Castle was built on the site of a Saxon church that was founded in AD 995. The big brass door knocker on the Cathedral dates back to the 12th century and was for the use of law breakers who could, in those more liberated days, seek sanctuary inside "God's Holy House".

Ride 4

Waskerley Way: Consett to Crawleyside, Durham

A magnificent railway path from Consett onto the wild moors.

Map: Landranger 1:50,000, Sheet number 87 and 88.

Distance: 24 miles (38½km) (total return).

Waymarked: Yes. A well-defined route.

Gradients: Easy.

Surface: Well-drained, solid, can be a bit muddy in a few places. Take a puncture repair kit.

Future proposals: N/A

Other cycle routes linking: The Waskerley way forms part of the proposed route linking the North Sea and the Irish sea. It also offers easy direct access to the following:

1. The Derwent Walk Railway Path.

2. The Consett and Sunderland Railway Path.

3. Lanchester Valley Railway Path.

Plus easy indirect access to:

4. South Tyne Cycleway.

5. North Tyne Country Park Cycle Way.

6. The Bowes Railway Path and The Tanfield Railway.

7. Deerness Valley Walk.

Bicycle hire: Rowland's Gill.

Shops and Refreshments: Plenty of *en route* or near-route stops.

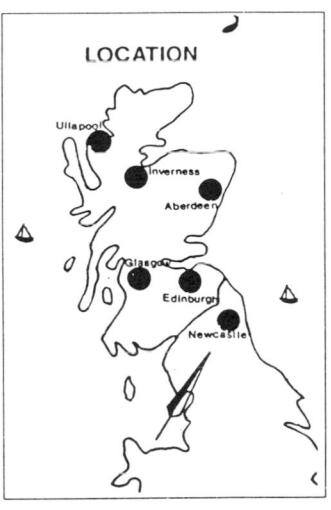

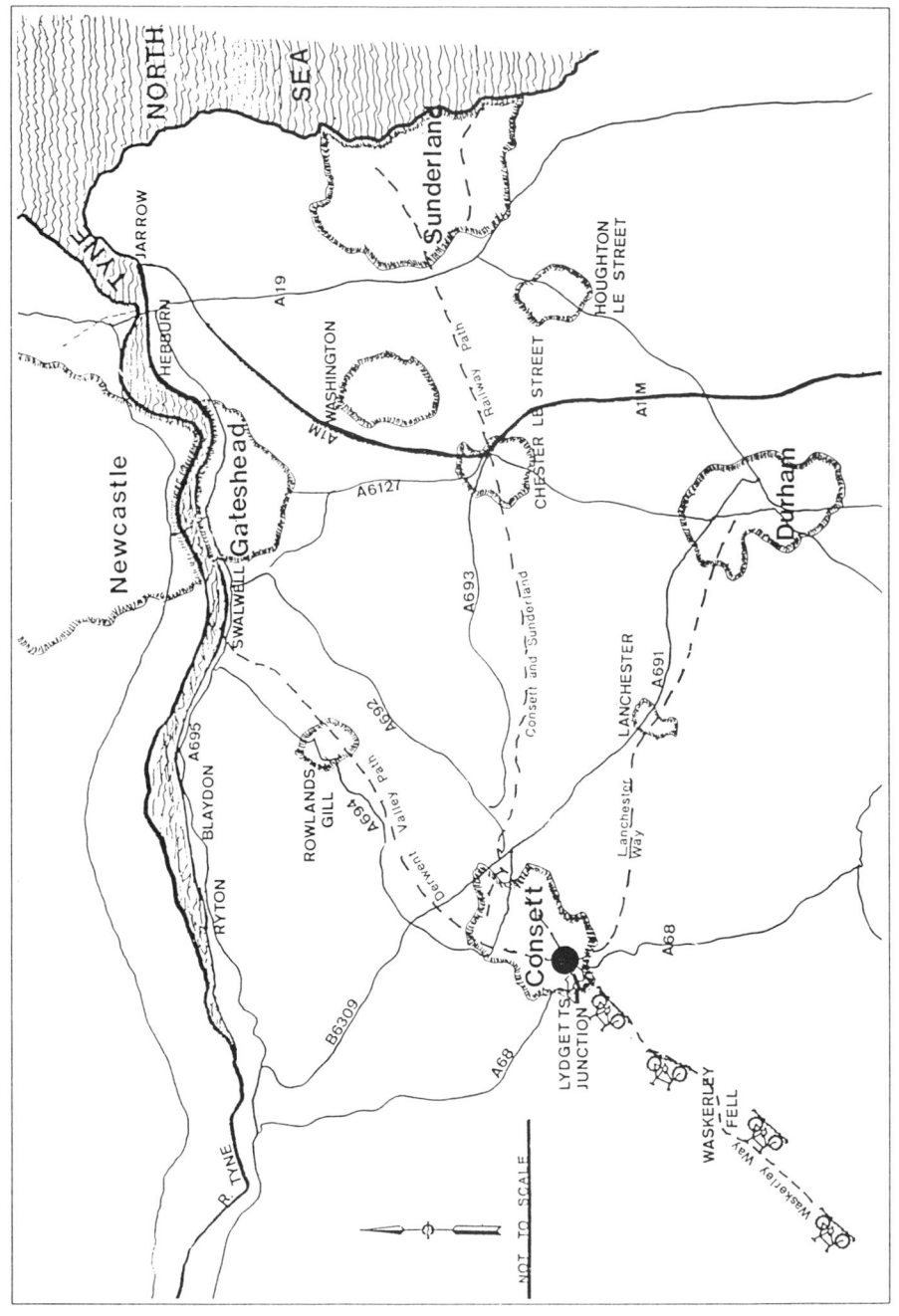

Introduction

The Waskerley Way is a twelve-mile cycle and recreational route utilising part of the disused track bed of the Stanhope and Tyne Railway. This old railway was originally opened in 1833 as a tramway, using horses for motive power. Its purpose was to bring the lead, coal, limestone and iron ore from Weardale and Medomsley down to the port at South Shields on the North Sea coast. The railway utilised inclined plains and winding engines in its earliest form, being modernised later on to become a fully modern steam railway line served by a few branches which still used the incline technology.

One of the stations of the line was called Rowley Station and even today it is still possible to catch a steam train at Rowley Station, but not on the Waskerley Way. Rowley Station is now an exhibit at the Beamish Northern England open Air Museum which is situated off the Consett and Sunderland Railway Path. This actually joins the Waskerley Way at Consett.

Passing over the 150 foot (45½ metre) viaduct at Howns Gill there is a stunning view of the distant moors and the the woody valley floor below. Then The Waskerley Way leaves the industrial area of Consett behind and heads out into a beautiful and barren high ground of the moors out to the west. It was from Howns Gill caves, below the viaduct, that the hard stone was quarried for use in the construction of the High Level Tyne Bridge to Newcastle.

Main Access Points

There are several access points along the route. At Lydgett's Junction Car Park and picnic area, just outside Consett, there is the unique junction of no less than four rail paths: the Waskerley Way, 12 miles (19½km), the Lanchester Valley Way, 10 miles (16km), the Derwent Valley Walk Rail Path, 11 miles (17½km) and the Consett and Sunderland Rail Path, 22 miles (35½km). Approaching Consett on the A692 after leaving the A68, look out for the unmarked turn on the right forming part of the staggered cross roads. The car park and picnic area are tucked away at the end of this road.

The Route

At Lydgett's Junction Car Park and picnic area, just outside Consett, the Waskerley Way heads out in a south-westerly direction and almost immediately onto Howns Gill viaduct. This viaduct was a later addition to the line, the third solution utilised to cross the valley of Howns Gill. The first effort involved two inclines but the gradients were so steep that only one wagon at a time could be hauled up and down. A normal train load of goods would take days to deliver by this method, so, in an effort to speed things up, a funicular railway system was constructed. This was not a great success, so the engineers were forced to do what they had originally tried to avoid and built the viaduct. They did a first class job. The Viaduct is a superb structure, towering more than a hundred and 50 feet (15 metres) over the valley floor. Another amazing 19th century engineering feat - try a bit of bird watching (from above the birds!)

Nearby

The original line was served by branches which used the incline technology. This was dependent on large steam engines to raise the loads in wooden wagons. One of these great old incline engines, the Weatherill Engine, is now a major exhibit in the National Railway Museum at York.

To the west of Crawleyside, at the western end of the line, is the oft forgotten Hunstanworth Moor. This is famous for Grouse shooting so if you resemble a grouse, keep well away. If you are not familiar with the appearance of grouse, they are rather unbecoming, inoffensive, reddish brown birds (check in the mirror if in any doubt). They live on top of the heather and, rather stupidly, they take to the air at the sound of beaters and gunfire.

On the moor you will see the distinctive turf covered "Butts". These are the hides where the sportsmen conceal themselves with their guns.

Ride 5

Consett and Sunderland Railway Path, County Durham (including the Tunstall Tramway)

A fine Railway Path exploring recent industrial history.

Map: Landranger 1:50,000, Sheet number 88.

Distance: 48 miles (77km) (total return).

Waymarked: Yes.

Gradients: Easy.

Surface: Well-drained solid tarmac and consolidated stone.

Future proposals: Constant maintenance and upkeep. Improvement of sections at Sunderland end.

Other cycle routes linking: The Consett and Sunderland Railway Path forms part of the proposed route linking the North Sea and the Irish sea. It also offers easy direct access to the following:

1. The Derwent Walk Railway Path.

2. The Waskerley Way.

Plus easy indirect access to:

3. North Tyne Country Park Cycle Way.

4. The Deerness Valley Walk.

Bicycle hire: Rowland's Gill. Sunderland.

Shops and Refreshments: Plenty of opportunities along the way.

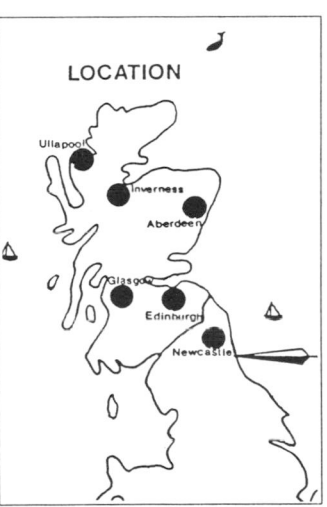

LOCATION

Introduction

The Consett and Sunderland Railway Path runs for 22 miles (35½km) from the great old steel town of Consett in the east to the famous old shipbuilding

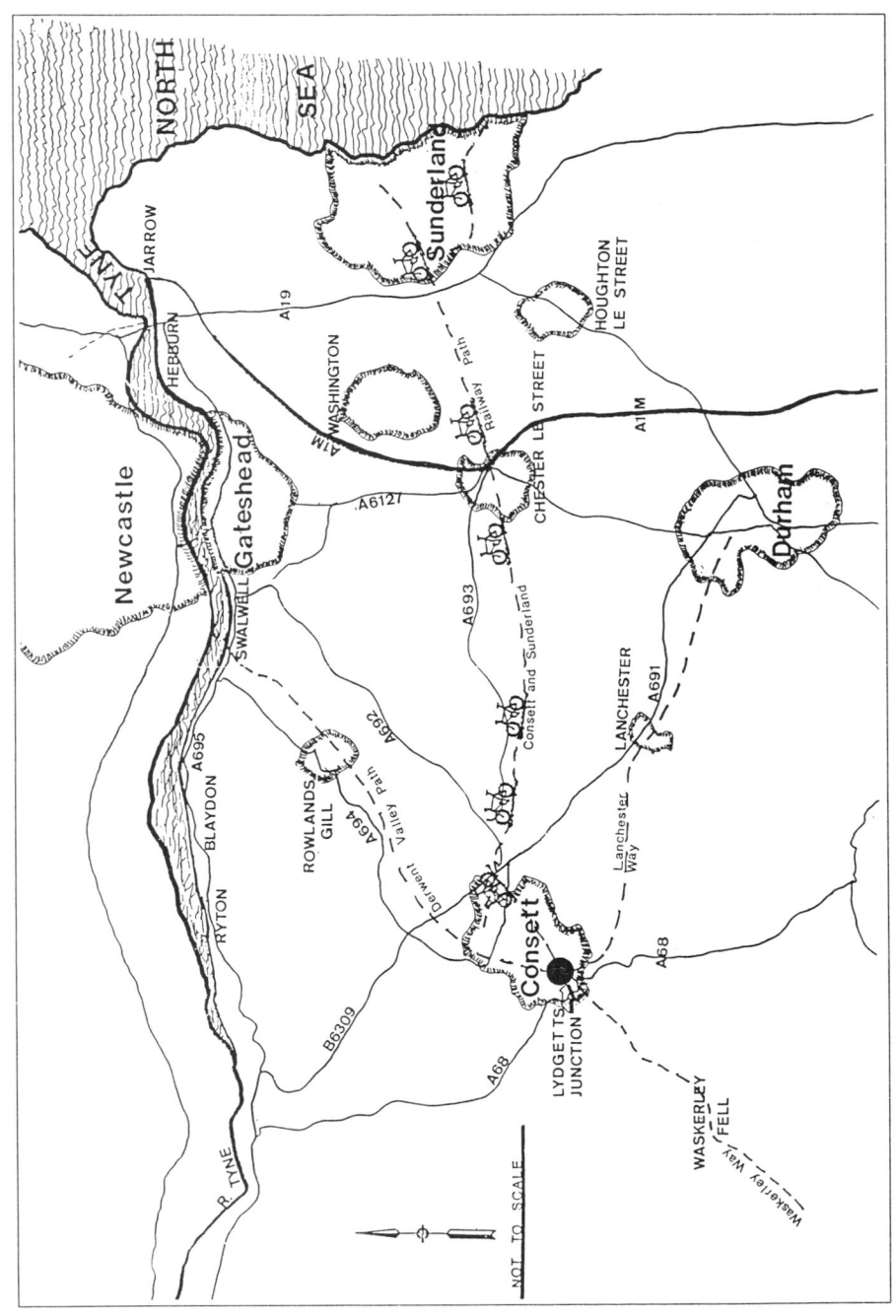

city of Sunderland in the west. It uses the disused track bed of one of Britain's oldest railways, the Stanhope and Tyne. This railway originally opened in 1834, later having two major improvement programmes in 1858 and then again in 1893. During the railway's history, both steam and horse power were utilised to carry the freight traffic, mainly raw materials going into the Consett Steel works and steel outward bound for the shipyards of Sunderland.

The Consett Steelworks was at one time the largest steel works complex in Europe and as such was the mainstay customer of the railway. It was therefore no great surprise that the closure of these works led to an almost immediate closure of the railway. In 1985, an initiative was taken and by 1990 the railway had been brought back to life as the recreational traffic-free route that we see today. Incorporated in the scheme is a trail of creative sculptures which includes work as diverse as a herd of grazing shorthorn cows made from scrap iron, through earthwork formations, and on to stone figures.

The historical and industrial archeological aspects of the railway's life history form the basis for a fascinating and educational insight into the modern history of the whole region and, as if in recognition of this, the

Towards Sunderland

Beamish North of England Open Air Museum is actually on the route. If you have not been there before and you have so much as a passing interest in modern industrial and social history, I would suggest that you make time for at least half a day's stop, if not a whole day.

Main Access Points

There are numerous access points along the route. At Lydgett's Junction Car Park and picnic area, just outside Consett, there is the unique junction of no less than four rail paths: the Waskerley Way, 12 miles (19½km), the Lanchester Valley Way, 10 miles (16km), the Derwent Valley Walk Rail Path, 11 miles (17½km), and the Consett and Sunderland Rail Path, 22 miles (35½km). To find the car park, assume you are approaching Consett on the A692 after leaving the A68. Look out for the unmarked turn on the right forming part of the staggered cross roads. The car park and picnic area is like a haven at the end of this road. Even if you do not intend to go down the Waskerley Way, ride the half mile (approx 1km) or so to Howns Gill Viaduct just to enjoy the view. (Only open your eyes if you have a head for heights.)

The Route

The whole route is easy to follow and well-signed. After leaving Consett and Leadgate, the railway path heads out into open countryside for a short while before returning to urbanisation at Annfield Plain and Stanley. The next section runs by the Beamish North of England Open air Museum and then on into Chester Le Street, Pelton and Fatfield before leading into the outskirts of Sunderland.

The route from Fatfield, south of Washington, onto the outskirts of Sunderland follows through the James Steel Country Park on existing pathways, crossing the River Wear at Cox. Once into Sunderland, cyclists can follow the narrow path on the old route of the Tunstall Tramway towards the coast.

Nearby

The Beamish North of England Open Air Museum is situated in the beautiful valley of the Beamish Burn. The Museum exhibits artefacts recovered from all parts of the north of England in order to demonstrate the fascinating industrial and social background of the region. Some of the exhibits are in daily use, such as the trams, the bandstand and the shops. Period costumes are worn by staff who man the shops and facilities. Have a look at the old school, the cottages, the pub, the chapel, the fairground and the station yard.

Ride 6

Derwent Walk Country Park: Consett to Swalwell - Tyne and Wear

A great family ride along a beautiful linear park railway path.

Map: Landranger 1:50,000, Sheet number 88.

Distance: 22 miles (35½km) (total return).

Waymarked: Yes at access points. The route is a railway track bed therefore it is self explanatory.

Gradients: Very mild.

Surface: Well-drained hard surfaces.

Future proposals: The Derwent Walk Country Park will eventually form an important part of the cross country cycle route from west to east coasts.

Other cycle routes linking: Easy or direct access to: the Consett and Sunderland Railway Path, the Waskerley Way, Deerness Valley Railway Walk, South Tyne Cycleway, North Tyne Country Park Cycle Way.

Bicycle hire: Rowland's Gill. Sunderland. Newcastle.

Shops and Refreshments: Plenty of opportunities near the route.

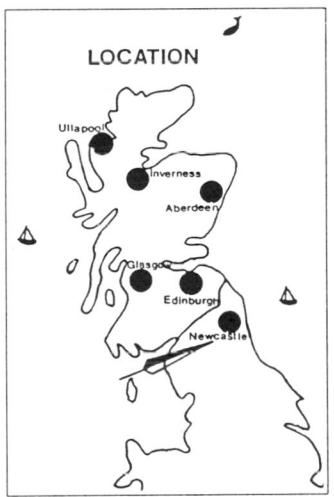

Introduction

The Derwent Valley Country Park is an 11 mile (17½km) linear recreational pathway with an excellent cycling surface. It leads from Consett in a north-easterly direction to Swalwell on the outskirts of Gateshead. The pathway is based on the track bed of a disused branch line of the old North Eastern Railway Company known as the Derwent Valley Line. It dates back to 1867, a time when the railway engineers were brimming with belief in the success of this great new age. The confidence and exuberance is reflected in the fact that the Derwent Valley Line, bearing in mind that it was no more than a short branch line, boasts no less than four large viaducts criss-crossing the

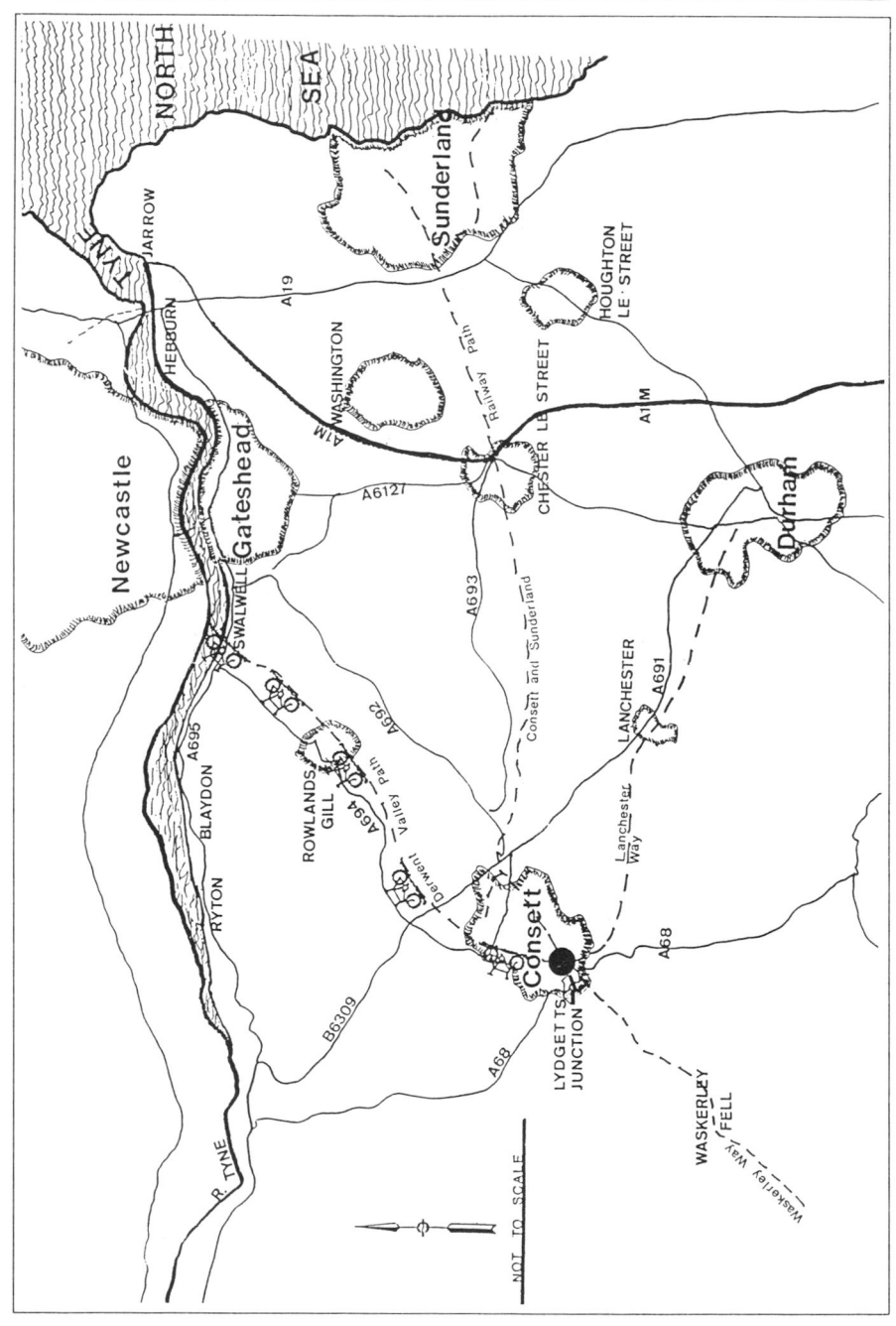

beautiful River Derwent along with numerous extravagant cuttings, up to 60 feet (18½ metres) in depth.

As it transpired, the confidence was fairly well-founded and the railway proved to be a commercial success, carrying millions of passengers and countless tons of freight based on regular traffic of coal, timber, bricks and iron ore to Newcastle and Consett. The downfall of the railway is attributed to the competition from road traffic and eventually the plug was pulled in 1962.

The track bed did not lie dormant for too long. It was reopened in 1972 as a public recreational route and linear park. Now, with so many years of good management, protection and caring attention, the whole linear park offers outstanding areas of natural beauty including woodlands, meadows, ponds, riverside locations and mellow undisturbed embankments rich with wild flowers. The route passes through a varied environment from open countryside, to industrial town, to commuter suburbs.

Main Access Points

The following access points have good car parking facilities:

Swalwell Visitor Centre; Thornley Woodland Centre; Rowlands Gill; Pontburn Wood; Ebchester; Shotley Bridge; Consett.

There are numerous access points along the route. At Lydgett's Junction Car Park and picnic area, just outside Consett, there is the unique junction of no less than four rail paths: the Waskerley Way, 12 miles (19½km), the Lanchester Valley Way, 10 miles (16km), the Derwent Valley Walk Rail Path, 11 miles (17½km) and the Consett and Sunderland Rail Path, 22 miles (35½km). To find this car park, assume that you are approaching Consett on the A692 after leaving the A68 and look out for the unmarked turn on the right forming part of the staggered cross roads.

The car park is at the end of this road and is an ideal picnic spot. While you are there, go down the Waskerley Way, ride the half mile (approx 1km) or so to Howns Gill Viaduct and enjoy the view. (Only open your eyes if you have a head for heights.)

The Route

From Consett to Swalwell, the path is either self-explanatory or waymarked clearly. Along the way there are either mature country views or interesting back yard aspects, in the towns and suburbs. The name of the pub at Shotley Bridge, "The Crown and Crossed Swords", is a reminder of the fact that 17th century sword makers settled here from Germany. At Ebchester is a picturesque National Trust Wood, and at Rowland's Gill, approximately half way along the route, there are good facilities for picnickers as well as information on the route and bicycle hire.

There is a wildlife observation hide at Far Pasture Wetlands, just beyond Rowland's Gill, and a bit further along is Thornley Wood Wildlife Centre. This offers a great deal of most informative detail on the local woodland habitat as well as two waymarked nature foot trails with interpretative boards. Swalwell Visitor Centre at the end of the route includes a delightful butterfly garden with duck-boarding over a large pond.

Viaduct at Rowland's Gill

Nearby

Beyond Swalwell is Gateshead and the River Tyne. Call into the Metro Centre. You will find that it is a colourful and entertaining urban experience. Just off the path, throughout its route, are several nature trails leading into woodlands or forming small circular walks within the country park. North of the nine arches viaduct is a path leading to Hollinside Manor. Here are the ruins of a thirteenth century manor house which fell into disuse in the 17th century. Now its main use is as a pleasant sheltered resting stop for tired walkers and cyclists.

Ride 7

Keelman's Way: South Tyne Riverside Cycle Route

A fascinating cycle route following the south bank of
The River Tyne

Map: Landranger 1:50,000, Sheet number 88.

Distance: 14 miles (22½km).

Return Distance: 28 miles (45km).

Waymarked: Yes.

Gradients: Easy flat riding.

Surface: Either tarmac road or pathway.

Future proposals: To reduce the "On road" sections.

Other cycle routes linking: Derwent Walk (Swalwell to Consett); North Tyne Country Park Cycleway.

Bicycle hire: Newcastle upon Tyne.

Shops and Refreshments: Plenty of choice along the route.

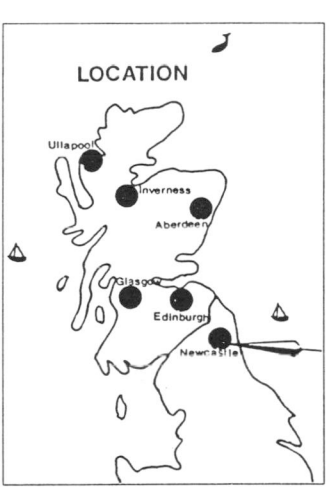

Introduction

The Keelman's Way is a fascinating on- and off-road route, following the south bank of the Tyne for a distance of fourteen miles, from Wylam in the west, to Hebburn Riverside Park in the east. A very easy link can be made onto the North Tyne Country Park Cycle Way and another easy link is available onto the Derwent Walk at Swalwell.

The route is a mix of off-road, mainly on the Riverside path, and on-road, mainly on quiet back streets. There is a short busy "A" road section, for which it is safest to use the pavement or walk.

The ride takes you through some fascinating urban scenes and has the added constant interest of the River Tyne as it peacefully heads down towards the

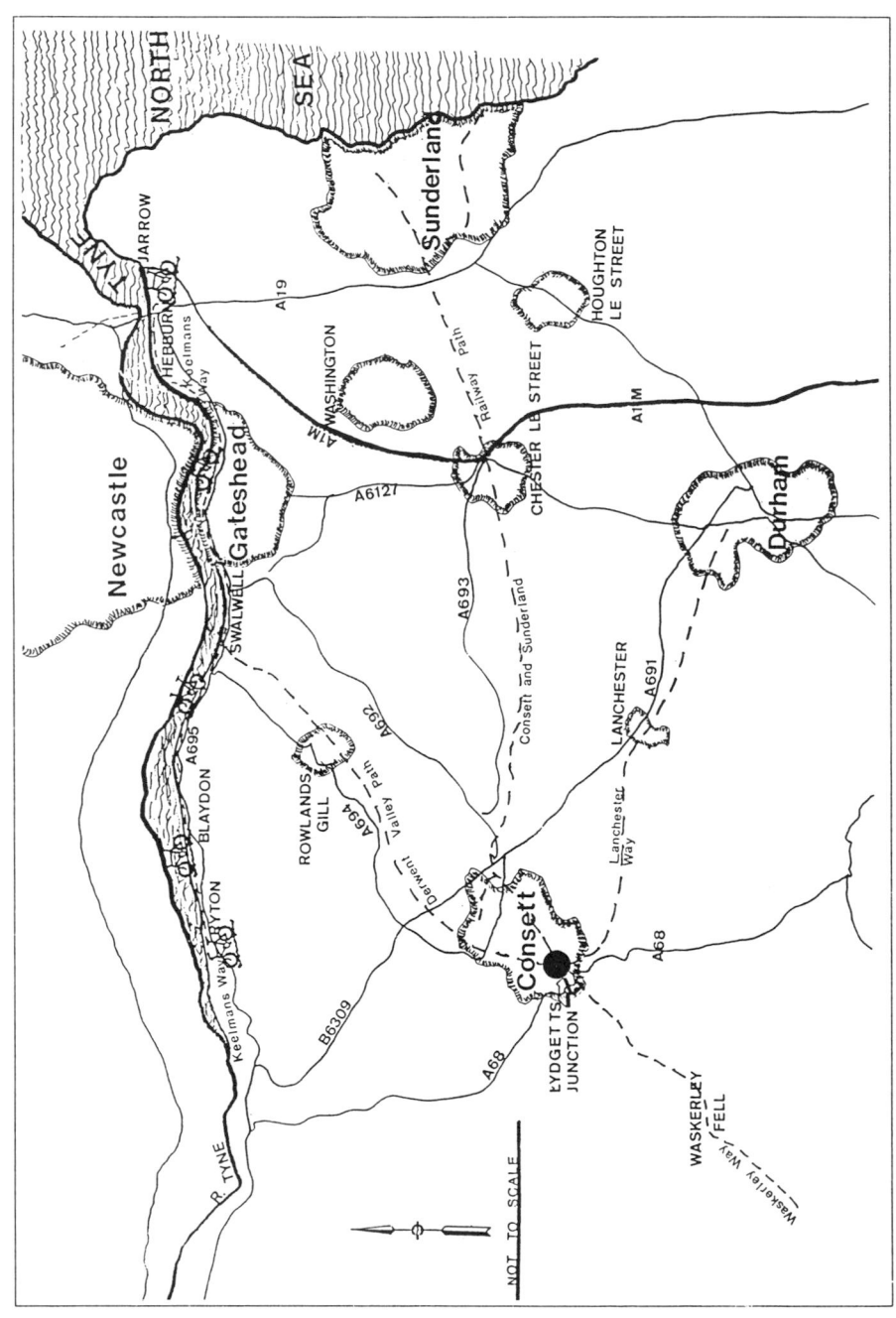

sea. There are plenty of good stopping off points and some very good shopping opportunities along the way. If you go on a Sunday, there is a good Sunday Market at Swalwell.

Main Access Points

The cycle route can be accessed from virtually any point along its course. The beginning in the west is Wylam Railway Station. In the east the beginning is at Hebburn Riverside Park

The Route

The Keelman's Way begins in the west, at Wylam Railway Station, and is off-road past Ryton until Newburn Bridge. If you just want a short ride, cross Newburn Bridge to return along the North Tyne Country Park Cycle Way to Wylam. To continue, follow the road up hill to the A695 and then after half a mile turn left, into a fine off-road section at Blaydon Burn. At Blaydon Haughs Industrial Estate, it is back onto quiet roads to Patterson Street, where you will rejoin the off-road path.

Newburn Bridge

At Derwenthaugh Marina, cross the railway and continue in front of the Derwent Lodge Pub. Pick up the off-road path at the railway bridge and continue along the south side of the railway, past the Metro Centre. At the road turn left and after going under the railway turn right to follow the river through Dunston where you should go left along Team Street, straight along Rose Street and left before the houses. Now you are back on the path.

At Friars Goose Marina, turn right along the road then left to rejoin the path. At the paints site, turn right past the football ground and left along Abbotsford Road. Turn left just before the houses and the path will take you to Hebburn Riverside Park.

The route is well-signed throughout.

Nearby

Roughly 13 miles (21km) of the route is in Gateshead, which was virtually destroyed in a massive fire in 1854. The town has grown and grown over the years and, until recently, seemed to show scant regard for the niceties of town planning. The mass of concrete slab structures may go down in history as features of architectural interest but are more likely to be monuments of a time when the names of John Poulson (Architect) and T. Dan Smith (entrepreneur?) were actively pursuing their professions. The more modern Metro Centre is a magnificent modern complex and is well worth a visit.

Ride 8

Wide Open and Seaton Burn to the Tyne Tunnel: Newcastle upon Tyne

A fine railway path linking Wide Open and Seaton Burn to The Tyne Pedestrian Tunnel and Jarrow.

Map: Landranger 1:50,000, Sheet number 88.

Distance: One-way Trip: 10 miles (16km); Return trip: 20 miles (32km).

Waymarked: Yes. Good waymarks throughout the length.

Gradients: Ranging from minimal to zero.

Surface: Good. Well-drained old railway track bed. Solid, rolled surfaces.

Future proposals: There are a proliferation of old tramways in the area and it is intended to create a network of cycle routes over a period of years.

Other cycle routes linking: South Tyne Cycleway.

Bicycle hire: Newcastle.

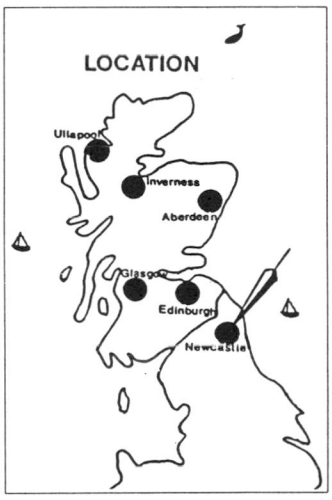

Shops and Refreshments: This route is predominantly through a built up area. There are numerous shops, pubs and other opportunities for sustenance along the route.

Introduction

Wide Open and Seaton Burn are situated to the north of the main Newcastle upon Tyne conurbation, just off the main A6125 Morpeth Road. The route goes from here to the Tyne Pedestrian and Cycle tunnel, which crosses under the river to emerge in Jarrow on the southern bank. The route takes in much of Newcastle's history and heritage.

The surface conditions are very good, being mainly solid, well-drained, purpose laid cycle paths, following the basic routes of old industrial tramways. The gradients are slight and the surroundings are delightful, making a thoroughly enjoyable ride.

Points of interest along the route include the Rising Sun Country Park and the Stephenson Railway Museum. There are a maze of bridle ways and surfaced wagon ways around the Rising Sun Country Park and the link from here to the Stephenson Railway Museum follows the course of the original Rising Sun Colliery wagon way.

Main Access Points
1. Jarrow at the entrance to the Tyne Tunnel.
2. Wide Open and Seaton Burn.
3. Rising Sun Country Park.

The Route
From Wide Open and Seaton Sluice, the route heads out to the east. It is clearly waymarked and very easy to follow. After crossing under the Tyne through the tunnel, you may wish to explore Jarrow before turning to retrace the route to Wide Open.

Nearby
Newcastle upon Tyne originally got its name from the 1172 Norman Castle. The massive 82 foot (25 metre) high keep is still a major feature of the city. A great place to taste Newcastle is in the area around the 17th Century timbered houses on the quayside. The city has always been blessed with visionary town planners and nowhere is this more easily seen than at the Central Railway Station. It stands on an expansive 17 acres (6½ hectares) of land and when Queen Victoria opened it in 1850, it boasted no less than 2 miles (3km) of platform. This openness spills over into the broad proportions of the town centre thoroughfares and streets, such as Grey Street. The great original vision of town planning came in the 1830s period, from the architect John Dobson. Modern vision seems equally impressive. There are over 1400 acres (565 hectares) of public open space, including the great town moor to the NW and Jesmond Dean to the NE.

Hadrian's wall once stretched across England for 73 miles (118km) and good remains can be seen at the modern start of the wall at Denton, on the A69.

There are six bridges crossing the Tyne in the space of less than one kilometre. The most famous is the 1928 suspension bridge with its coat

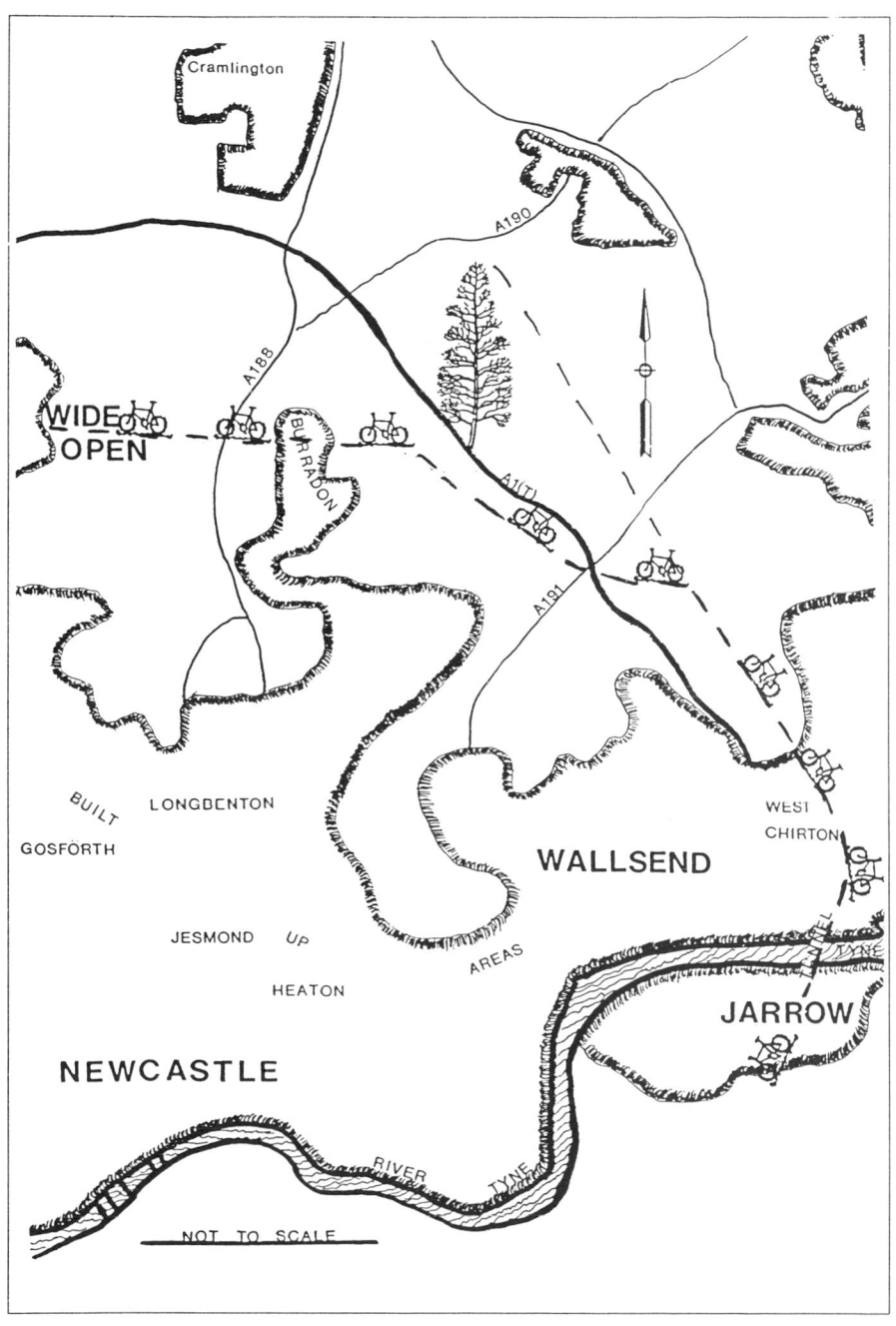

hanger arch, built to carry the A1 trunk road. The two-tiered high-level bridge carries a railway on top of the lower road deck and the Swing Bridge, built in 1876, swings open, pivoted on a gigantic man-made island, to allow ships to pass. To the west are the King Edward VII railway bridge of 1906, and the Redeugh Road Bridge of 1900. The modern bridge of the 1970s era carries the bulk of the motor traffic.

Wallsend was the original terminus of Hadrian's Wall. It was here, in the once world-famous shipyards, that the magnificent liner *RMS Mauretania* was launched in 1902. She held the transatlantic record for 22 years.

Ride 9

Harwood Forest: North Northumberland

A circular ride through the peace and isolation of Harwood Forest.

Map: Landranger 1:50,000, Sheet number 81.

Distances: Total length of forest roads: Over 25 miles (40km); The round trip from Harwood: 18 miles (29km).

Waymarked: Forestry reassurance "cycling markers".

Gradients: The southern part of the forest is relatively easy. There are some climbs around the Simonside Hills in the northern part of the forest.

Surface: Good, well-drained, solid and stony forest roads.

Future proposals: N/A.

Other cycle routes linking: N/A.

Bicycle hire: Newcastle upon Tyne. Forestry Enterprises.

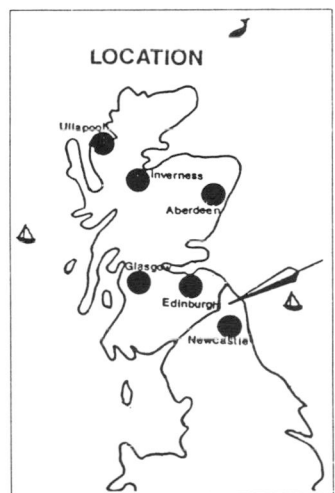

Shops and Refreshments: None. Take a sandwich and a drink.

Introduction

Harwood Forest is part of the Rothbury Forest District and is situated in the peace and tranquillity of north Northumberland, an area often overlooked in favour of the Kielder and Southern Scottish Forests. Harwood is located in the open landscapes on the eastern boundary of the Northumberland National Park, west of the B6342, south of Rothbury and north of the A696. The southern part of the forest is relatively level and well-drained, the ideal forestry conditions. The northern part includes the Simonside Hills and therefore presents a very different type of riding for those who are looking for this type of challenge.

The forest is mainly planted with a selection of Spruce, Pine and Larch and is well into its second rotation. There is a good range of differences in the various areas of the forest, so there is a constantly changing scene for the cyclist. In the south there is a minor public road which can form part of a route if required. Although the traffic along this road is fairly light, the road is very straight, and therefore vehicles can be moving surprisingly fast.

From time to time the forest is used for car rallies and other automotive events, so check carefully for any local warning notices. The nearby towns of Rothbury and Otterburn are both well worth visiting.

Main Access Points

The ride can be approached from either Rothbury in the north or from the B6342 in the south. There is car parking at either end. The riding in the northern part of the forest is steep on the Simonside Hills but the reward is the possibility of marvellous views on a clear day. The southern part of the forest enjoys more manageable gradients.

From Rothbury, take the bridge crossing the River Coquet to the south and turn right onto the minor public road heading west. Turn left at the hamlet

Harwood Forest

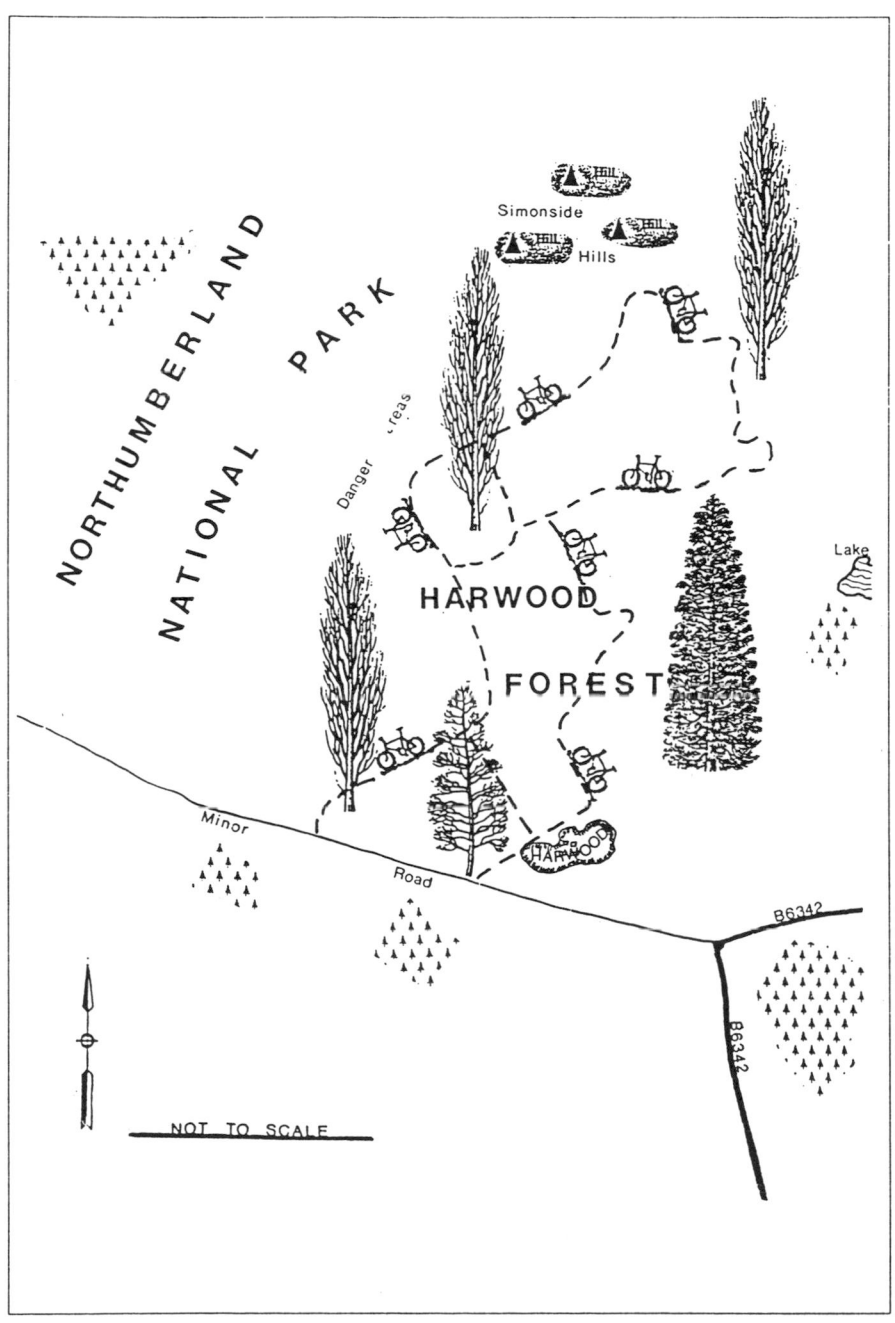

of Newtown and left again at Great Tosson. After a short distance you will be able to join the forest ride on your right, heading south.

From the south and the A696(T), take the B6342 heading north and follow this for six or seven miles until the road takes a sharp right turn. Here take the minor public road to the left, heading west. Parking is in lay-bys off the forest roads, near the hamlet of Harwood.

The Route

The Simonside Hills, in the northern part of the forest, present some serious climbing, so a circular route in the southern and central part of the forest is suggested. The forest road heads in roughly a northerly direction away from Harwood Hamlet. The exact route is really up to the individual choice, but as can be seen by the map, there are five or six loops which can be ridden. These range from a short loop via Harwood and the public road, to a fairly comprehensive forest sortie taking in the delightful streams of Fallowlees Burn, Newbiggin Burn, Chartner Burn and Blanch Burn.

Nearby

Rothbury is a charming old market town with a population of only 1700 serving the River Coquet Valley area. This is a quiet and peaceful place with a dignified atmosphere, enhanced by the local stone which is very much in evidence as a building material.

Otterburn is a lovely old town with a population of about 1500. It is situated to the south-west of Harwood Forest. The woollen mill is quite famous for its tweeds and still uses water to power its machinery. Otterburn is also noted for a vicious border battle in 1388. The old song "The Battle of Chevy Chase" recounts the gory details. (The Scots won).

Ride 10

Kielder Water: North Northumberland

Ride around the largest man-made lake in Europe, situated in the midst of the dauntingly beautiful Kielder Forest.

Map: Landranger 1:50,000, Sheet number 80.

Distances: Around the reservoir, 17 miles (27km); Bull Crag Peninsula Tour: 6 miles (10km); full ride including bull crag: 23 miles (37km)

Waymarked: Self explanatory and very clearly way-marked in both directions.

Gradients: There are a few ups and downs but nothing that should worry you too much.

Surface: Well-drained solid. Either tarmac path or forestry track. Mainly easy going. (Harder work in the forest sections.)

Future proposals: Good ongoing maintenance.

Other cycle routes linking: Good access to other waymarked rides in the forest.

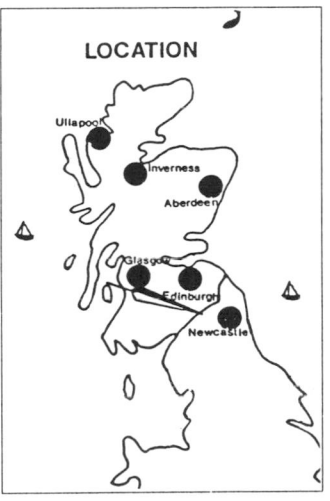

Bicycle hire: Kielder Castle and Leapish Barn.

Shops and Refreshments: Good facilities at centres on the south-western shores.

Warning: Some of this ride is on public road. Beware of the traffic.

Introduction

Kielder Water is a magnificent man-made lake and boasts no less than 27 miles (43km) of shoreline. It is situated in the heart of the Kielder Forest, by Kielder Castle in the ancient border area of Northumberland. Here, in the midst of the Cheviot Hills, the lake takes its water from the surrounding high ground. The storage capacity of Kielder Water is measured in millions of litres and the deepest parts of Kielder are more than 50 feet (15 metres).

The dam that holds it all in place is built from the upper deposits pulled off

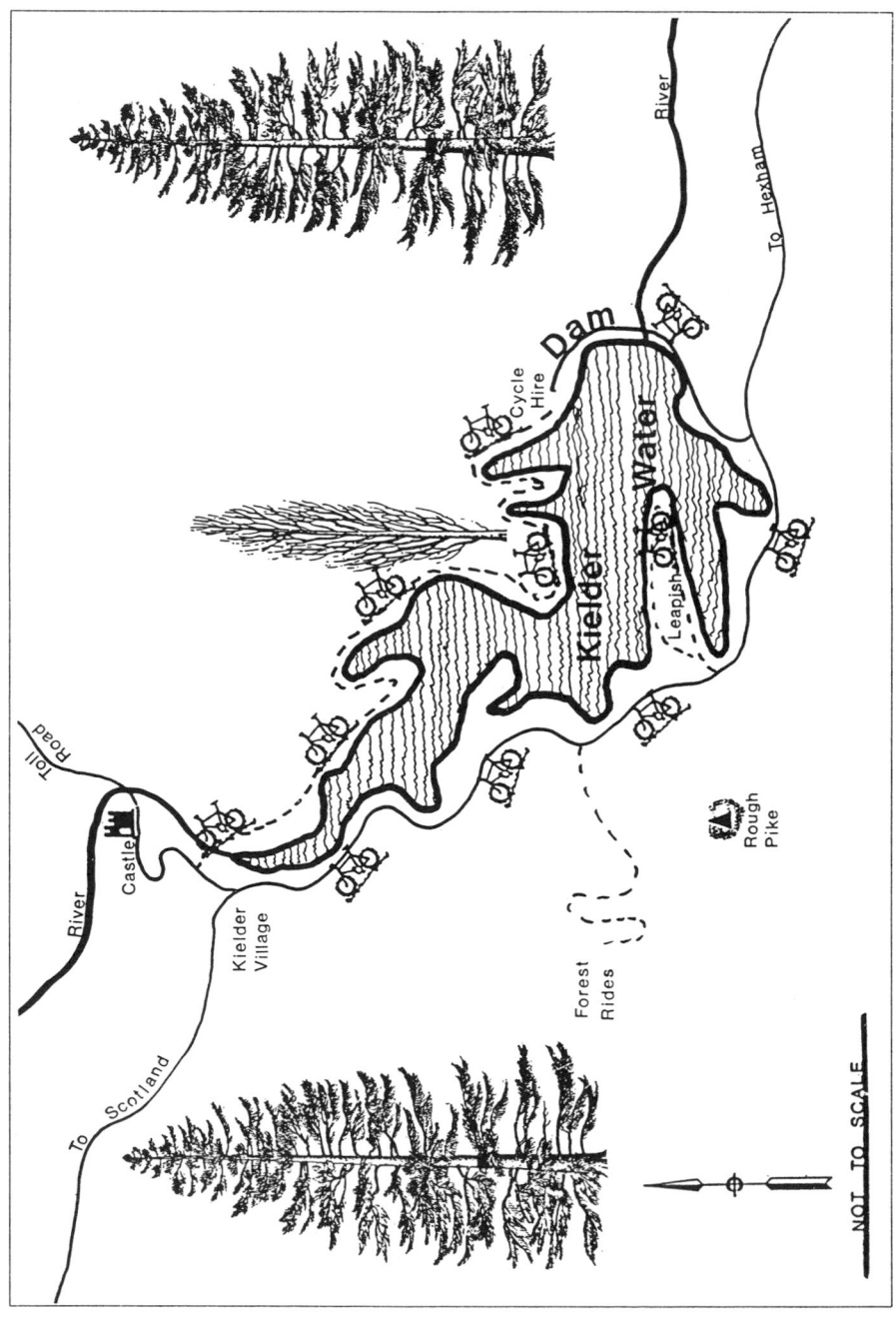

the land which is now the lake bed. The treatment works at Kielder deals with many millions of gallons of water a day to serve major local towns and cities. There are other attractions.

If you get bored with your bicycle, try a bit of wind surfing, sailing, canoeing, motor boating, rowing or fishing. For a more gentle pursuit, pop into the Kielder Heavy Horse Company or take a gentle stroll from the Kielder Castle Visitor Centre, the starting point for a range of nature trails and scenic walks. Take a cruise on the Osprey or for the energetic, a session at Leapish Water Slide Park. Hire a horse, take a Land Rover safari or enjoy a game of crazy golf.

All this for a cycle track? Well not quite, but not bad service from Northumbrian Water. The cycling is great fun. Leisurely and casual, a superb 17 mile (27km) water side (or near) circuit of the lake. About half the ride is on made up tarmac road or pathway and the other half on forestry track. Everything is at hand for your comfort. Refreshments, Pubs, Toilets, Playgrounds, Picnic Tables and even hides for a bit of bird watching.

Main Access Points

There are several clearly marked car parks around the south-western shores of Kielder Water and all of these give access to the cycle path. Favourite starting points are Kielder Castle in the north and Leapish Water Slide Park in the south.

The Route

There are several routes to choose from, depending on your starting point and time available, but as a rule of thumb, a cyclist taking a leisurely continuous ride will cover a mile every five or six minutes. The total trip around Kielder Water is roughly seventeen miles, obviously more if you loop into the forest, so a complete circle will take roughly an hour and a half to two hours. A really energetic cyclist could get round the whole reservoir in very little time at all, perhaps even less than that, but I assume that we're not all in such a hurry. Take your time and enjoy your surroundings. Add on a bit of stop-over time for picnics, visiting a pub, picking a pallet of strawberries or just having a lie down and you can work out your own routes near enough to suit the time available to you.

Apart from the straightforward round trip of the lake (red waymarks) the waymarks also offer a choice of four other rides. Three of these are fairly hard work, (yellow, green and orange waymarks) taking you up into the hills to the west or the north. The fourth ride (purple waymarks) takes you on a delightful loop around the Bull Crag peninsula that protrudes into the southern part of the lake.

Nearby

Kielder Castle is only half a mile from the north-western tip of Kielder Water and is a delightful spot. This is also the home of the very interesting Border Forest Museum. Around the reservoir are many points of interest and great viewing points. In the general Border Forest area, there are several excellent waymarked rides designed to cater for all shapes and sizes of cyclist.

The steamer pier at Leapish

Ride 11
Craik Forest: Scottish Borders

One of the undiscovered forests of the Border country. Great cycling in magnificent, unspoilt, wild surroundings.

Map: Landranger 1:50,000, Sheet number 79.

Distances: Total length of trails: Green Route - 10 miles (16km); All Routes - 30 miles (80½km).

Waymarked: Yes.

Gradients: There are climbs on all of the waymarked routes at Craik, even the "easy" route. Take your time, enjoy your surroundings and remember, what goes up must ... etc.

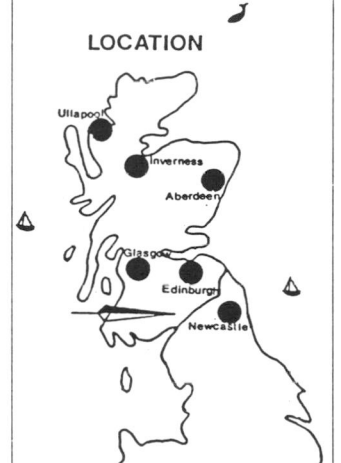

Surface: The easy routes are well-drained and enjoy hard forestry track surfaces. There are the usual loose and muddy ground problems on the harder routes.

Future proposals: As per Ride 12.

Other cycle routes linking: There are plenty of forestry roads in the area which are available for cycling. The roads in this area are generally very quiet, especially the unclassified roads.

Bicycle hire: Craik trekking centre.

Shops and Refreshments: Take a sandwich and a flask.

Introduction

The Craik Forest, situated just north of the England and Scotland border, is one of the undiscovered forests in this delightful region. It is not on the mainstream tourist route, being well away from the main thoroughfares, and is often ignored by the traveller, who is more intent on heading for the better known areas of Scotland to the north or for Northumberland's border forests, Kielder and Hadrian's wall to the south. Craik offers some superb cycling for the dedicated mountain biker or for the family group, all in absolutely magnificent wild and unspoilt surroundings.

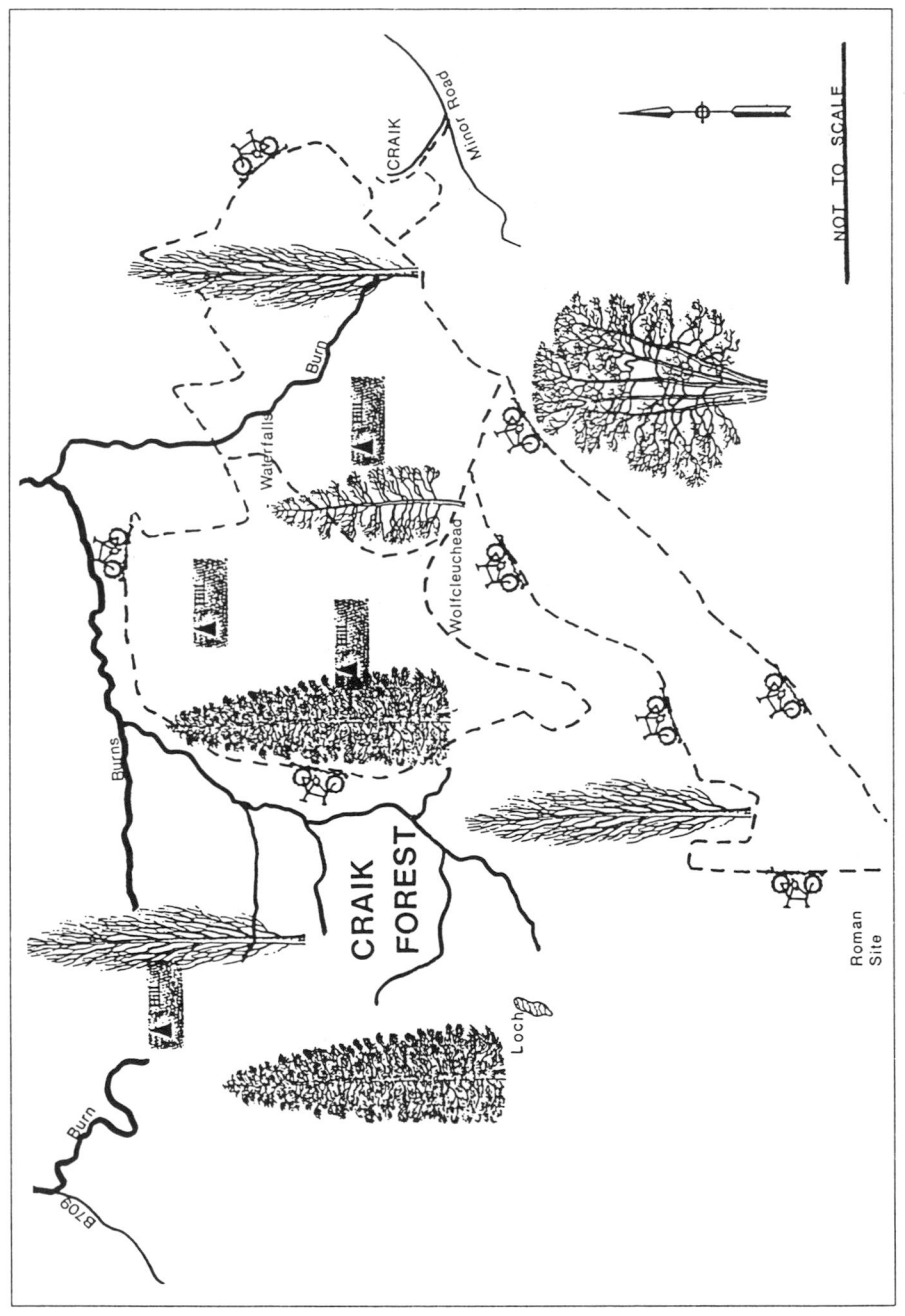

Tourist Board statistics rate this Border Country as the least visited area of Scotland, with less than five per cent of tourists settling in the region for more than just a passing visit. Although this is bad news for the local economy, it is good news for the tourists who do bother to visit, particularly the cyclists. There are few places in Britain today where such peaceful solitude can be found.

The Romans found Craik and their passing presence is very much in evidence, with remains of a Roman Road, an early warning signal post and an ancient culvert. Amongst other historic remains are the Wolfcleuchead, reputed to be a covenanters hiding place in the middle ages, and for something slightly less spooky, the Loupin, a mysterious small carved tryst stone, where lovers can meet and make pacts.

The forest itself is over 10,000 acres (4046 Hectares) in size and was originally planted in the early 1950s amidst rolling countryside, with elevations ranging between 500 and 1000 feet (150 and 300 metres) above sea level, so the rides tend to be anything but totally flat. An easy contour-hugging route has been waymarked as well as a series of circuit rides, some reaching quite high into the forest. If you do decide to venture into the deeper parts of the forest, head north from Craik car park up the Aithouse Burn and after about a mile you will come across the amazing Wolfcleuchead Waterfall. This is a fine spot to sit and simply enjoy the true beauty of the place, perhaps imagining the days when the old woodland, which was on this site, was populated with wolves, instead of the current inhabitants of deer, hawks, squirrels and hares.

Main Access Points

Craik village car park is situated off the unclassified road, south of the B711, west of Hawick. Look out for information regarding the use of the forest for car rallies or motorcycle enduro events.

The Route

The waymarked routes all set out from the car park at Craik village. They are clearly waymarked and interpretative information is available. The green waymarks represent the easier routes: the red waymarks should be followed only by the experienced and preferably the fit.

For less energetic activity, visit the Craik Policy woodland where you will see a lovely collection of interesting tree species including a 150 year old Scots Pine.

If you want a change from pure forest riding, one of the most pleasant rides in the vicinity is not in the forest itself, but up and down the beautiful Borthwick Water Valley Approach Road as it leads away from the forest and back towards the B711. This is not a through route for vehicles, so enjoys very light traffic flow.

Nearby

The charming old sheep market town of Hawick is famous worldwide for its knitwear. Call into the Wilton Lodge museum where you will see a whole large section devoted to the history of the local woollen industry. One exhibit is claimed to be the world most speedily produced sweater, which was completed in only 275 minutes (just over four and a half hours) after the wool was keeping the sheep warm.

Border violence is never far away from these areas and there are few better reminders that the Scottish are Scottish and the English are English than the Horse Monument in the High Street. This commemorates the valour of the local youth who rallied in the year 1514 to defeat a heavily armed English raiding party.

Plenty of shade in the forest

Ride 12

The Forest of Ae: South-West Scotland

A range of forest rides along the contoured tracks by bustling burns.

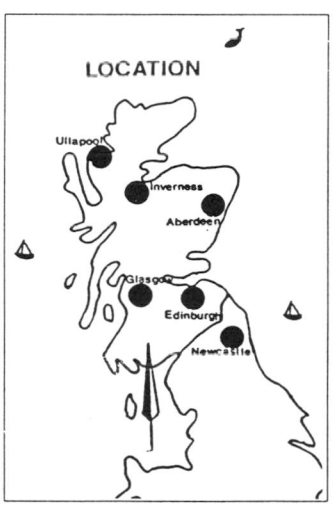

Map: Landranger 1:50,000, Sheet number 78.

Distance: Forest trails: 15 miles (24km).

Waymarked: Yes. A range of waymarked trails.

Gradients: Check the latest interpretative information boards and leaflets in order to choose the route that is best suited to your mood! The easiest trails stay close to The Waters of Ae.

Surface: Ranging from solid forest roads to less solid (possibly quite muddy) tracks. The contour track is a well made up forestry road.

Future proposals: The forest is always changing and the policy of the Forestry Commission is constantly to enhance the environment for wildlife and natural beauty.

Other cycle routes linking: N/A.

Bicycle hire: Dumfries.

Shops and Refreshments: Take a snack and a drink with you.

Introduction

Situated on the exposed and wind blown lands north of Dumfries, the Forest of Ae has an unusual beauty of its own. Ae is a modern forest, most of it planted in the 1950s. Timber production, which reached a high of 49,000 cubic metres in 1991, is hoped to rise to nearly 100,000 cubic metres by 2006. Careful management is ensuring that a wide range of natural inhabitants are

allowed to thrive and have the opportunity to occupy a broad choice of diverse surroundings. An instance of this policy is seen in the landscape planning which ensures that any adjoining forestry areas have a minimum of a ten year age difference and, wherever possible, special features, such as rocky outcrops, are kept clear and protected.

Part of the art of forest management is deciding when the trees might be at high risk from being blown over by the local winds and in order to assess this risk, land is divided into wind hazard classifications. Major factors for consideration are the prevailing winds, the geographical location, the local exposure and the soil quality.

Here in the forest of Ae the lands are fairly exposed, especially at high points, and the soil type is not particularly supportive when wet. Because of this, the Spruce trees which form the majority of the planting are felled at the age of 35-40 years, at a height of 55-65 feet (17-20 metres).

To the south of the main car park is an interesting open air museum collection of forestry ploughs. These were specially developed to cut drainage ditches and water courses when the forest was originally laid out. The careful drainage and the control of water are possibly the most essential elements of good landscaping. Bird life is particularly rich in the forest of Ae

and, amongst other species, it is now common to see buzzards with their magnificent broad wings and feathered legs. Also, keep a good look out for kestrels, sparrow hawks, goshawks and merlins as well as the odd wise old owl.

Main Access Point

The main Forest Car Park is well-signed from the road by Ae village. It is situated beside the Water of Ae and is an excellent picnic spot. The Forest itself is sign-posted from the main A701T, a left turn when travelling north-east out of Dumfries.

The Route

Start your ride from the main car park, beside the Water of Ae, which is sign posted from the road near Ae village. The cycle routes are waymarked from here but because they are often varied to suit the working operation of the Forest, reference should be made to any interpretative maps and information available at the car park, at the time of your visit.

Broadly, the rides are designed initially to follow the very pretty Water of Ae via the contour track that follows the valley. For a pleasant ride without too much exertion, follow the road south towards Ae village and take the route from there, up Goukstane Burn and Braidlane Burn. If you feel in need of more exercise, there are plenty of alternative routes, some of which will take you deep into the forest.

Nearby

Dumfries is an ancient town on the banks of the Nith where the river is crossed by no less than five bridges. The oldest bridge, with six arches, dates back to 1426. It is called Devorgilla's Bridge, named after Lady Devorgilla who founded New Abbey, five miles to the south.

The great scribe Robert Burns lived in Dumfries from 1791 until he died here in 1796. It was here that he wrote his most internationally famous piece, song "Auld Lang Syne". He is buried in the mausoleum in St Michael's churchyard.

Ride 13

Mabie Forest: South-West Scotland

A ride through a mature forest to the Forest Nature Reserve of Lochaber Loch.

Map: Landranger 1:50,000, Sheet number 84.

Distance: Forest: 22 easy miles (35½km) or 3½ miles (5½km) of demanding riding - only if you want it.

Waymarked: Yes: Green very easy. Purple and Blue moderately easy. Red for serious sporting work.

Gradients: Vary from hardly any on the Green (easiest) route to quite steep on the Red (Demanding) route.

Surface: Forest road and track. Well-drained, solid. (The Red Route is loose and can be hard going).

Future proposals: Constant maintenance.

Other cycle routes linking: There are other numerous waymarked forest routes in the Galloway Forest Park.

Bicycle hire: Dumfries.

Shops and Refreshments: None close by.

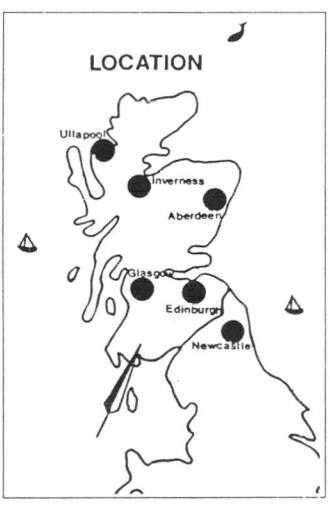

Introduction

Although Mabie Forest is a comparative newcomer to the Forestry Commission, having only been in their ownership since 1943, references to it can be found as far back as 1240, when it was included in the Charters of the Abbey of Holm Cultran in Cumberland. Historically, forestry has been a major activity here since the early 1800s and some of the largest trees date back 100 years or more. Close to Mabie House, now a hotel, are some very interesting old plantings which incorporate a great variety of different tree species, some of which are also now planted in the fascinating arboretum by the public picnic place. Constant active management of the arboretum ensures an ever changing and increasingly varied selection.

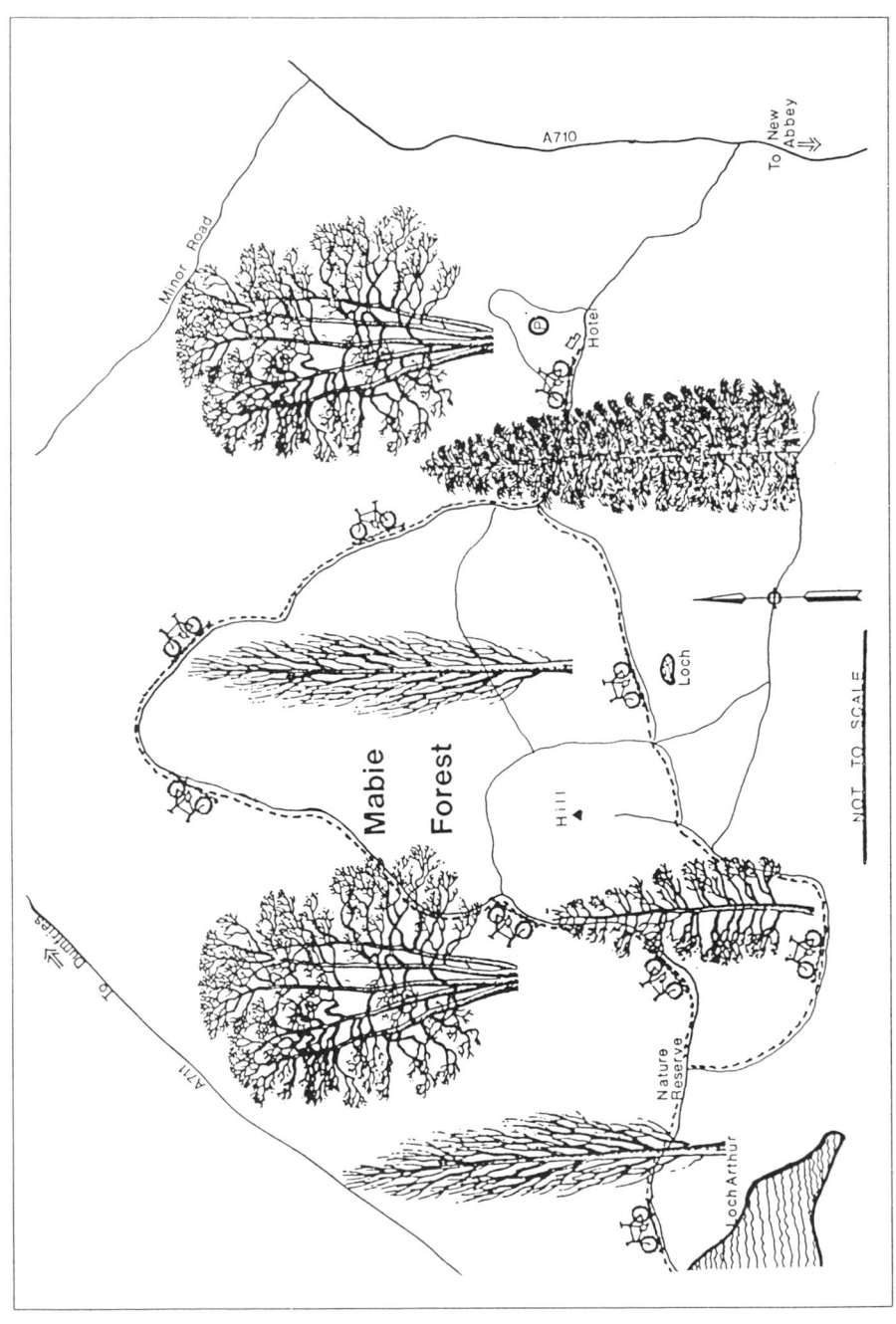

For a quick lesson in forestry, go no further than the car park. Half an hour spent here, reading the labels on the nearby trees, and you will be able to identify virtually all the trees in the forest. While at the car park, cross the small bridge over to the picnic area and visit the site of the old sawmill. Here is an interesting display demonstrating how the water-driven sawmill worked when it was introduced in 1840.

Main Access Points

The car park by the Mabie House Hotel. Leave Dumfries on the A710 and look out for the forest sign post to the right after about 4 miles (6½km).

The Routes

There are four waymarked routes at Mabie. The short Woodhead route is an easy 4 mile (6½km) introduction to the forest. Follow the green waymarks at the foot of Woodhead Hill. Two slightly more ambitious routes, waymarked Purple and Blue, both take in the Forest Nature Reserve of Lochaber Loch. These routes are 8 and 10 miles respectively, the purple and the blue

The rich undergrowth adds to the charm of Mabie

routes some public road. Finally, for the fit sporting cyclist, there is a three and a half mile hill route waymarked red, taking in Marthrown Hill, the very heart of Mabie.

Nearby

Dumfries is 4 miles (6½km) to the north of the forest and boasts five separate bridge crossings of the River Nith. One of these bridges is known as Devorgilla's.

New Abbey is a village a couple of miles (approx 3km) to the south of Mabie Forest and it is famed for the ruins of the Cistercian Abbey, which was founded in 1273 by Devorgilla. She was the mother of the Vassal King, John Balliol.

The historians have worked out that when her husband (John Balliol Senior) died, she inherited his great wealth and became one of the wealthiest women in Europe, owning not only most of Galloway but a great deal of England and Normandy as well, along with numerous estates and castles.

Devorgilla was so upset about her husband's demise that she kept his embalmed heart in a silver and ivory casket at her side until the day she died. It was buried with her in her grave in front of the Abbey's altar and it was because of this that the Abbey came to be known as "Dulce Cor" which, roughly translated from the Latin to modern English, is "Sweet Heart", hence the common expression. One of Devorgilla's parting gestures was to utilise some of her wealth to found Balliol College in Oxford, named in her husband's memory.

Ride 14

Dalbeattie Forest, Galloway Forest Park: South-West Scotland

A figure-of-eight ride in the forest.

Map: Landranger 1:50,000, Sheet number 84.

Distance : Forest 18 miles (29km).

Waymarked: Green and Purple. green for the 7 mile (11km) Moyle Hill Section which is generally easier than the purple 11 mile (17½km) Ironhash Hill Section.

Gradients: Less steep gradients on the green waymarked section.

Surface: Good forestry trail and road surfaces. Well-drained and solid.

Future proposals: Forestry Commission policy of constant ongoing maintenance.

Other cycle routes linking: There are many more waymarked cycle trails in the Galloway Forest Park. Full details can be obtained from the information point at the nearby Mabie Forest.

Bicycle hire: Dumfries.

Shops and Refreshments: Dalbeattie, Kippford or Rockcliffe.

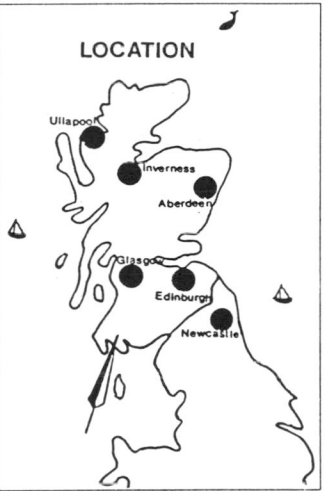

Introduction

Tucked away in the gap of land between Dalbeattie and the Rough Firth, Dalbeattie forest is one of those lovely, oft forgotten places. The A710 coastal route passing by Kippford and Rockcliffe is a popular leisure drive in its own right, though it is more usually associated with the sea than with the forest.

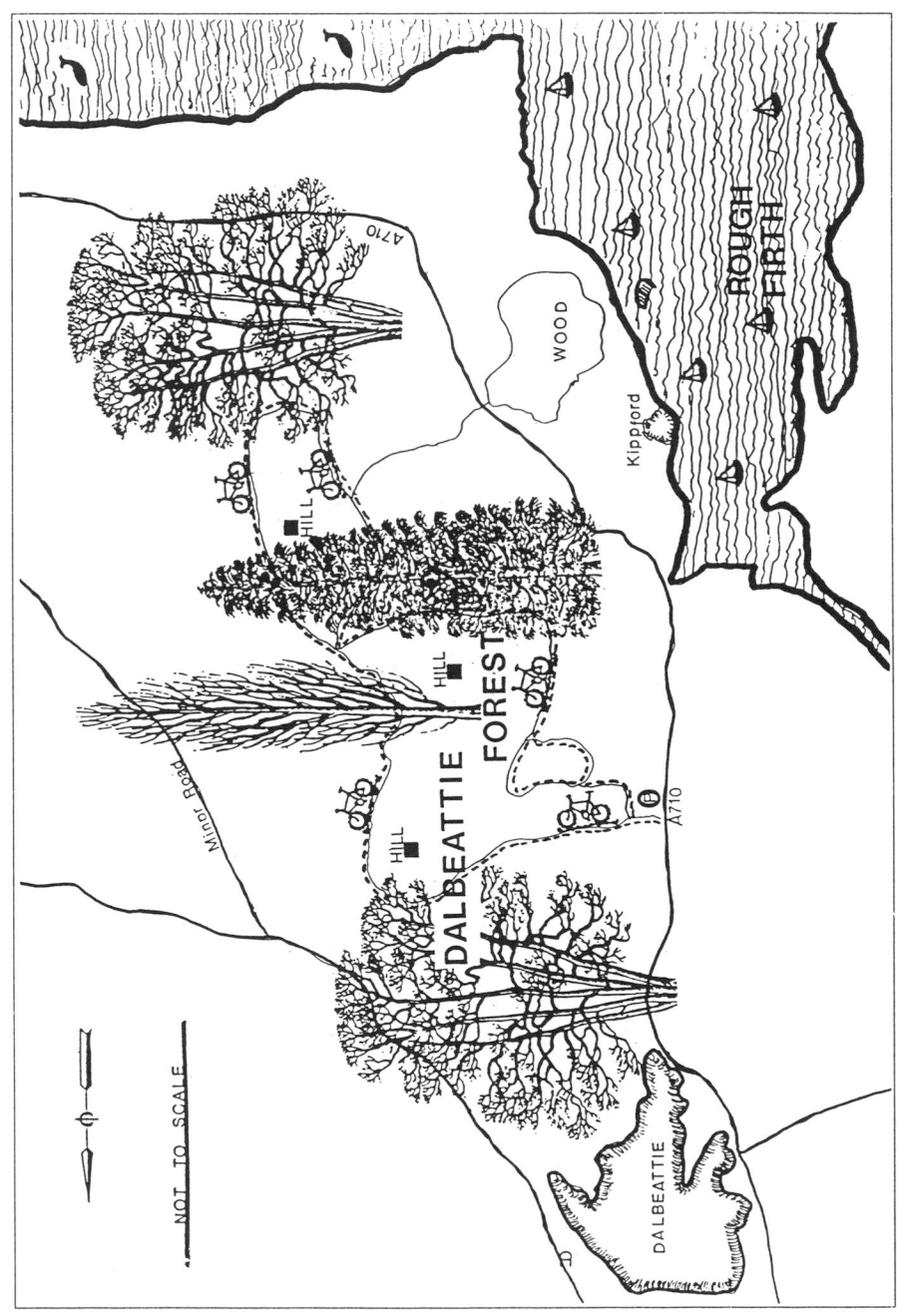

When the Forestry Commission acquired Dalbeattie forest lands in the early 1920s, the planting was sparse and a great deal of it was rough grazing pasture and rocky granite outcrops. A smattering of now-disused quarries produced the very hardy and salt resistant Dalbeattie Granite, which was a favourite choice for use in harbour construction. Because the land is low lying and the soil is rich, broadleaved trees were planted and they have flourished well, only set back occasionally by inclement climatic conditions, particularly the severe gales of the seventies and eighties.

The figure of eight ride around the forest is fairly easy, particularly the first green waymarked 7 mile (11km) circle. Apart from cycling, walking and pony trekking, Dalbeattie is sometimes a venue for car rallies, so watch out for any local notices to that effect.

Main Access Points

Take the A710 south from Dalbeattie. Richorn Plantation car park is on the left-hand side. The easier of the two waymarked rides starts and finishes here. The slightly more energetic Ironhash Hill route is joined near the southern extreme of the Moyle Hill route. See how you feel when you get there?

New Beginnings

The Route

From the car park at Richorn Plantation, pick up the green waymarks into Dalbeattie Forest. These will take you in a rough half circle centred around Moyle Hill. Behind the hill you can opt to continue with the green waymarks for a very pleasant and easy ride back to Richorn Plantation. If you prefer, take up the purple waymarks which will take you around the circular route centred on Ironhash Hill, which at this point is the high ground in front of you.

If you take the purple route and complete the figure of eight, the total figure of eight distance is 18 miles (29km). The green route alone is just 7 miles (11km).

Nearby

The attractive coastal resorts of Kippford and Rockcliffe are situated just to the west of the ride with good car parks at both resorts. The Jubilee Path is a pleasant walk at high level overlooking the estuary waters of the Rough Firth and Rough Island. Both the walk and the island are National Trust property. At low tide it is possible to walk out to Rough Island across the muddy estuary of the Firth on a shingle spit which is better known as the "Rack to Rough Island". The views are magnificent.

Rockcliffe is noted for its delightfully sheltered sandy beach. Kippford is a yachting centre with a safe low water anchorage for small keeled boats.

Ride 15

Raider's Road, Glen Trool Forest Park: South-West Scotland

A loch-side route and a ride through a beautiful mature forest.

Maps: Landranger 1:50,000, Sheet numbers 77, 83 and 84.

Distances (Approx): Raiders Road one-way: 10 miles (16km); Clatteringshaws loch-side route: 5 miles (8km); The circuit route, (returning through New Galloway): 28 miles (45km).

Waymarked: The ride is clearly marked.

Gradients: What goes up must come down but nothing too daunting. Enjoy the views.

Surface: Good well-drained forest vehicular toll road.

Future proposals: Forestry Commission's policy of constant maintenance and improvement.

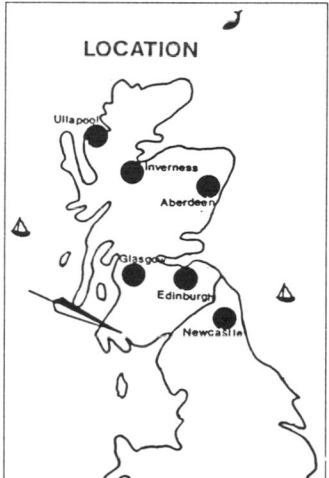

Other cycle routes linking: Try making a circular route by taking the forest drive from Clatteringshaws Forest Wildlife Centre, south and then returning via the A762 north, alongside the very beautiful Loch Ken, to New Galloway and then the A712 west to return to the visitor centre.

Bicycle hire: New Galloway.

Shops and Refreshments: At Clatteringshaws Forest Wildlife Centre. Also at New Galloway.

Introduction

The Raiders' Road Forest Drive extends for over 10 miles (16km) from the A712 at the Clatteringshaws Forest Wildlife Centre. This is situated 6 miles (9½km) west of New Galloway. The southern end of the Raiders Road is on the A762, 5 miles (8km) to the south of New Galloway. A toll road for cars

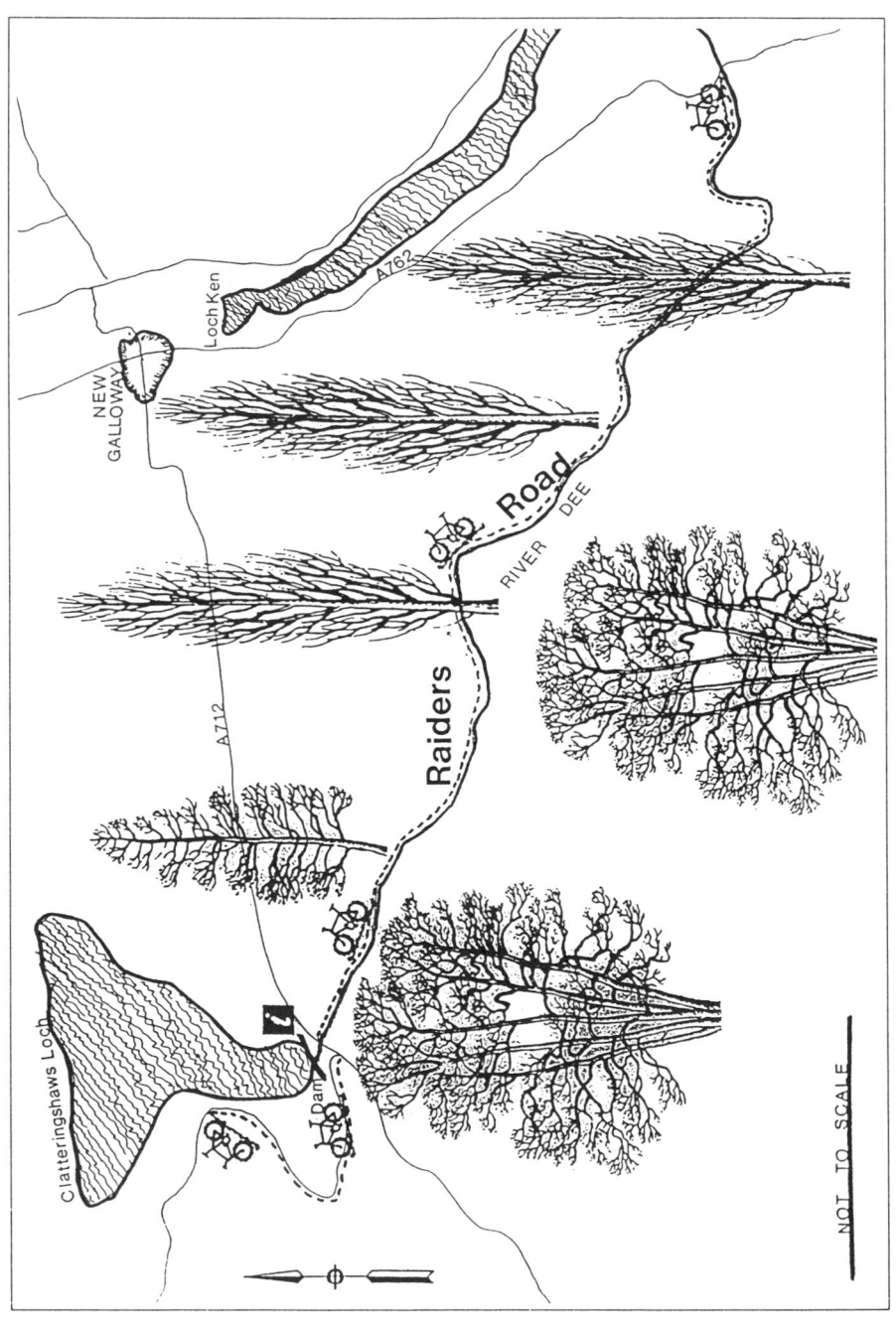

and a free through route for bicycles, Raiders' Road Forest Drive is not heavily used by motor traffic. Even during peak months, those cars that are using the route normally travel at a sedate and safe pace, which is a speed that I would recommend to all cyclists wishing to make the best of the magnificence of these surroundings.

Heading in the other direction from Clatteringshaws Forest Wildlife Centre is the waymarked route around the beautiful Clatteringshaws Loch. This is best treated as a return route, following the Loch to the point where the trail turns away from the Loch to head east.

Clatteringshaws forest is situated in the southern part of the mighty 135,000 acre (55,000 hectare) Glen Trool Forest Park which is famed for its absolute profusion of woody glens, lochs and daunting peaks, dominated by the Cairnsmore of Fleet at 2331 feet (680 metres). Also ever present is the rugged Merrick which, at 2764 feet (843 metres), is the highest point of the "Awful Hand" range and the highest point in the southern Scottish mainland. It was from these very peaks that Robert the Bruce and his men initiated the fight for the independence of the Scots by hurling rocks at English soldiers, who cowered in retreat at this unusual onslaught.

Glen Trool Forest Park comprises four forests. The other three are Carrick, Glentrool and Kirroughtree. There are very many waymarked routes throughout the Forest Park and further information can be obtained from any one of the visitor centres at either Glen Trool, Kirroughtree or Clatteringshaw. The Clatteringshaw Forest Wildlife Centre is well worth a visit, offering food, drink and general information as well as an excellent and highly informative presentation.

Main Access Points
Join the Raiders' Road Forest Drive and the Clatteringshaws loch-side ride at the Clatteringshaws Forest Wildlife Centre.

The Route
The Clatteringshaws loch-side route is accessed by leaving the Wildlife Centre to the east and turning right onto the loch-side path just beyond the dam. There is a waymarked return route but it does involve the use of potentially busy roads, so you may treat the loch-side route as a return trip.

The Raiders' Road Forest Drive can be treated either as a linear return route or, for those willing to accept a bit of public "A" road riding, the Raiders' can be one side of a triangular route, incorporating a scenic trip alongside Loch Ken on the A762 and a visit to New Galloway.

Start at the Clatteringshaws Forest Wildlife Centre and head off in a south-easterly direction along the Raiders' Road. The trail will wind through the forest keeping the busy waters of the River Dee (or "Black Waters of Dee") on your right. Just after passing Stroan Loch, the trail turns north and just over a mile later, you will emerge onto the A762. Either retrace the route, or continue north along the A762, turning left in New Galloway to return to the Wildlife centre.

For the Clatteringshaws Loch section, turn right out of the wildlife centre and turn right again along the loch-side road after a few hundred yards. Once you have ridden to the end of the Loch, where the road backs off to the left, retrace your steps to the wildlife centre.

Nearby

The whole of this part of Scotland is outstanding for its natural beauty and rugged landscapes. There are very many famous tourist attractions and a visit to a tourist information centre will furnish you with plenty of good ideas. Don't forget all the other waymarked forest rides.

Loch Ken

Ride 16

Barr to Loch Doon, through Carrick Forest: South-West Scotland

A magnificent through ride on easy forestry roads passing five lochs.

Maps: Landranger 1:50,000, Sheet numbers 76 and 77.

Distance: 19 miles (30½km).

Waymarked: Yes.

Gradients: There are ups and there are downs, but nothing too horrific.

Surface: The forest roads are solid, good enough for the narrow tyres of touring bicycles and are generally well-drained.

Future proposals: The Forestry Commission has a policy of constant maintenance and is keen to promote leisure activities.

Other cycle routes linking: There are plenty of forestry roads in the area which are available for cycling. There are information centres at Stinchar Bridge and at Pinvalley near Balloch Burn.

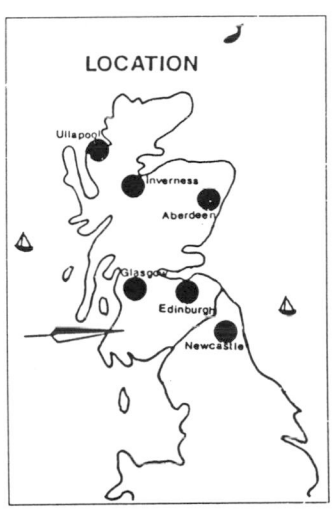

Bicycle hire: Ayr.

Shops and Refreshments: There is a very welcoming inn at Barr. Otherwise, you are by yourself.

Introduction

The gross area of Carrick Forest is nearly 47,000 acres. It spans over 8 miles (13km) on a north-south axis and over twelve miles (19½km) on an east-west axis. Over half the area is planted with trees and plans exist to plant most of

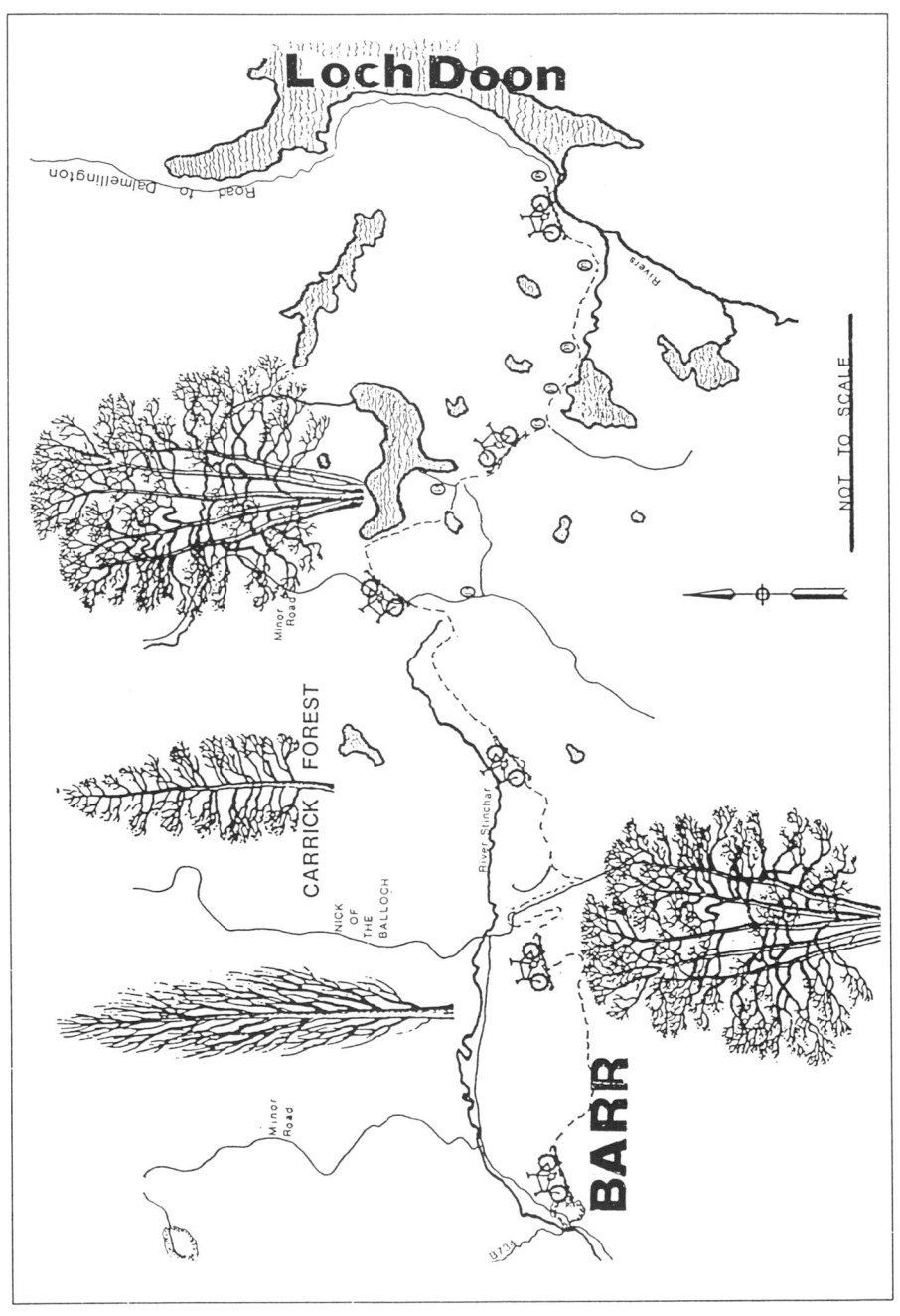

the remaining acres in the foreseeable future. At any given time the landscaping and tree felling schedules are planned in detail for a period thirty years into the future. Included as a major consideration within these plans are ongoing improvement and creation of leisure associated facilities.

The Forestry Commission and the forest industry are important in local employment terms. The forest park also creates a vast amount of timber processing work for the big mills at Irvine, Troon, Dalmellington and Dumfries. The Forestry Commission has a policy of welcoming visitors into the forest, thus creating a good tourist trade in the area.

The ride from Loch Doon to Barr is truly beautiful and is exceptional in its relative ease and accessibility. Take your time and enjoy the experience, linger when you spot a particularly fine view there are plenty to see. Try to identify some of the amazing range of wildlife and plant species.

Doon Castle (photo: courtesy of Scottish Borders Tourist Board)

Main Access Points

If you are not starting at Barr or at Loch Doon, two good access points are found where the minor public road crosses the route at Stinchar Bridge, or on the Nick o' the Balloch at Pinvalley. There are good car parks and information at both these points.

The Route

Starting at Dalmellington, follow the A713 one mile south and then take the minor public road which clings to the western shore of Loch Doon. Follow the sign-posts for the cycle route near the car park which is situated just before the southern end of the loch and follow the waymarked route approximately 19 miles (30½km) into Barr.

On route you will pass the small Loch Gower followed by the larger Loch Riecawr, both to the south. Again on the left, after a while, you will pass the small Loch Skelloch and the much larger Loch Bradan on the right. The waymarks and signs will lead you between Eldrick Hill and Black Hill, through the Balloch plantation and over the minor road which runs north to Tairlow and on via the forest road known as Aqueduct Road. For a short distance you will join the minor public road known as Nick o' the Balloch before completing the final leg into Barr around Balloch Burn and Pinmullan Burn.

Such is the variety on offer, that you could cycle this route every day for a year and still be guaranteed a new surprise or a different view. This ride is a fantastic experience, enjoy it!

Nearby

The whole area enjoys tremendous scenic beauty. You could easily lose yourself for a week just exploring the various lochs, valleys and hills throughout the forest. In many places along the route, there are good picnic spots mostly having brilliant views and a few simple facilities. Loch Bradan is regularly stocked with fish and fishing permits can be obtained on a weekly or daily basis.

Carrick Forest is just a small part of the Galloway Forest Park most of which extends to the south of here. There is an excellent visitor centre at Glen Trool.

Ride 17
Peebles to Peel Bridge: Tweed Valley

A lovely riverside ride along the Tweed Valley from Peebles

Map: Landranger 1:50,000, Sheet number 73.

Distance: One-way trip: 22 miles (35½km); Return trip : 44 miles (71km).

Waymarked: "The Tweed Cycle Way".

Gradients: Nothing to worry about.

Surface: Tarmac.

Future proposals: N/A.

Other cycle routes linking: The Tweed Cycleway.

Bicycle hire: Edinburgh.

Shops and Refreshments: Peebles and Traquair. There are a couple of pubs near the route but to be sure, take your own sustenance.

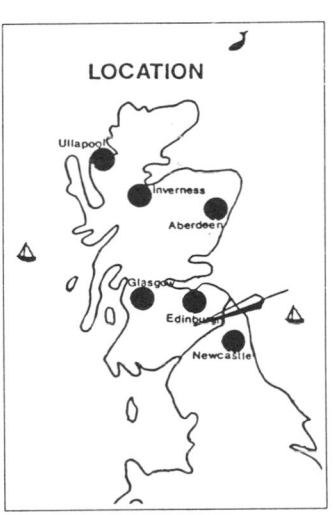

Warning: Unlike most of the rides in this guide, this route is entirely dependent on minor public roads. The traffic level is normally very light but beware.

Introduction

This very pleasant riverside ride follows the Tweed Valley via minor roads to Peel, near Melrose. Here you can turn back or, if you are brave, follow the main road to Galashiels and Melrose. The ride follows one of the most traffic-free sections of the Tweed Cycleway. Along the way are the two major Forests, Cardrona and Elibank & Traquair and just beyond Peel Bridge is Yair Hill Forest. These three forests combine with Glentress Forest, which is just east of Peebles on the far side of the Tweed, to make up the heart of the Tweed Valley Forest Group.

There are great walks in all of these forests as well as many miles of excellent waymarked cycle trails. The Tweed rises in the southern Uplands of Scotland, only a mile from another of Scotland's great rivers, the Clyde. The two

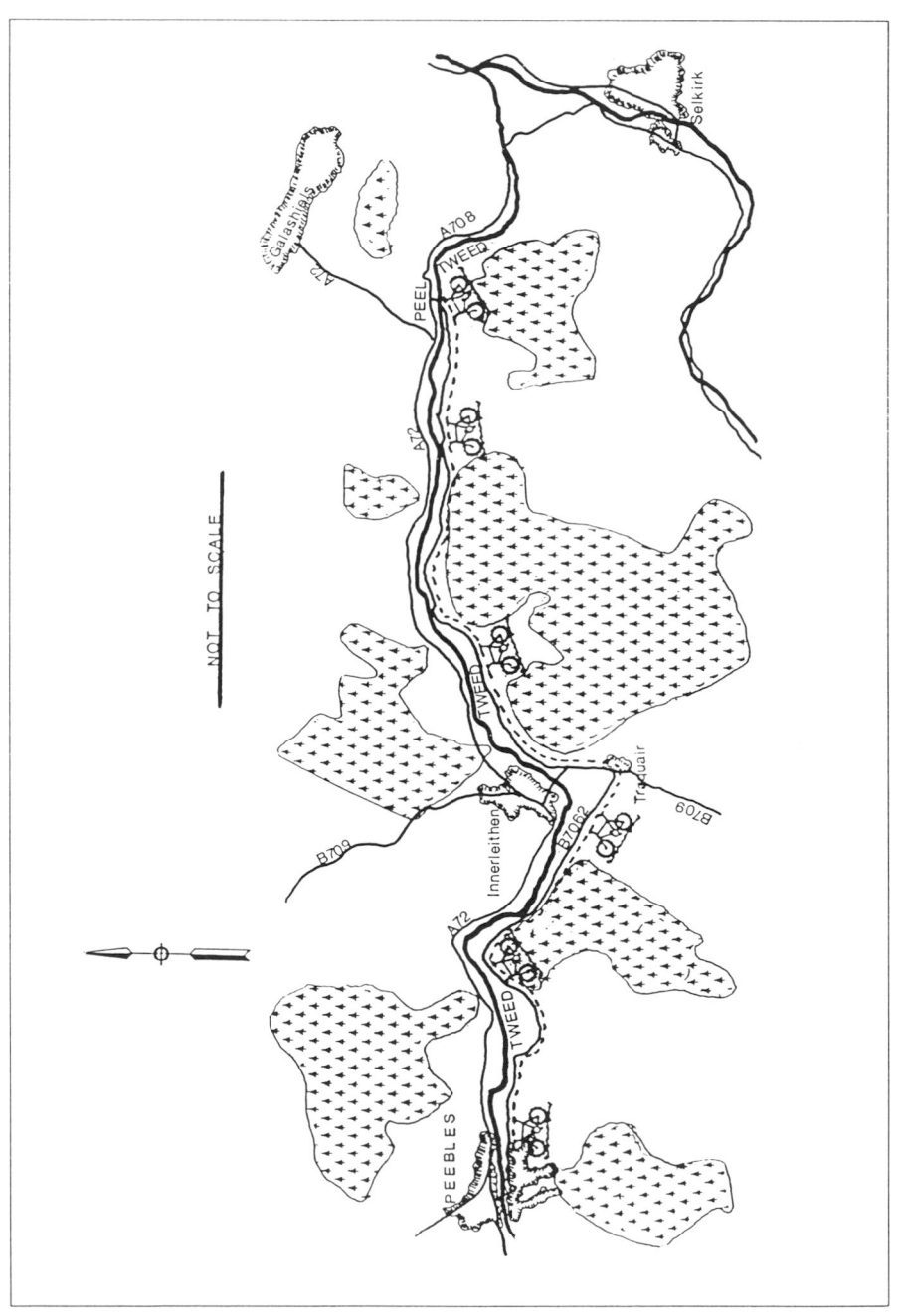

great rivers run a virtually parallel course, before finally deciding on their individual destinies.

This is a relaxing, easy ride along tarmac surfaced minor roads and offers some delightful views of the Tweed and the surrounding rolling hills. Traquair House is well worth a visit if it is open. The little windows and the tiny turrets are delightful architectural details and the grounds are quite beautiful in the autumn. It is claimed that no less than twenty-seven English or Scottish monarchs have stayed in Traquair House, including Bonnie Prince Charles.

Main Access Points

The route begins at Peebles. Cross the bridge out of the town onto the south side of the Tweed and follow the B7062 towards Traquair.

The Route

From the centre of Peebles, cross the Tweed and head out to the west on the B7062. The road bends and twists along, passing the double gatehouses of Traquair House and the Cardrona Forest, to the war memorial at Traquair.

On the way to Peebles? (photo: courtesy of Scottish Borders Tourist Board)

Turn left here onto the B709 and follow the road around until you are faced with a very minor road on a left-hand bend. Carry straight on along the minor road. The Tweed is below you on your left.

Carry on past the Elibank and Traquair Forest to Peel.

If you do decide to brave your way across the main road to Galashiels and Melrose, two interesting towns, turn right at Peel Bridge and follow the A707 to Yair. Just before Yair Bridge, turn left onto the B7060 and then turn left onto minor roads twice again. This road will take you into Galashiels.

Nearby

Peebles is a lovely country town famed for tweeds, knitwear and salmon fishing. The Bridge dates back to the 15th century. Two famous brothers who were born in the town were William Chambers (1800-1883) and Robert Chambers (1802-1871). They were the publishers of the first Chambers Dictionaries and Encyclopedias.

Ride 18

Longniddry Cycle Way and Musselburgh Link Route: Edinburgh Area

A ride along a delightful railway path to a coastal ride on a shared use footpath. A short road link.

Map: Landranger 1:50,000, Sheet number 66.

Distance: 16 miles (26km).

Waymarked: Yes.

Gradients: Minimal. Easy going.

Surface: Consolidated Stone.

Future proposals: Constant Maintenance.

Other cycle routes linking: N/A.

Bicycle hire: Edinburgh.

Shops and Refreshments: Longniddry, Haddington and Musselburgh.

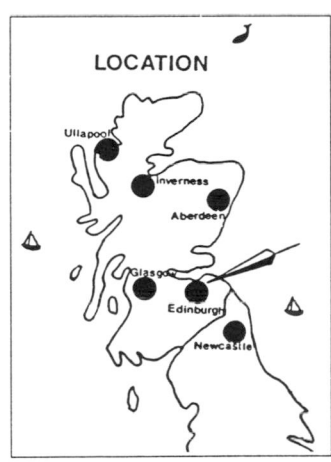

Introduction

The Longniddry cycle path follows the disused trackway of the Longniddry to Haddington branch railway and has been a popular recreational route since it was revamped in 1986/87 by East Lothian District Council. The railway was originally opened in 1846 by the old North British Railway Company. It was generally quite successful in its earlier years, but business and use declined steadily until it was eventually closed by British Railways in 1968.

The 7km cycle way is ideal for a quick thrash, up and down, to exercise and loosen up tired and under-used muscles or for a whole day's peaceful

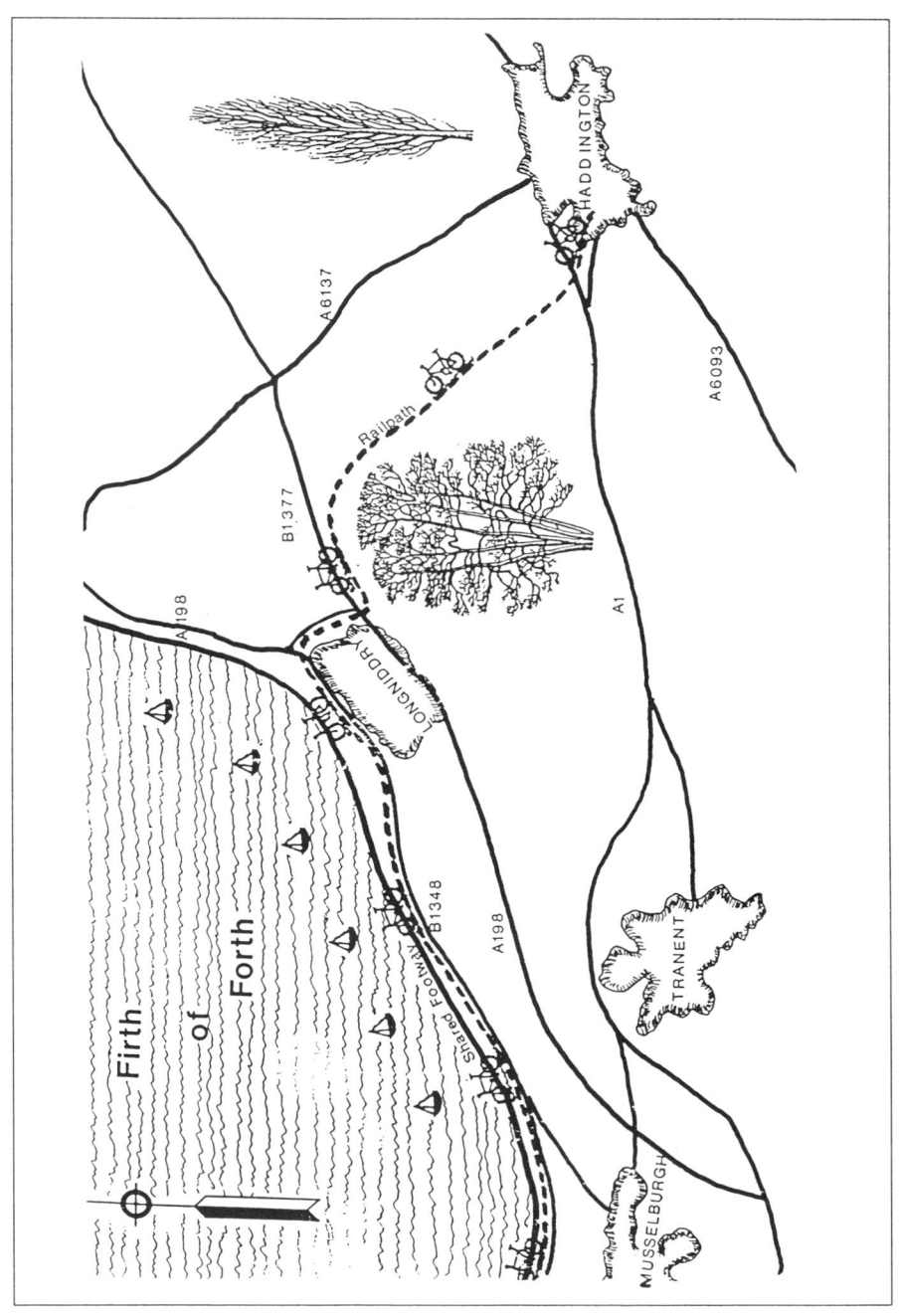

enjoyment with a picnic. The surface is first class for cycling and the gradients are slight. The route is entirely off-road and the link to Musselburgh is along a shared use seaside footpath and is a delightful ride in its own right.

Haddington is a gracious and elegant old town. The streets are generously wide and the buildings enjoy classic proportions. The town was laid out in the 12th century in a triangular pattern. The lines of High Street, Market Street and Hardgate still mark the original town boundaries. The 15th century St Mary's Church is known as the "Lamp of Lothian" because of a lamp that hung in its tower for years before its restoration.

Main Access Points
Alderston Road, Haddington.

Cottyburn Picnic Site, Setonhill.

Longniddry Station. (B1377)

Musselburgh Harbour. (Head east)

The Route
Starting at the cycle path in Alderston Road, Haddington, it is simply a matter of cycling until you can cycle no more. At this point you will find

yourself at Longniddry Station off the B1377, or thereabouts. Spend some time in Longniddry. 500 years of coal mining came to an end in the 1920s when the coal ran out. Now Longniddry flourishes as a dormitory of Edinburgh. Follow the A198 down to the rocky shoreline at Gosford Sands, follow the road to the west keeping the sea on your right and you will soon join a shared use footpath that will lead you to the harbour at Musselburgh. Turn around and retrace your route.

Along the railway path route it is possible sometimes to see roe deer in adjoining fields. The embankments have been left largely to their own devies and flourish with wild flowers and wildlife.

Nearby

Golf, golf, golf. The links run for miles and miles along this coast, the turf perfectly matched to the demands of the game. One of the more famous golf links is known as Muirfield and the British Open has been regularly played here. A couple of miles to the east of Longniddry are the picturesque remains of the 16th century Red House Castle. Two miles to the north of Haddington is Athelstaneford. Here is a plaque marking the spot where the St Andrew's Cross appeared in the sky before the Picts and Scots battled with the Northumbrian Army which was led by the Saxon King, Athlestan. Just to the east of Longniddry is the old port of Aberlady, which is no longer any use to shipping, having silted up in the 19th century.

Ride 19

Pencaitland Railway Path (West Saltoun to Crossgatehall): Edinburgh Area

A ride following track beds of two railway paths on the outskirts of Edinburgh.

Map: Landranger 1:50,000, Sheet number 66.

Distances: West Saltoun to Whitecraig: 7½ miles (12km); Return ride: 15 miles (24km).

Waymarked: Yes.

Gradients: Negligible.

Surface: Solid, well-drained. Easy going.

Future proposals: Ongoing maintenance.

Other cycle routes linking: Edinburgh commuter network.

Bicycle hire: Edinburgh.

Shops and Refreshments: At built up areas along the route.

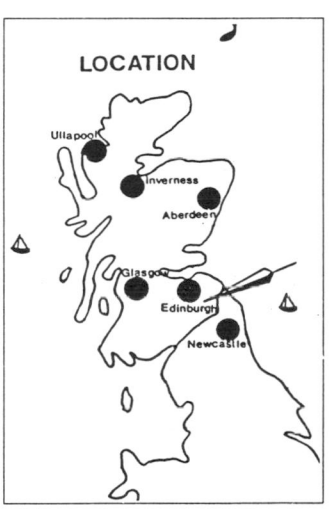

Introduction

The Pencaitland Railway Path has been established as a recreational route since its closure as a railway. The cycle path follows the track bed of two railways which had subsequently merged to become one. The biggest, the North British Railway Company, built the western part of the line and bought out the company that built the eastern section, the Gifford and Garrard Light Railway Company.

There is a large distillery at Glenkinchie, just up the Kinvhie Burn from the

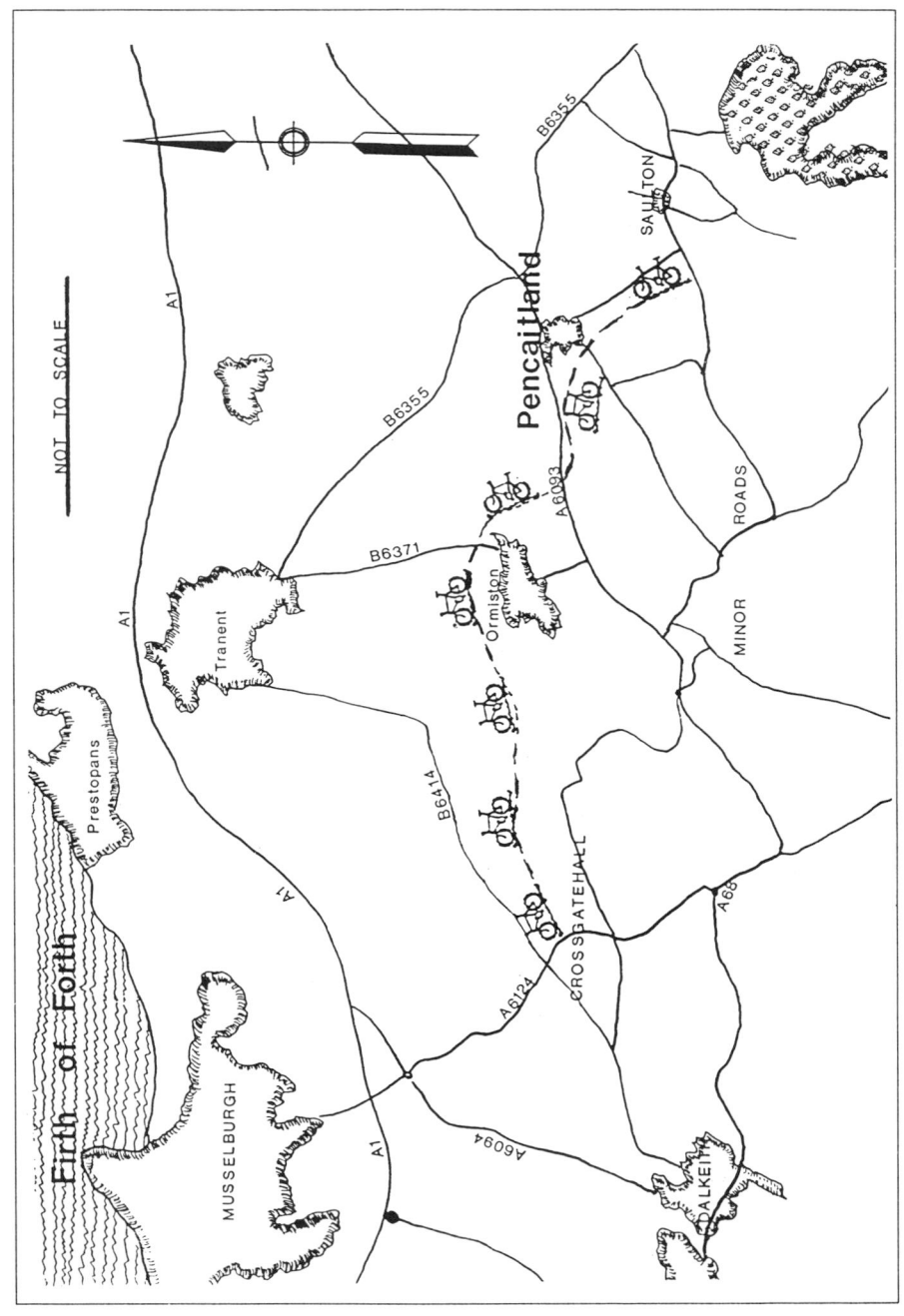

Leaving Ormiston Station

path, and it is certain that they used the services of the line. However, the main purpose of the railway was to serve the coal mines that were once active all along the route. In simple terms, the mining activities began in the 19th century, closed as uneconomical in the 1930s, reopened in the 1950s and closed as uneconomical in the 1960s.

The fortunes of the railway closely followed the fortunes of the mines and now there is little evidence of this heavily based industrial past. An expert eye will recognise the familiar shape of the slag heaps but these are now part of the landscape, maturing and returning to the gentle handling of mother nature. The Railway Path now enjoys all the characteristics of a rural route, the steep sides of the embankments and cuttings offering superb havens for all types of wild plants, birds and little creatures.

Main Access Points
West Saltoun (off B6355); west of Pencaitland (A6093); Ormiston (B6371); Crossgatehall (A6124); Whitecraig (A6094)

The Route

After joining the railway path at West Saltoun, opposite the old station, you may become aware of the unmistakable odours emanating from the Glenkinchie Distillery. This is soon left behind as the path is swallowed into deep cuttings and on into shady woods. The rural feel of the railway is strong at this point and it is an excellent place to picnic. Interpretative information boards tell of the passing of the mines from time to time along the route, noticeably more regularly as the path nears the outskirts of Edinburgh. The railway crosses the River Tyne beyond West Pencaitland. The eagle-eyed will spot the change of construction and differences of architectural finishes at the join of the old narrow gauge and standard gauge lines near Ormiston.

Beyond here the industrial past of the line becomes more apparent, but it is here that the path is at its most beautiful in the summer, with rich banks of colourful wild flowers and thickets of flowering summer fruit. The going is good for cycling all along the route.

Nearby

The surrounding countryside is not quite "Scottish" in character, more resembling the lush rolling green patchworks that are normally associated with the rich soils of southern England. If you are visiting the area, make sure that you take time to have a really good look at Edinburgh. Its guide books will tell a full story but it is a very interesting and beautiful city.

Ride 20

Penicuik to Sheriffhall or Musselburgh: Edinburgh Area

An enjoyable 12½ mile (20km) Railway Path and Cycle Route from Penicuik, a town south of Edinburgh.

Map: Landranger 1:50,000, Sheet number 66.

Distances: To Sheriffhall: 9½ miles (15km); To Musselburgh: 12½ miles (20km); Return fom Sheriffhall: 19 miles (30km).

Waymarked: Yes, good signposting.

Gradients: None worth considering.

Surface: All solid and well-drained.

Future proposals: The local participating authority have a policy of continual improvement, as funds and access allow.

Other cycle routes linking: At Musselburgh join the route to Longniddry or the Innocent Railway Path into the central area of Edinburgh.

LOCATION

Bicycle hire: Edinburgh.

Shops and Refreshments: There are plenty of built up areas along the route offering a good selection of shops and pubs near The Route.

Warning: Carry a torch for the tunnel sections if you do not have lights.

Introduction

This ride is largely based on the abandoned route and the old track bed of the Edinburgh to Peebles railway line which closed for business in 1969. It is quite rural in feel but retains a good many interesting historic features. There are a couple of tunnels, interesting bridges, aqueducts and wooded

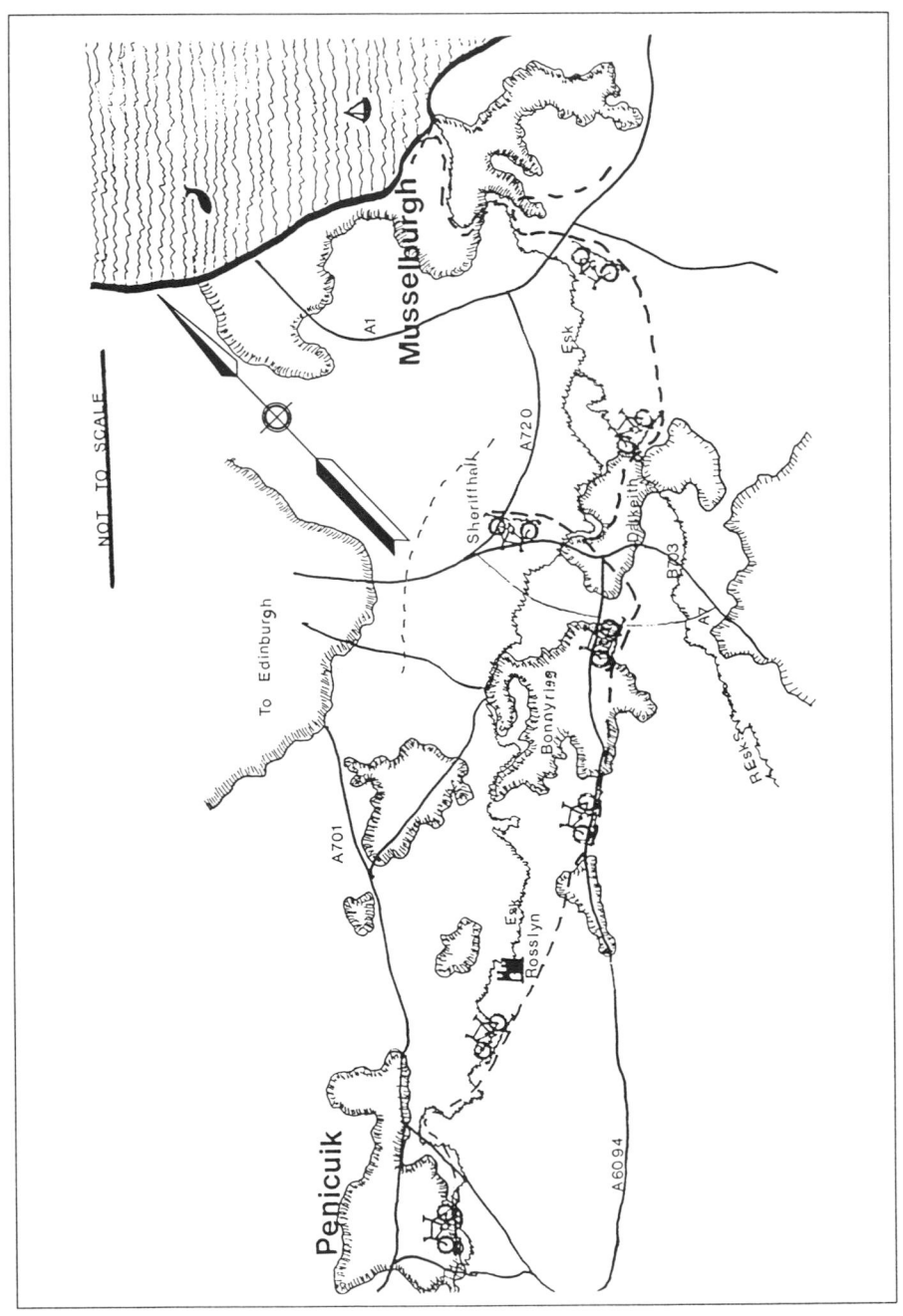

cuttings. It is generally an excellent environment for wildlife and anybody interested in the natural vegetation of railway cuttings can have a ball here.

This is a popular route with cyclists, an enjoyable and interesting ride. The option to go to Musselburgh will give you the chance to join the route of the Innocent Railway Path which will take you into the central Edinburgh area.

There are many interesting points along the route including a castle, two tunnels, two aqueducts and the site of an old gunpowder factory.

Main Access Points

Valleyfield and Eskmill Road, Penicuik; Auchendinny, south of Dalmore Mill (B7026); Lea Farm, Rosslyn; B7003 Rosewell; north of Hawthornden Cemetery; Dundas Street, Bonnyrigg (B704); Cemetery Road, Dalkeith. (By the water tower).

The Route

Starting in Penicuik at the Valleyfield and Eskmill Road access point, the track initially passes a sewage works. Do not worry, it is the only one on the

Penicuik

route. You will soon come to Auchendinny Station, and after a pretty iron bridge and a tunnel, to Dalmore Paper Mill. This is the last paper mill in an area that was famed for the product. The early mills in the area used the water power from the Esk.

There is another tunnel and a viaduct before you pass Rosslyn Glen Country Park. There was a gunpowder mill here until 1953 which first supplied munitions for the Napoleonic Wars and last supplied them for the second World War. When the gunpowder mill was manufacturing, the railway was covered with a spark proof corrugated tin tunnel!

After Rosslyn Castle Station the route continues through woodland to Bonnyrigg Station and Eskbank. Signs will guide you to Cemetery Road and here you have a choice.

To continue on to Musselburgh, follow the signed route through Dalkeith. The route after Dalkeith is on a disused railway line, a riverside track and a short road section. To continue to Sheriffhall, rejoin the railway line at Cemetery Road by the old water tower and cross the beautiful Dalkeith Viaduct, which crosses 60 feet over the River Esk in a grand sweeping single span.

Nearby

Penicuik is the home of Edinburgh Crystal Glassware. The visitor centre is situated just off the A701 and there are regular guided tours around the manufacturing plant. Bulls and young children are discouraged from the tours.

Rosslyn Castle is located just off the route. The Castle is private but the grounds are a pleasant place to relax for a while.

Ride 21

Balerno to Slateford Railway Path along the banks of the Water of Leith: Edinburgh Area

A very pleasant 10 mile return ride on a well-surfaced Railway Path alongside the Water of Leith.

Map: Landranger 1:50,000, Sheet number 66.

Distance: Total return trip, 10 miles (16km).

Waymarked: Yes, but some of the signs are difficult to see.

Gradients: Negligible.

Surface: Rolled stone and ash. Solid and well-drained.

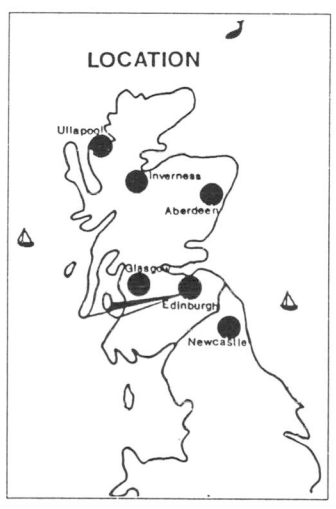

LOCATION

Future proposals: Plans are in hand to open up the whole route from Balerno to Leith, but these will take a bit of time to come to fruition. If you do not mind a bit of on road riding, The Water of Leith can be followed all of the way to Leith. The route is a little bit complicated at the present time. Broadly there are four other prepared off-road sections which are not presently interconnected. These are as follows: Slateford to Roseburn, Roseburn to Stockbridge, Stockbridge to Bonnington, Bonnington to Leith. The links between these routes are all on fairly quiet back roads but the link across Slateford involves mixing with heavy traffic.

Other cycle routes linking: N/A

Bicycle hire: Edinburgh.

Shops and Refreshments: The route passes through mainly residential areas. There are plenty of shops and pubs.

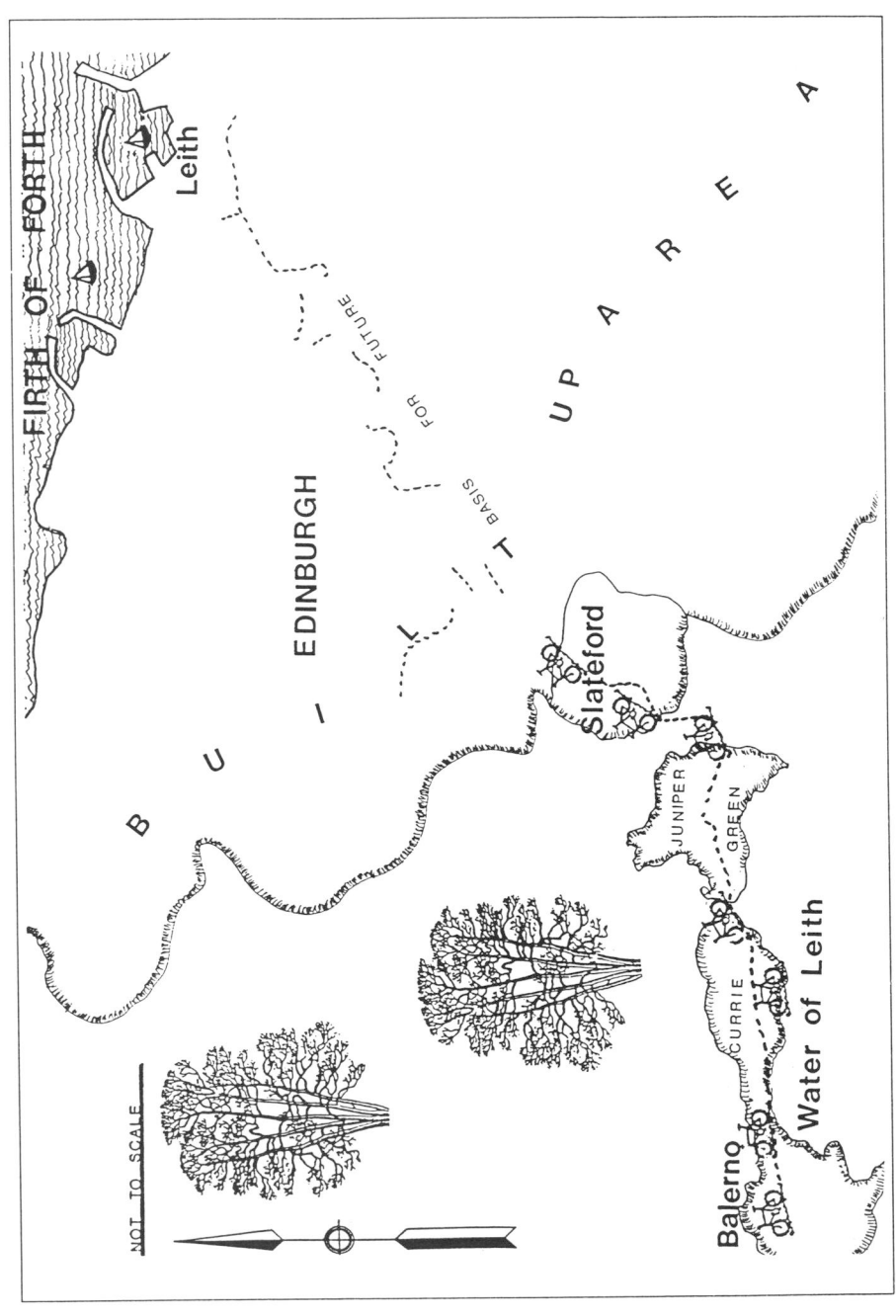

Introduction

The Water of Leith, sometimes described as Edinburgh's own trout stream, rises in the heather covered Pentland Hills above East Colzium. It firstly serves one of Edinburgh's major compensation reservoirs, Harperrig, before flowing on, replenished from many brooks and streams, to the outskirts of Edinburgh amongst the desirable commuter properties at Balerno. It is here that our ride starts.

The Water of Leith flows on through Currie and Juniper Green to Slateford where our ride ends. The Water continues through the ever more industrial areas of Edinburgh before flowing out into the Firth of Forth at Leith. A great deal of Edinburgh's early industry was started by utilising the power from the Water of Leith in a long line of water mills.

There was a time before this industry when the Water of Leith provided sparkling clean and clear water to central Edinburgh. An Act of Scottish Parliament in the year 1617 defined the standard pint jug measurement as "Three pounds seven ouncches troye of clean rynand water from the Water of Leith"

Inevitably and sadly, the industrial and residential growth that tended to follow the Water of Leith upstream from Edinburgh, provided sufficient pollution to poison the river until it was little more than an open sewer. It is only in recent years that this trend has been reversed and it is cause for celebration that the Water can now maintain a healthy stock of trout.

Main Access Points
Bridge Road, Balerno; Kirkgate, Currie; Baberton Loan, Juniper Green; Gilespie Road, Colinton (B701); Lanark Road, Kingsknowe (A70); Union Canal Towpath, Slateford.

Note: The access points are marked but some of the signs are difficult to see or have been the victims of vandalism.

The Route
The ride follows the disused track bed of the Balerno Branch Railway. After joining the railway path at Balerno (through a gap in the wall) the path leads down alongside the Water of Leith to the villages of Currie and Juniper Green. Balerno, Currie and Juniper Green have all been declared conservation areas by the local planning authorities.

After Juniper Green the route passes by Colinton, where the remains of Colinton Castle now form part of the grounds of Merchiston Castle School, and finally on to Slateford where it meets the Union Canal. From this point, retrace your route to Balerno.

Nearby
Visit Malleny Gardens in Balerno. They offer a good shrub rose display and a pleasant woodland walk.

The Hillend Ski Slope is one of Britain's longest dry ski slopes. The only tip that comes to mind is to avoid skiing over your thumb – if you do you will probably break it as I did. Apart from being useful for skiers, the chair lift is a good way of getting up the Pentland Hills.

Ride 22

The Innocent Railway Path: Edinburgh

A city ride from Musselburgh to Holyrood Park, in central
Edinburgh. A railway path and a river path.

Map: Landranger 1:50,000, Sheet number 66.

Distance: 16 miles (26km).

Waymarked: Yes.

Gradients: Easily manageable.

Surface: Solid, well-drained.

Future proposals: Constant maintenance, possible extension.

Other cycle routes linking: Edinburgh commuter routes.

Bicycle hire: Edinburgh.

Shops and Refreshments: Plenty of places.

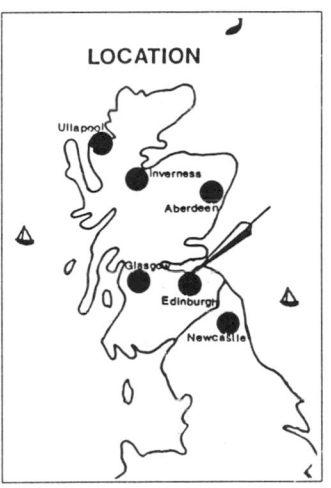

Introduction

There's a rumour in Edinburgh that the Innocent Railway is the oldest
railway in the world. This warning is offered because I can imagine the
situation that you might find yourself in, if you listen to too much local
folklore and find yourself in the company of the resident bar room historian:
"I went for a bike ride along the oldest railway in the world the other day.
The Innocent Railway, near Edinburgh."

The bar room historian interrupts. (Smirking). "That's not the oldest railway in
the world! The oldest is the Stockton and Darlington, near er.... Stockton
and... er... Darlington."

Let me stop you there before this develops into an unruly brawl.

The Innocent is not the oldest railway in the world as is popularly claimed

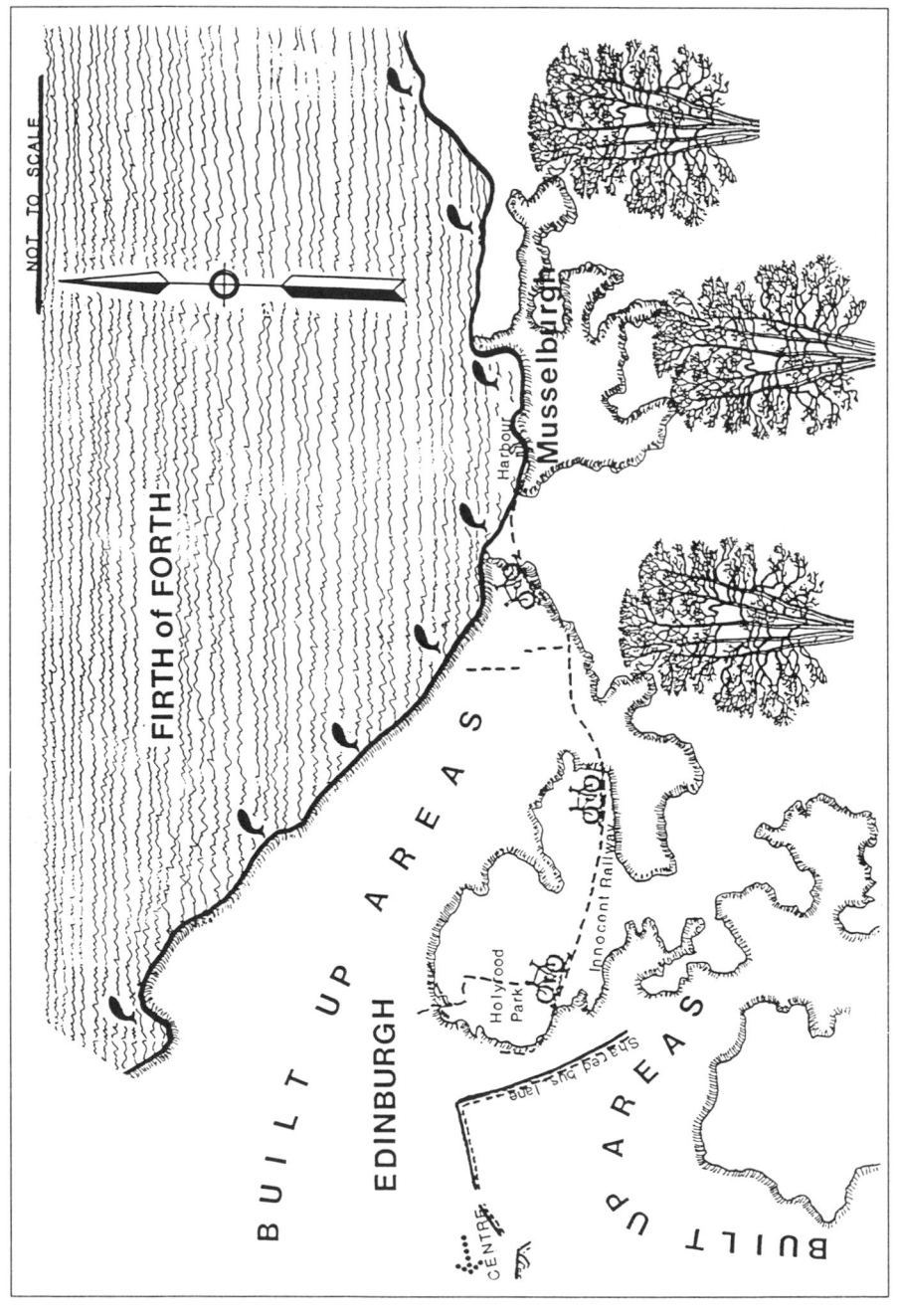

locally and nor is the Stockton and Darlington Railway, although it was amongst the first to carry Steam Trains commercially. The oldest railway in the world to carry a steam engine is generally agreed to be the Penydarren Tramway in Wales. Here the Cornishman, Trevithick, demonstrated his steam engine in 1804.

Having cleared up that point, the Innocent Railway is very very old. It is so old that it predates the introduction of Steam Engines to Scotland. If this sounds a bit like inventing Fluffy Dice before Ford Cortinas or inventing currant buns before the currant tree was propagated it is not really as daft as it initially sounds. The Innocent Railway was originally built for horse drawn trams.

The railway was opened in 1831 for the purpose of carrying the high quality coal from the mines around Dalkeith, then owned by the Duke of Buccleuch, to the furnaces and firesides of Edinburgh. Although the main motive power was originally the horse, there was a steep section at the Edinburgh end of the route that used a steam driven cable tow through the steep tunnel leading into St Leonard's Goods Yard. Now that all that is clarified, let's try the bicycle ride.

Hiding in the hedge

Main Access Points

East Parkside and by Samson's ribs in Holyrood Park; Duddingston Road West; Duddingston Row; Duddingston Park South; The Jewel.

The Route

The route leaves Holyrood Park on the old track bed of the Innocent Railway and follows this until joining the line of Niddrie Burn to Brunstane. If you look over from the path towards Duddingston Loch, you will look over the Scottish Wildlife Trust Reserve of Bawsinch.

If you look carefully in this section, you will see the remains of the original bridge over Braid burn. Further on, an interesting comparison can be made between the wildlife and vegetation near Prestonfield and Duddingston golf courses and the wildlife and vegetation in the Bingham Neighbourhood Park.

The routes into Musselburgh are signed on quiet roads.

Nearby

Holyrood Palace near the beginning of the path is one of the most important historic buildings in Britain. The history of the Palace is entwined with the oft tragic history of the Stuarts. The earliest recorded building on the site of the palace was the guest house of the nearby Abbey. It was this building that James IV extended in the 15th century to form the basis of the Palace that we see today, most of which was built for Charles II. Mary Queen of Scots lived here from 1561 to 1567. Her son, James VI of Scotland, was said to have been in Holyrood Palace when in 1603 he learnt that he had also become James I of England. Bonnie Prince Charles lived in the Palace briefly in 1745 and George IV was a visitor in 1822. The present Queen has State Apartments in the Palace.

Ride 23

The Forth Road Bridge: Edinburgh to North Queensferry

A marvellous and fascinating ride crossing the giant Forth Road Bridge, to North Queensferry in Fife.

Map: Landranger 1:50,000, Sheet number 64 and 65.

Distance: One-way, Gyle to North Queensferry: 10 miles (16km); Return trip: 20 miles (32km).

Waymarked: The route is sign posted and marked extensively with cycling symbols.

Gradients: No serious sustained gradients.

Surface: All solid and well-drained surfaces ranging from crushed stone to tarmac and concrete.

Future proposals: Linking the route to further commuter routes into Edinburgh and linking the Railway Path, just south of Kirkliston into the Almond Walkway (Cycle path).

Other cycle routes linking: River Almond Walkway just south of Kirkliston.

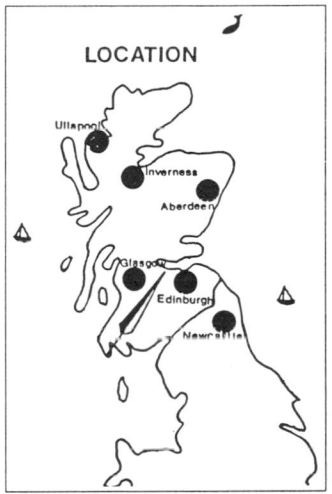

LOCATION

Bicycle hire: Edinburgh.

Shops and Refreshments: There are plenty of opportunities.

Warning: In windy conditions, the Cycle Path across the Forth Road bridge is very exposed. If you have a serious fear of heights or falling off bridges this route might test your courage. As lorries and bunches of cars pass by on the main roadway, there is a noticeable swinging sensation of the cycle path.

Introduction

The route is a great mixture of traffic-free cycling ranging from a shared use footpath on the A8(T), a recreational railway path between Newbridge and the Forth Estuary and a dedicated pedestrian and cycling path crossing the massive Forth Road Bridge.

The bridge is actually crossed on the maintenance spans, which are separate from the main road spans, and double as pedestrian and cycle paths. Do not worry if the bridge wobbles a little as you ride along, especially in windy conditions; the movement is all part of the design.

The recreational railway path from Newbridge is built on the old track bed of a railway. It passes through woods, open farmland and cuttings for a distance of nearly 4½ miles (7km). The A8(T) section utilises a safe shared pedestrian and cycle path, well away from the rushing traffic.

Main Access Points

The ride can be accessed from almost any point along its route. There are good car parking opportunities at either end, particularly in North Queensferry and in the road services here. This is a very pleasant return trip in either direction.

A private bridge for bicycles

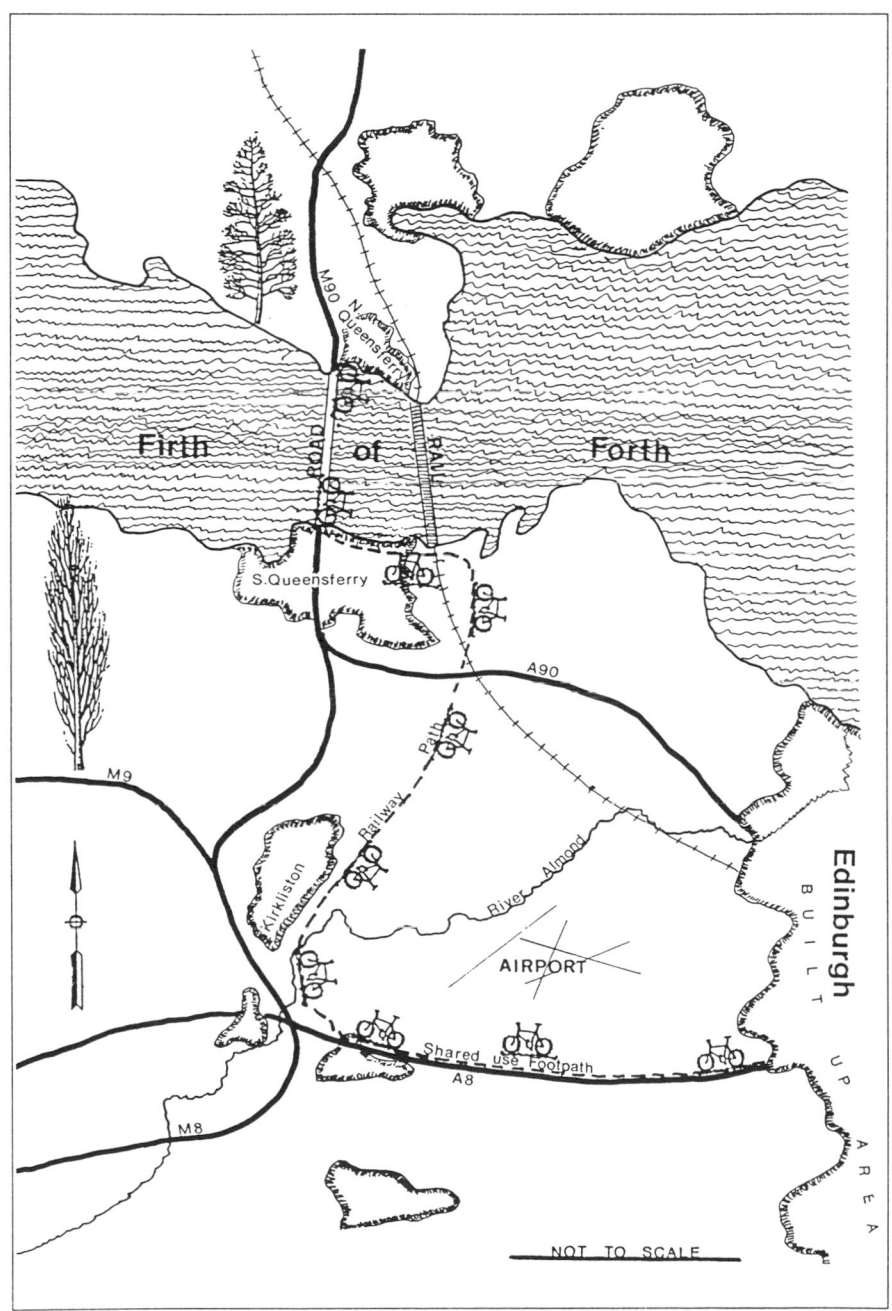

The Route

From Gyle, cycle along the A8(T) shared use footpath towards Newbridge. The Airport and the Royal Highland Show Ground are on the right. Near the A8/M9 junction in Newbridge, follow the signs for the Railway Path off to your right. This path will take you past the sewage works, across the River Almond, through the eastern edge of Kirkliston and past the eastern outskirts of Dalmeny. The great bridges across the Forth will heave into view.

Pass under a massive land span of the Forth Rail Bridge and onto the cycle path of the Forth Road Bridge at South Queensferry. At the far end of the bridge, keep to the minor public roads into North Queensferry.

Nearby

The Forth Rail Bridge was completed in 1890. Built using the joint funds of four railway companies, it has a total length of just over one mile. Built on the cantilever principle, the bridge is strong enough to take the heaviest rolling stock that has ever been introduced on the British railway system. The clear spans between the towers are 1,710 feet (156 metres) each. In construction, the cantilevers were self supporting balanced overhangs before joining for mutual support.

The Forth Road Bridge was completed in 1964. It is 1½ miles long and towers to 512 feet over the Firth of Forth. A ferry plied the river from Queensferry for 800 years before the bridge opened. The Queen in Queensferry was Queen Margaret of Scotland (1489-1541).

Ride 24

Livingston and the Almond River Valley: West Lothian

A great day out on the pathways of a new town and along a river valley.

Map: Landranger 1:50,000, Sheet number 65.

Distance: Over 25 miles (40km) of pleasant riding.

Waymarked: Name association test!

Gradients: Nothing too extreme, easiest near the river.

Surface: Concretes and tarmac. Superb mainly hard made up surfaces.

Future proposals: In addition to the continued development and extension of the cycle way network in the town, a long distance cycle route is currently being developed, to run from Glasgow to Edinburgh via Coatbridge, Bathgate and Balerno. When completed it will run through Livingston and take in the Valley of The River Almond.

Other cycle routes linking: See above.

Bicycle hire: Edinburgh.

Shops and Refreshments: Plenty.

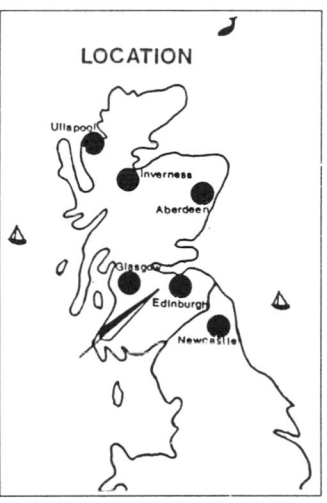

Introduction

For a great day out, cycling just for the sheer hell of it and exploring a bright and progressive town, go to Livingston. There are plenty of points of interest, not the least of which is the cycling facility itself.

The refreshing aspect of cycling in Livingston is the way that the rule book has been thrown away in order to accommodate a cycling policy into the infrastructure. At a council meeting in 1987 a question was asked in terms similar to this: "Where are our traffic-free cycling trails?" The answer was clear and unambiguous.

"We have not got any!" A commendable attack of free and clear thinking and the answer was clear. The decision was made: "Change the bye-laws and let the bikes onto the footpaths!"

Virtually overnight, Livingston was proudly claiming the best traffic-free cycling network in the country. Anywhere pedestrians could go, cyclists could join them. You can take your bicycle anywhere with the thoughtful proviso that you should not ride over footbridges for fear of getting blown off your bicycle in the strong, gusty local wind patterns. There are also conditions and recommendations appertaining to not running into pedestrians including pregnant women, old ladies and toddlers. The safety code reference about wearing cycle helmets presumably is to protect the poor cyclists from the flaying umbrellas of those old ladies who were not alert enough to jump out of your way.

Apart from its novel ideas about cycling on the footpaths, it is a prerequisite of navigation in Livingston that the cyclist is an expert in the art of name association. A few examples are the names of Walter Scott's novels eg: Ivanhoe or Durward, the names of famous Scottish scientists eg: Kelvin or Maxwell and the names of Australian towns eg: Melbourne or Fremantle. The street names are arranged in groups of these associated names and great fun can be had in trying to figure out which names belong to which groups. With whom or with what would you associate "Lizzie Brice's Roundabout"?

To quote a leaflet printed by the Lothian Regional Council..."Although cyclists are not banned from the road system of Livingston, for the majority of journeys it should not be necessary to use it. Indeed, for most journeys within the town, the segregated footpath/cycle way network is more direct and safer"...

Main Access Points

Anywhere at all in Livingston. Just get onto the footpath and off you go! Look at the nearest road name and find out which group you are in. Are you amongst social innovators such as Owen or Morris perhaps? One more helpful safety recommendation from the helpful Livingston Regional Council... "Don't make any sudden swerves or start zig-zagging"... Presumably they fear that you may fall off your bicycle!

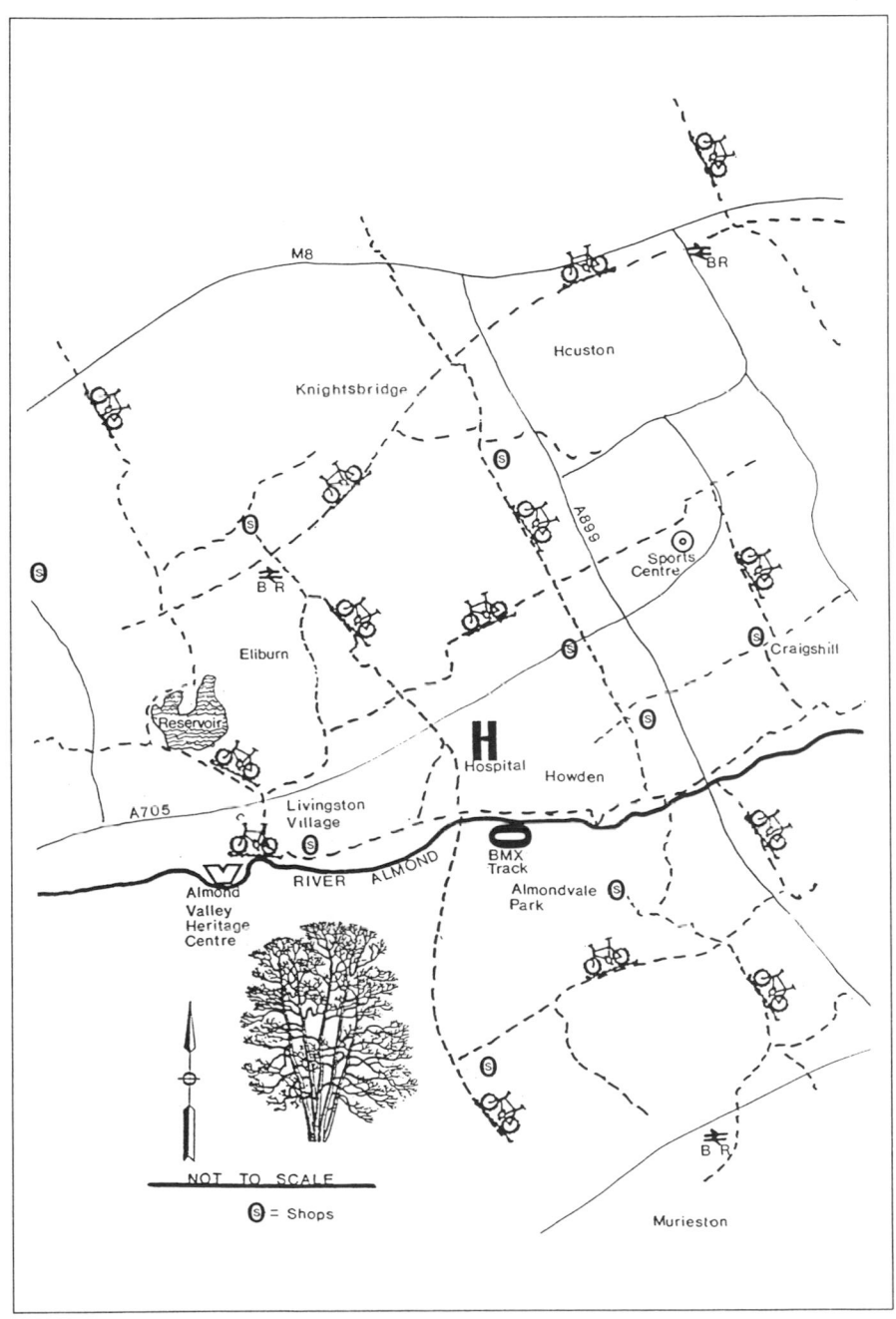

NOT TO SCALE

⑤ = Shops

The Route

There are formal bicycle routes linking the various districts of the town and "the route" rather depends on where you want to go. As a suggestion, try visiting the Almond Valley Heritage Centre near Livingston village. It's worth paying the small entry fee for this 16 acre open air museum of the agricultural and industrial past of the area. Take the 3 mile (5km) cycle path that begins at the old Livingston village. This takes you past Almondvale Park along the River Almond. Have a game of pitch and putt or carry on through Livingston and on to Mid Calder.

Livingston village

Nearby

There are plenty of good off-road cycling opportunities in the area, some of which are included in this guide. To the north of Livingston is Linlithgow and the fine palace that used to be the home of Mary Queen of Scots who was born there in 1542. To the south are the Pentland and Moorfoot Hills, areas of great rolling beauty that are well worth a visit.

Ride 25

The Airdrie to Bathgate Railway Path: West Lothian and Strathclyde

A fine railway path ride between two towns in Central Scotland.

Map: Landranger 1:50,000, Sheet numbers 64 and 65.

Distances: Return: 30 miles (48km); One-way: 15 miles (24km).

Waymarked: This is an easy route to follow. It has good waymarks and map boards.

Gradients: An ex-railway line, so very easy with hardly noticeable gradients.

Surface: Tarmac and consolidated rolled stone. The path is well-drained throughout the route.

Future proposals: This will form part of a continuous Glasgow to Edinburgh corridor which, in turn, will become a section of a whole cross Scotland route from the Clyde coast to the Firth of Forth. It is also proposed to link into the Livingston network.

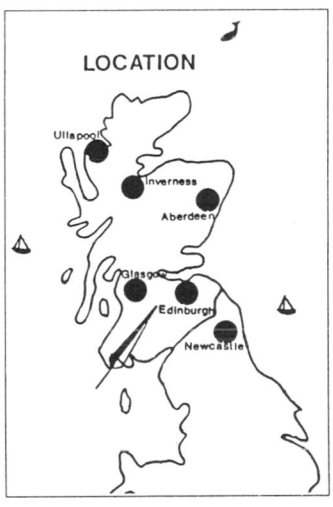

LOCATION

Other cycle routes linking: There is a sign posted route into the Livingston network and the Almond Valley Walkway.

Bicycle hire: Edinburgh.

Shops and Refreshments: Plenty of opportunities along the route.

Introduction

The Airdrie to Bathgate Railway Path follows part of the route and track bed of the disused Northern British Railway Company's line, which once formed one of the major transport links between the great cities of Glasgow and Edinburgh. The line was abandoned after nationalisation and has only recently been updated to provide this fine, public recreational pathway. In the longer term, the rail path will form part of the ambitious Cross-Scotland

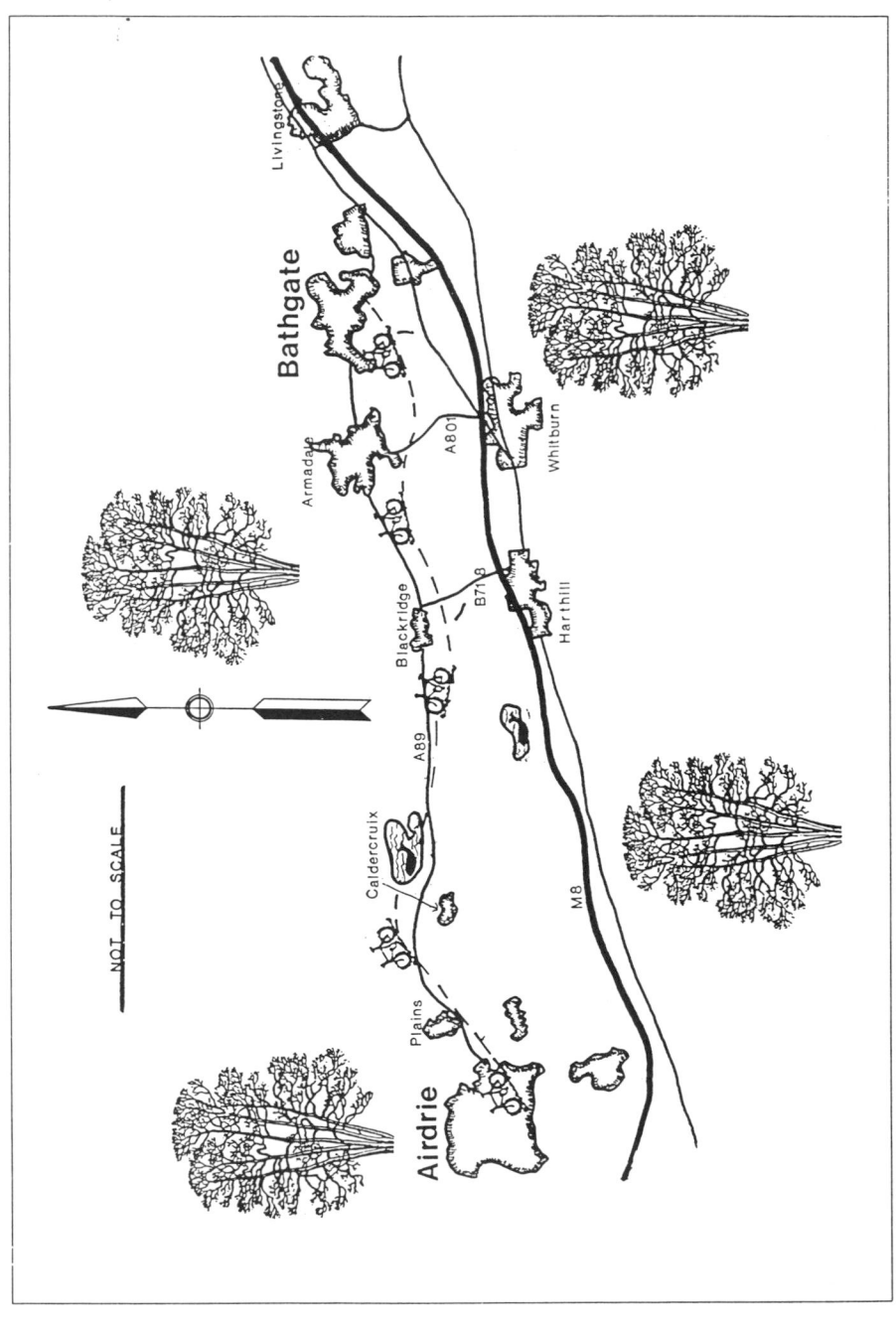

Route, which will link the eastern Clyde coast with the Firth of Forth beyond Edinburgh.

The path's surface is purpose built for cycling, walking and movement of wheelchairs and because of its railway origins enjoys level gradients and a well-drained substructure. It offers a clear 15 mile (24km) stretch of easy, traffic-free cycling, all on a tarmac or consolidated surface, where both the novice cyclist or the hardened enthusiast can capture equal pleasure. A novice rider should easily and comfortably cover the route one-way in under two hours cycling.

The town of Airdrie, with a population of 37,000, is on the eastern outskirts of Glasgow. Rome was built on seven hills and that is probably the only similarity that it has with Airdrie. Here the ride begins, in genuine railway style, from the platform of Drumgelloch station.

Bathgate is served by Junction 3a of the M8 Motorway and is now a fresh modern town, after suffering in the past from the closure of a large British Leyland manufacturing plant. The population is less than Airdrie at 14,500. Trains run regularly from here to Edinburgh and will carry your bicycle, subject to the normal availability of space.

A great cycling surface

Main Access Points

Bathgate, Armadale, Blackridge, Hillend Reservoir, Caldercruix, Plains and Airdrie.

The Route

From Drumgelloch Station platform, the path soon leaves Airdrie into open country, past Plains village and on to Caldercruix. All the time the A89 is close at hand to the left. Just before Caldercruix, on the right, the path squeezes between the A89 and the picturesque Hillend Reservoir before crossing under the road once again and traversing the border from Strathclyde into Lothian. After passing Blackridge, the path peacefully sets off into open rolling countryside and under three more major roads before emerging into the bustle of Bathgate. The ride is easy to follow, being clearly waymarked all along the route and interpretive maps are sited at regular intervals.

Refreshments can be taken in any of the towns or villages along the way and there are plenty of quiet, peaceful picnic spots which are ideal for a few minutes breather. Even within the bounds of built up areas, there is a real rural feel to this railway path, largely because of the proliferation of cuttings, an inheritance of the old Victorian railway engineers' skills.

Nearby

The large conurbations of Edinburgh and Glasgow are both well worth day visits. Nearer to the path are the very different towns of Bathgate and Airdrie. Bathgate is now very much a residential and light industrial centre, standing in pleasant rolling countryside. Airdrie has a more industrial feel, being an old mining town, but its roots are very much in the middle ages.

Historically, Airdrie supplied the coal that powered the great steel mills of Motherwell. The steel in turn was used to build the great ships at Clydebank. Airdrie's modern growth, therefore, is attributable to the sprawling effect of this industrialisation in the greater Glasgow area but despite the effects of this onslaught over the years Airdrie still retains the lovely atmosphere of an old market town. From the highest point, Airdrie Hill, it is supposed to be possible to see Arran in the Firth of Clyde some fifty miles away, but you will need a very clear day.

Ride 26

The Forth and Clyde Canal,Castlecary to Falkirk: Glasgow Area

A 14 mile (22km) return trip ride along the revitalised towpaths of the old Forth and Clyde Canal.

Maps: Landranger 1:50,000, Sheet numbers 64 and 65.

Distance: Total return trip: 14 miles (22km).

Waymarked: Follow the towpath.

Gradients: None.

Surface: Solid well-drained ash, clinker and stone. There are some sections that are still potentially muddy so this ride is best tackled after a dry spell.

Future proposals: Constant improvement of the towpath.

Other cycle routes linking: Not at the present time but, the Union Canal is very nearby at Falkirk.

Bicycle hire: Edinburgh.

Shops and Refreshments: There are numerous built-up areas along the route.

LOCATION

Introduction

The Forth and Clyde Canal is a proper ship canal, originally designed and built to take tall masted ships all the way across this central part of Scotland, from the Forth to the Clyde (hence the name). Sadly, it was closed in 1962, for no better reason than the fact that it was in the way of modern development at that time. When it was originally completed in the early 19th Century, it was an instant success, quickly becoming one of the busiest trans-Scotland routes for shipping. It also carried coal and raw materials from the rich seams around Falkirk and Cumbernauld into the industrial might of Glasgow.

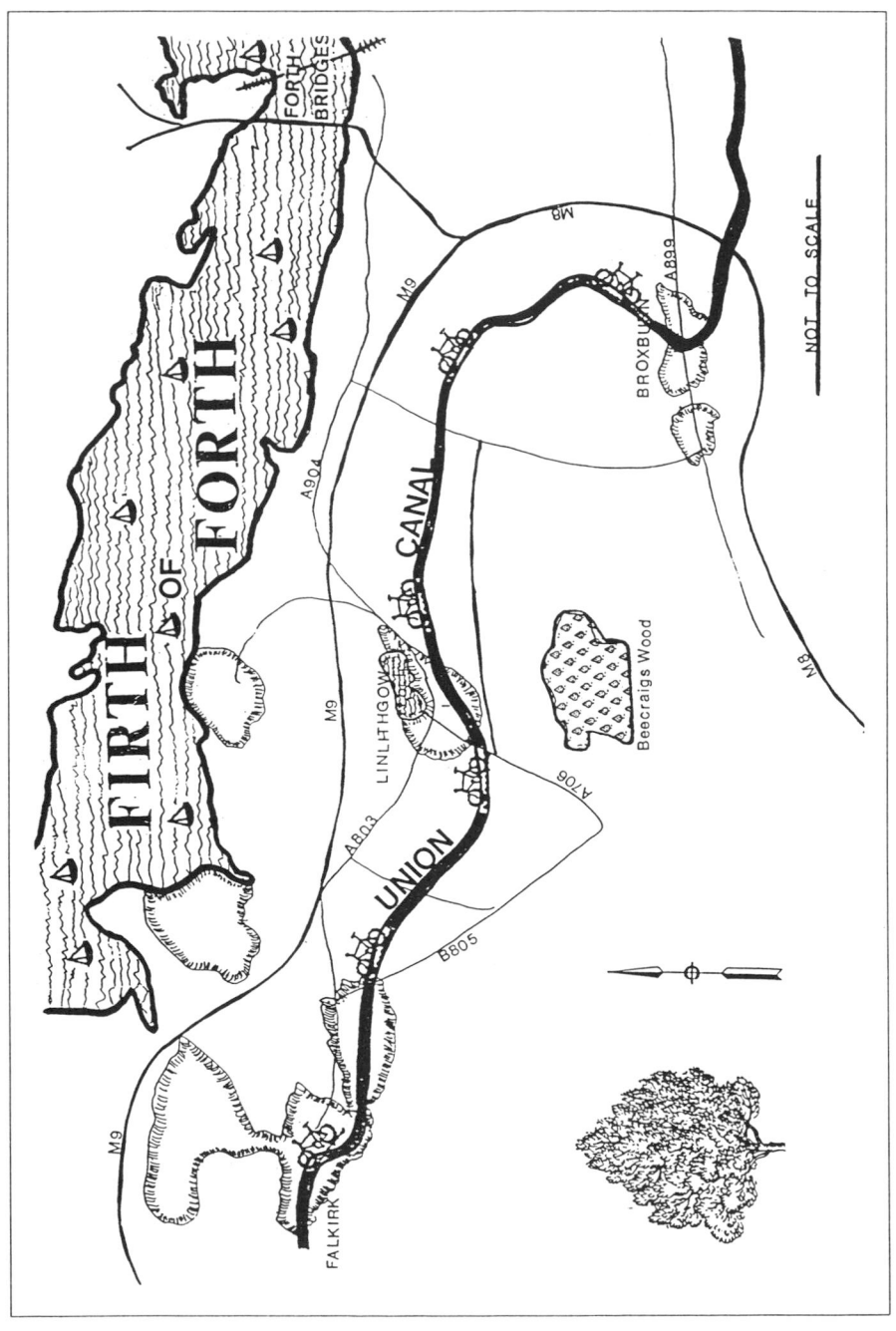

At Falkirk the canal linked into The Union Canal, via a now defunct eleven lock flight. West of Falkirk it slipped into the Forth at Grangemouth. Thus there were good links to Edinburgh and the east.

The waterway fell into an almost hopeless state of disrepair, until a series of local initiatives led to its revitalisation as a recreational route. Unfortunately, the canal is still below par in certain places, although it is hoped that future projects may overcome that problem.

The towpath is heavily used as a recreational route by local cyclists and a constant programme of groundwork is improving the facility all the time. Like the Union Canal, the Forth and Clyde is really more of a linear recreational park than it is a canal for boating purposes.

The route passes through some delightful countryside, mostly farmland and small urbanisation, as it makes its lazy way into the north-east of Glasgow and joins up with the Clyde at Bowling Basin. Industrial archeologists will be interested in the various moving bridge structures that allowed the tall ships to pass; unfortunately, modern developers have not been sympathetic to the route and all of the expensive newer bridge structures are immovable.

Dereliction at Glasgow

Main Access Points
Just off the B816 at Castlecary; Bonnybridge; east of the B902 in Falkirk.

The Route
Join the canal just off the B816 at Castlecary, east of the Motorway. Good parking is available. Here the canal is at its summit level. The route is reasonably self explanatory, just follow the towpath in an easterly direction. There is some lovely open countryside before Bonnybridge, after which the canal creeps into the urbanisation of Falkirk. Just beyond Falkirk, the towpath stops; turn around here and retrace your route.

There are further stretches of towpath which are useable closer to and within the environs of Glasgow.

Nearby
Bonnybridge and Falkirk are both industrial towns and both have Roman remains in the form of an old defensive wall. Castlecary is the site of an old Roman Fort that formed part of the wall but its name actually comes from a 15th century tower that was destroyed by fire in 1715.

Ride 27

Glasgow to Irvine and Ardrossan

A cycle route linking the centre of Glasgow to the west coast via safe on and off-road commuter cycle routes and a fine railway path.

Maps: Landranger 1:50,000, Sheet numbers 63, 64 and 70.

Distances: From Glasgow to Irvine: 33 miles (53km); to Ardrossan: 35 miles (56km); to Kilbirnie: 21 miles (34km); full return trip: 77 miles (124km).

Waymarked: Yes. There are very clear waymarks all along the route.

Gradients: Nothing to worry about. No terribly difficult gradients.

Surface: All solid, mainly tarmac, well-drained.

Future proposals: Policy of constant improvement. Eventually it is hoped to link Ardrossan with Greenock via a coastal route.

Other nearby Cycle Routes: Glasgow to Greenock Route. Isle of Arran. Isle of Cumbrae.

Bicycle hire: Glasgow, Irvine.

Shops and Refreshments: There are plenty of opportunities to pick up sustenance along or near to the route.

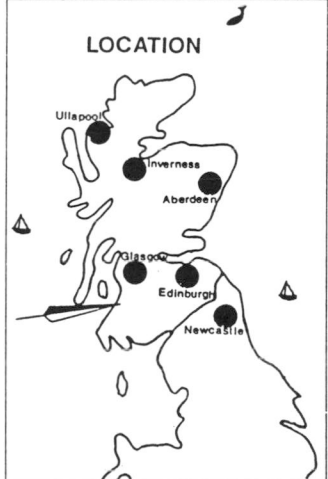

Introduction

This superb cycle way network has been developed as a safe recreational route. The participating local authorities ask users to look upon it as a linear park for recreation, local commuting and general enjoyment. They have good justification in this description as the cycle way is full of beauty and interest. It comprises a cleverly designed mixture of railway paths, waterside paths, minor roads and shared use avenues. There is a minimum of contact with motor traffic, thus ensuring that it is a safe facility for family recreation.

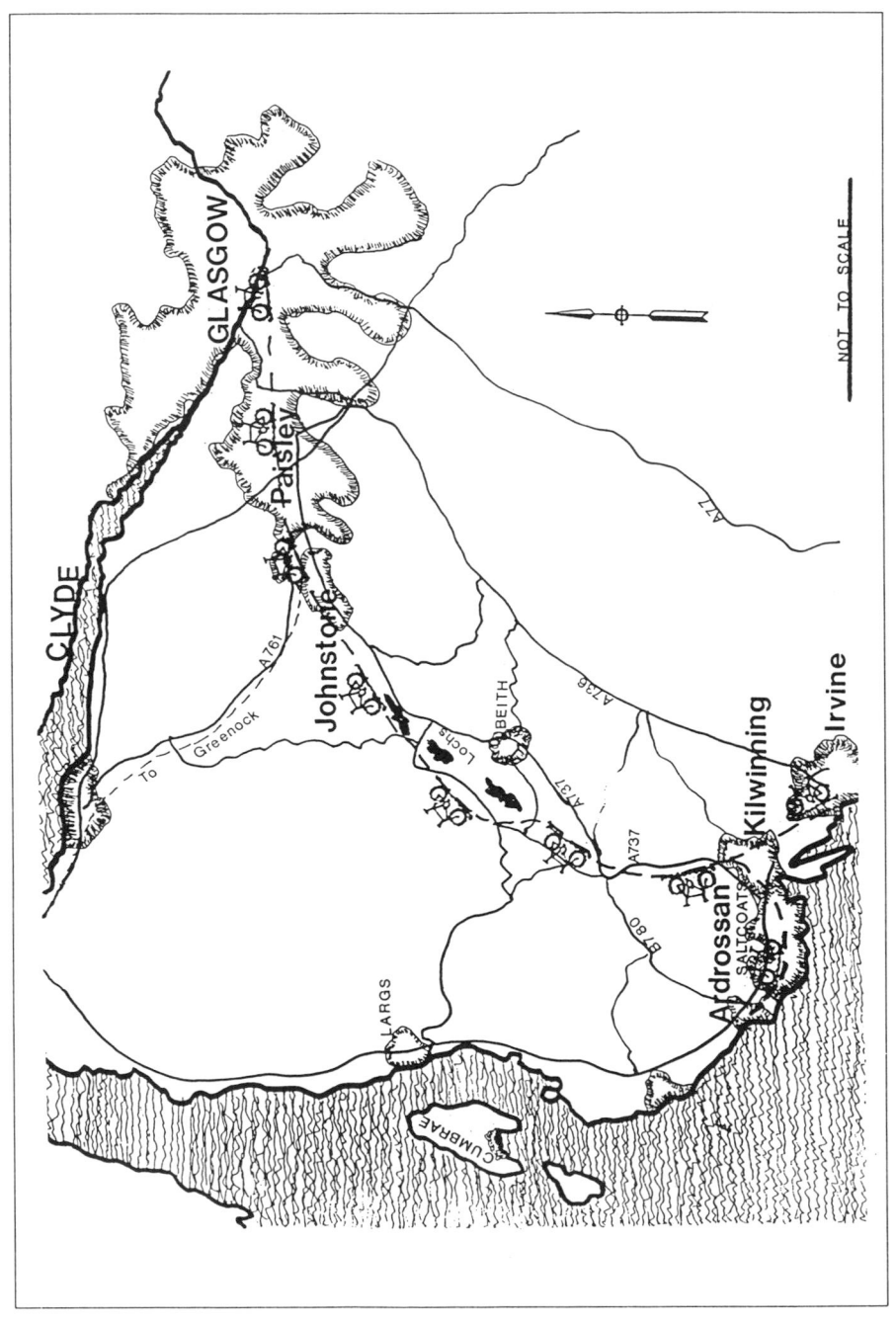

Amongst the numerous places of interest along the route are three coastal towns, Irvine, Saltcoats and Ardrossan. Try to pay a visit to all of them; they each have something to offer. Ardrossan is a seaport and the home of the ferry terminal to Arran (cycles travel free on Caledonian MacBrayne Ferries). Saltcoats has a delightful, recently restored promenade and Irvine has a super pedestrianised cobbled street of pretty rendered cottages, a lovely little harbour area, a maritime museum and the Magnum Centre which is billed as Europe's biggest leisure centre (Take your swimming gear).

A further encouragement to cyclists is the policy of Strathclyde Transport, allowing bicycles to travel free of charge on their electric local service trains (which are orange).

Main Access Points

There are many access points along the route. This is a short listing mentioning just a few of them.

Bells Bridge in Glasgow (by the Scottish Exhibition Centre).

Bellhouston Park, Govan.

Ross Hall Park (near Crookston station).

Paisley (Canal Street Station).

Johnstone (south of Bypass)

Lochwinnoch (good car parking by the Loch).

Kilbirnie Loch (Loch shore Distributor Road).

Kilwinning (north of A78(T), west of A737.

Irvine (Beach Park).

Ardrossan (South Beach).

The Route

The first part of the route, from Bell's Bridge in the centre of Glasgow, is shared with the Glasgow to Clyde Coast (Greenock) route. You are guided out of the city by safe well-waymarked lanes and off-road paths, passing through Bellhouston Park and Ross Hall Park on the way to Paisley. After passing through Paisley, the route passes through Elderslie and reaches Johnstone where a fork separates the two Clyde coast cycle routes. Go right for Port Glasgow and Greenock, keep left for Irvine, Saltcoats and Ardrossan.

The route passes through Kilbarchan, north of Howwood, and then alongside the lovely Castle Semple Loch to Lochwinnoch. You can hire a boat here or try a bit of fishing. You will then pass close to Barr Loch and Kilbirnie

Loch before joining minor roads at Glengarnock. The route into Kilwinning is through pleasant countryside.

At Kilwinning, either fork right for Saltcoats and Ardrossan or carry on to the left for Irvine.

Bells Bridge

Nearby

Kilwinning is noted for the great medieval Abbey which was built between 1140 and 1191. It had survived numerous onslaughts during the Reformation, before finally succumbing to the might of the armies of the Earls of Arran, Argyll and Glencaim in 1560.

Just outside Kilwinning is Eglinton Country Park, a thousand acres of riverside parkland in the grounds of Eglinton Castle. It was here that there was a great jousting tournament as late as 1839 which was re-enacted in great style in 1989. There is a good cafe here.

Ride 28

Great Cumbrae Island: Firth of Clyde

A coastal circuit ride around a small attractive island only
five minutes by ferry from the mainland.

Map: Landranger 1:50,000, Sheet number 63.

Distance: 10 miles (16km) around the island.

Waymarked: When you come off the ferry follow the
signs to Millport. The coast road is the A860.

Gradients: The coast road is easy. There are some
steep climbs inland.

Surface: Tarmac.

Future proposals: N/A

Other cycle routes linking: N/A

Bicycle hire: Millport.

Shops and Refreshments: Plenty.

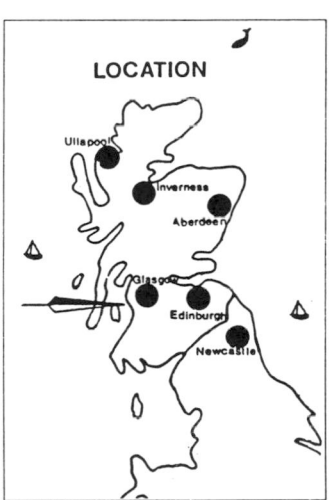

Introduction

Five minutes ferry ride is all it takes and you are in a new world, a world
that is known by cartographers as Great Cumbrae Island but always described locally as Big Cumbrae, presumably to differentiate it from Little
Cumbrae Island which is proclaimed locally as Wee Cumbrae. Wee Cumbrae is not occupied and is visited only by a few individuals such as
fishermen, yachtsmen, and divers.

Big Cumbrae, on the other hand, is a thriving holiday and touring centre.
Within its five square miles it has great beaches, a bustling little fishing
harbour, a marine station and aquarium, an eighteen hole golf course and
many welcoming pubs and eating houses for thirsty or hungry cyclists. A
wide variety of wild and marine life includes a thriving rabbit population,

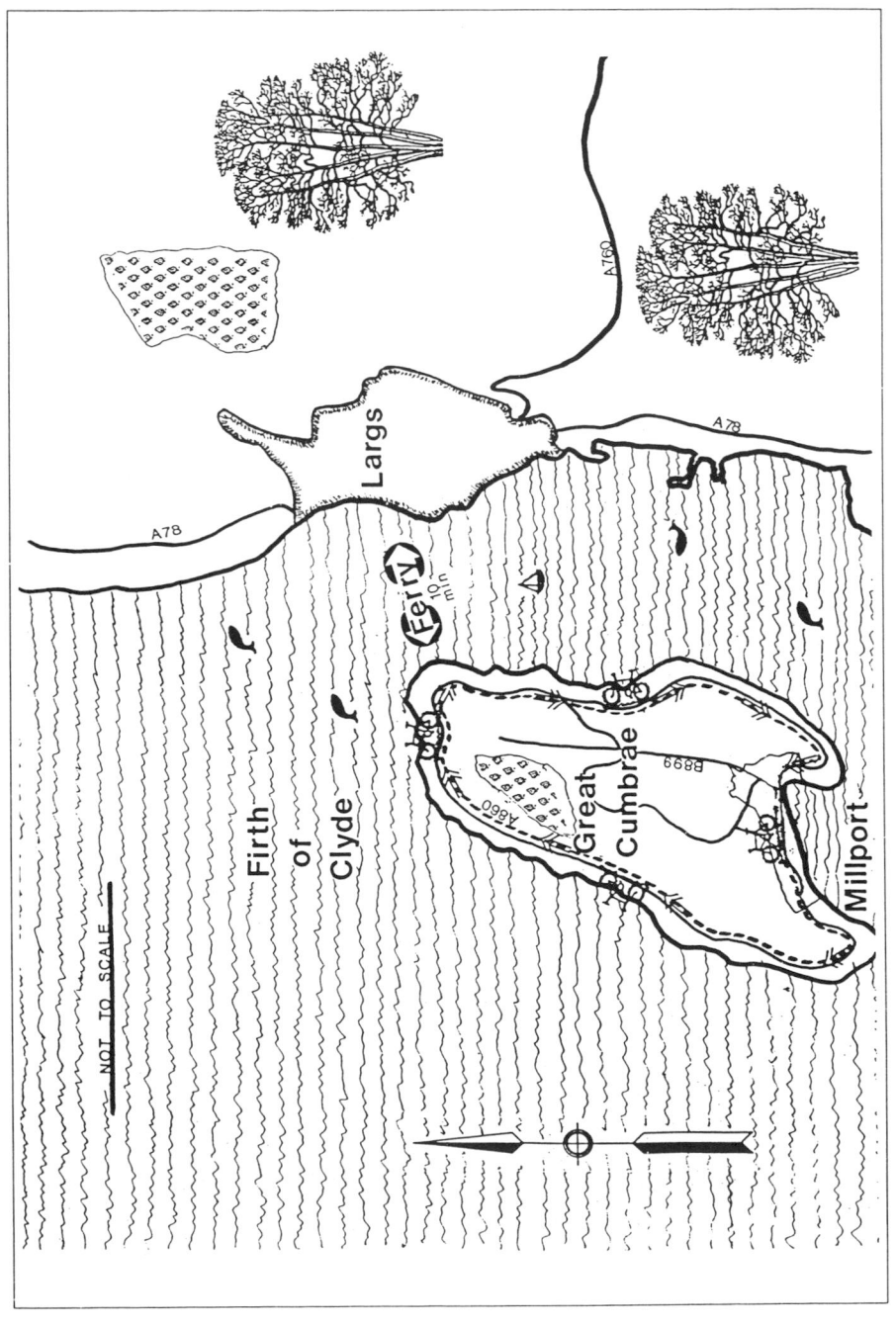

squirrels, magnificent sea birds and harmless basking sharks that are often seen close to the shore.

Big Cumbrae is situated a couple of miles off the east Scottish Ayrshire coast in the Firth of Clyde, midway between Largs and the Isle of Bute, yet only half an hour from Glasgow. Millport is the main settlement and its impressive centrepiece is the Cathedral of The Isles. This is Scotland's smallest cathedral. There are also some interesting shops and restaurants in the town.

Cumbrae ferry at Largs

Main Access Points

Once you are off the ferry and onto the Island turn left, keep on the coast road and after about four miles of easy cycling, you will arrive at Millport.

The Route

The A860 coast road is 10 miles (16km) long and enjoys marvellous views from virtually every inch of its length. Although it is classified as an "A" road, it does not carry the weight of traffic which is more normally associated with this classification. The going is easy, the surface is good and there are plenty of pleasant stopping off places. There are also roads running away from the coast as well as an inner circle road which, after a steep climb reaches the height 415 feet at Glaid Stone, the Island's highest point.

Nearby

The Island is accessed by ferry from Largs, a typical seaside town with a long esplanade with whelk stalls, amusement arcades, sticks of rock and "kiss me quick" hats. A monument, known locally as The Pencil commemorates the Battle of Largs (1263). The Scottish, under Alexander III, successfully defended the town and coastline against an attempted invasion by the Vikings, who were commanded by the Norwegian King, Haakon. The National Water Sports Centre operates in the sound off Millport. The internationally famed Inverclyde National Sports Training Centre is situated just inland behind Largs. This is used to train sports coaches and a few sportsmen and women who demonstrate exceptional ability and promise.

Ride 29
Glasgow to Greenock

A cycle route linking Glasgow to the west Clyde coast at Greenock.

Map: Landranger 1:50,000, Sheet numbers 63 and 64.

Distances: Glasgow to Greenock: 25 miles (40km); Glasgow to Johnstone: 12 miles (19½km); Full return ride: 50 miles (80km).

Waymarked: Yes. Good sign posting and waymarks throughout.

Gradients: No major sustained climbs, mainly railway path.

Surface: Consolidated stone, tarmac and concrete.

Future proposals: Apart from constant maintenance of the existing cycle route, there are various links that presently use roads which will be improved or rerouted. There is also a proposal to complete a coastal link, down the west coast towards Irvine.

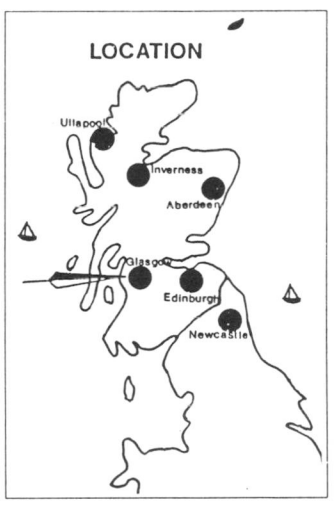

Other cycle routes linking: The beginning of the Route in Glasgow is also the beginning of the cycle route via Paisley to Irvine and Ardrossan as well as the cycle route to Loch Lomond and Killin, the Edinburgh route and the commuter route to Cumbernauld.

Bicycle hire: Glasgow.

Shops and Refreshments: There are plenty of opportunities. The route passes through a lot of built up areas.

Introduction

The route follows the commuter cycle way out of Glasgow, some of it in cycle lanes, some off-road, some through pleasant public parks, some on quiet roads and some on footpaths of busier roads, shared with pedestrians. At Johnstone, the route joins the Johnstone to Greenock Railway Path, which follows the disused track bed of the old railway that runs towards the Clyde

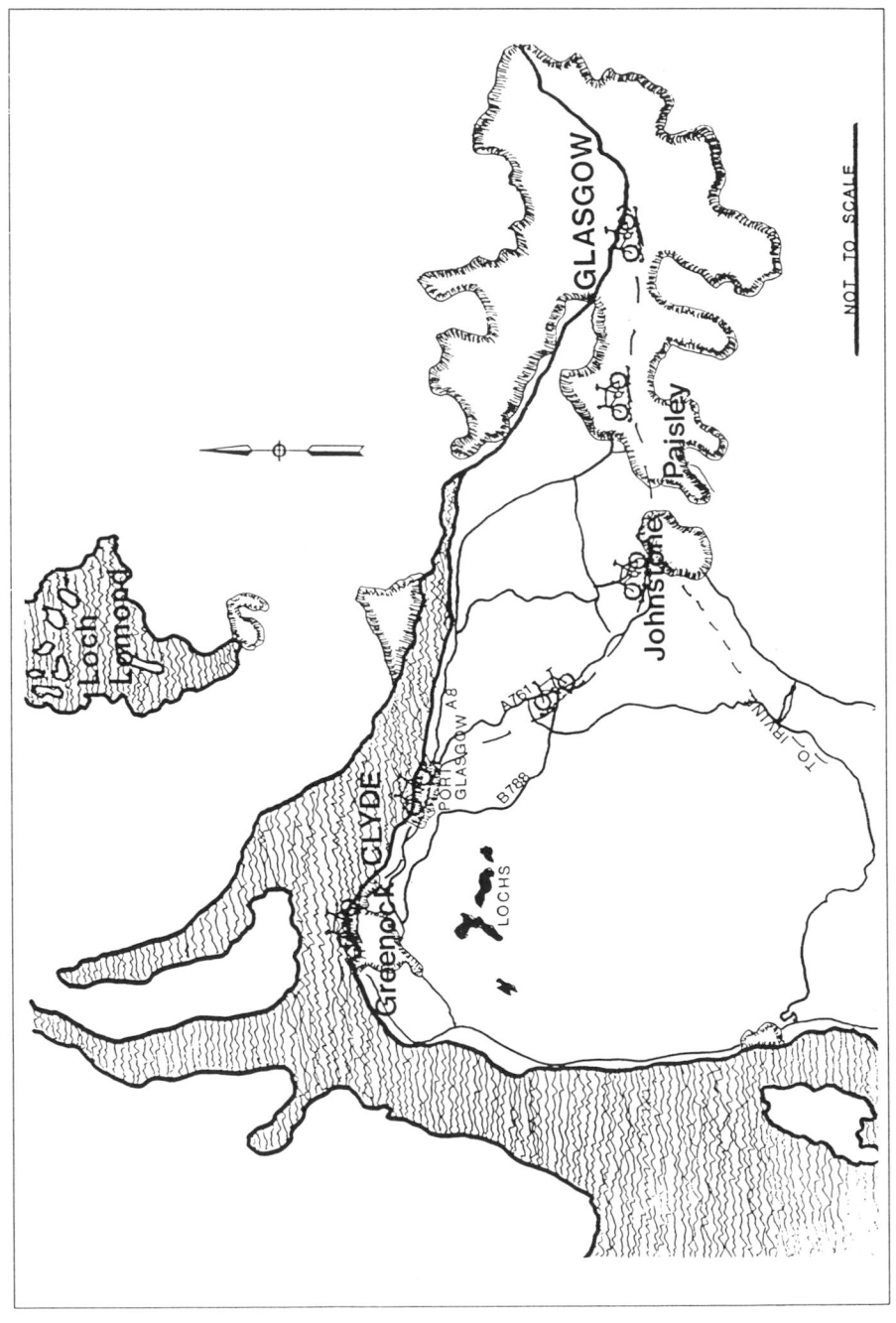

estuary coast and once served the industrial demands of the Port Glasgow area.

Along the route, it is possible to take an easy diversion ride, along quiet lanes and private roads, to the Clyde-Muirshiel Country Park Centre on the shores of the very popular and beautiful Loch Thom.

A further encouragement to cyclists is the policy of Strathclyde Transport, allowing bicycles to travel free of charge on their distinctive orange-coloured electric local service trains.

The Glasgow to Greenock route at Port Glasgow

The Route

The first part of the route, from Bell's Bridge in the centre of Glasgow, is shared with the Glasgow to West Coast (Irvine) route. You are guided out of the city by safe well-waymarked lanes and off-road paths passing through Bellhouston Park and Ross Hall Park on the way to Paisley. After passing through Paisley, the route goes through Elderslie and reaches Johnstone where a fork separates the two Clyde coast cycle routes. Go right for Port Glasgow and Greenock, keep left for Irvine, Saltcoats and Ardrossan.

After the junction, the route passes Bishopton before following the southern reaches of the Clyde past Port Glasgow and onto Greenock. On this leg of the path, you will often be at high level above the industrial wastelands of a virtually defunct shipbuilding past.

Nearby

The evidence of a great shipbuilding industry on the Clyde is obvious as you proceed along the route. The main towns have a sense of having seen better times and nowhere is this more marked than in Greenock, the birthplace of James Watt, and in Port Glasgow, which boasts one of the finest examples of 16th century architecture, Newark Castle.

Main Access Points

There are many access points along the route. In Glasgow, the route begins at the Scottish Conference and Exhibition Centre, and the Clyde is crossed via nearby Bell's Bridge, which was built as part of the Glasgow Garden Festival. The route can also be easily accessed at twenty or more points along the way. Some of the more obvious points are at its terminus in Greenock, Port Glasgow, Kilmacolm, Quarriers village and Bridge of Weir. Also, at the western end are the following:

1. Bellhouston Park, Govan.

2. Ross Hall Park (near Crookston station).

3. Paisley (Canal Street Station).

4. Johnstone (south and north of the bypass and near the hospital).

Ride 30

The Lochan Ghleannain Loop: Loch Ard Forest, North of Glasgow

A magnificent range of forest rides and a recommended loch-side route.

Map: Landranger 1:50,000, Sheet numbers 56 and 57.

Distance: 9 miles (14½km) (Many more miles of easy routes from Milton Car Park.)

Waymarked: Yes. Different colours for different routes. Follow red markers around Lochan Ghleannain Loop and Loch Ard South.

Gradients: None of the routes are completely flat but all but one route in the Loch Ard Forest offer fairly easy riding. If you want to avoid steep gradients stick to Loch Ard and avoid the Green Route.

Surface: The easier routes are mainly on compacted forest roads and paths.

Future proposals: Constant maintenance.

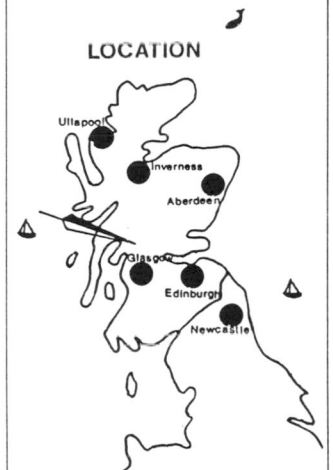

LOCATION

Other cycle routes linking: Balloch to Aberfoyle and Callander to Balquhidder sections of the Glasgow to Killin Cycleway.

Bicycle hire: At the Queen Elizabeth Forest Park Visitor Centre.

Shops and Refreshments: Plenty of opportunities but not within the forest.

Introduction

The Queen Elizabeth ll Forest Park is situated between the Highlands in the north and the Forth Valley in the south and within it are the three separate forests of Strathyre, Achray and Loch Ard. All of these offer waymarked cycle trails. This is an incredible landscape of lochs, conifers and mountains encompassing or adjoining Loch Lomond, Loch Ard, Loch Achray and Loch

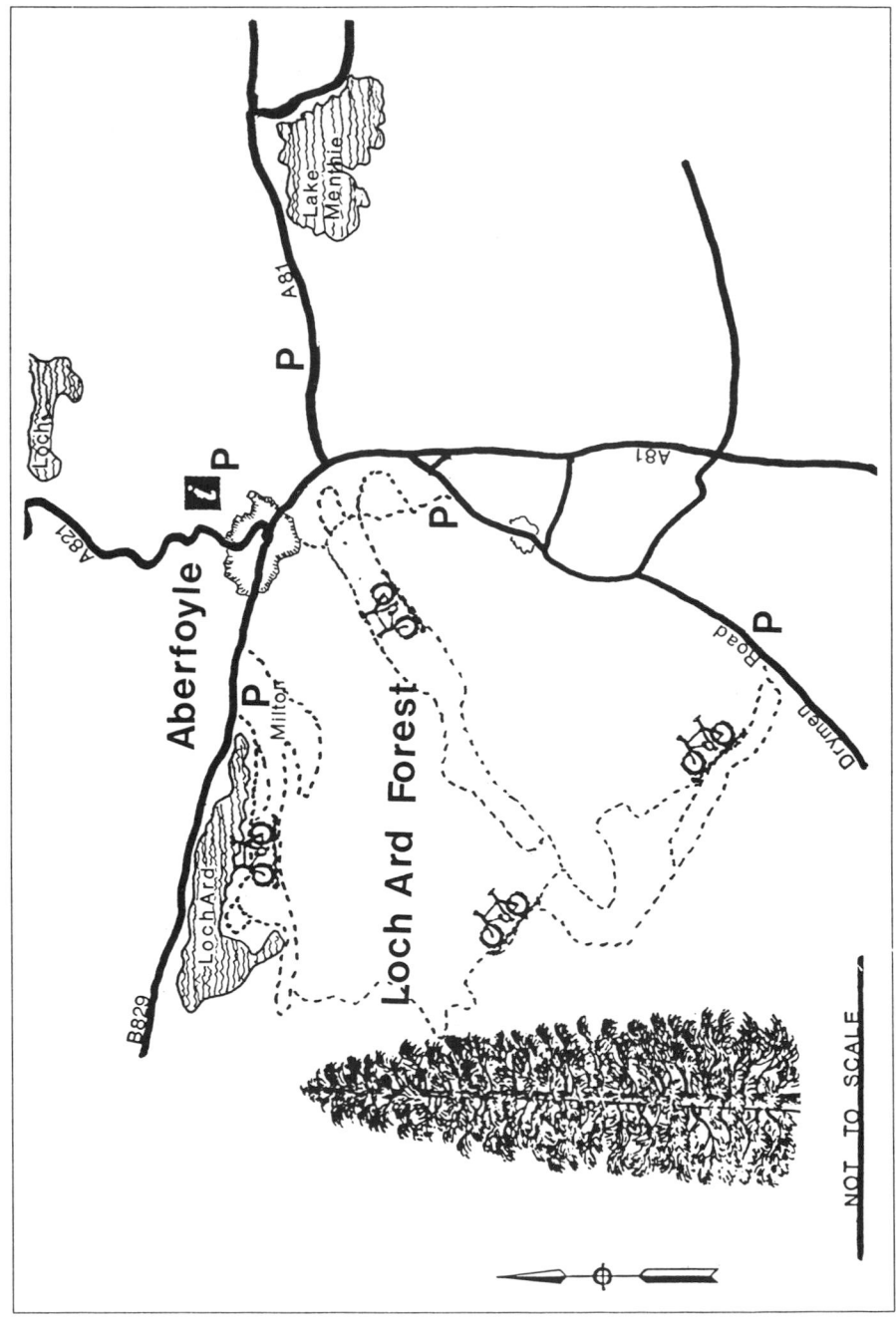

Lubnaig as well as the great mountains of Ben Venue at 2393 feet (729 metres), Ben A'an and Ben Ledi at 2973 feet (907 metres).

Aberfoyle is one of the major centres of the Forest Park. The community has developed around forestry and tourism. The introduction of tourism is not a recent phenomenon but one that has grown steadily since the main road to the north, known as Duke's Pass, was built by the Duke of Montrose in the 19th century.

The three individual forests each have their own special characteristics and this is very relevant to the cycling conditions.

Sporting cyclists, who are seeking challenging gradients and rougher surfaces, should aim for Achray where there is plenty of high ground and great views. Here there are three waymarked trails of $13\frac{1}{2}$, 7 and $4\frac{1}{2}$ miles ($21\frac{1}{2}$, 11 and 7km) but they are not good news for the beginner or the family group.

Strathyre Forest links into the beautiful Callander to Balquhidder section of the Glasgow to Killin cycle way (see entry) and offers a range of forest conditions to suit everyone's requirements. The waymarked cycle trails here are categorised as easy, moderate or demanding. These categorisations are based on the sort of gradients and surface conditions that you are likely to encounter, so they broadly translate to the availability of uphill, downhill, flat, rough or smooth conditions. If you are planning a ride along the Callander to Balquhidder route and just want a change, or perhaps a picnic, there are three or four waymarked paths linking onto the glorious Loch Lubnaig loch-side pathway. There are some lovely quiet spots in this forest.

Loch Ard forest is a great choice for a full range of routes. There are miles and miles of easy forestry tracks which will suit families and non-sporting riders. In all, there are six waymarked routes in Loch Ard Forest, all guaranteeing beautifully wild surroundings and great views. Family riders beware, the green waymarked trail is a $15\frac{1}{2}$ mile (25km) route, tailored to the fit, sporting rider. It goes deep into the forest and includes steep climbs and descents. The other five routes are all gentle and undemanding, ideal for those who just prefer to potter along and enjoy the surroundings.

The wildlife population is quite varied but particularly profound are roe deer, hares, foxes and countless rabbits. This is one of the few places where grey squirrels and red squirrels live side by side. By night you can see plenty of badgers.

Main Access Points

Strathyre Forest is best approached from the Strathyre Forest information centre where there is good car parking. Alternatively at Strathyre Forest Cabins by way of the Callander to Balquhidder section of the Glasgow to Killin Cycle Way.

Achray Forest is served by the Queen Elizabeth Visitor Centre.

Loch Ard Forest is served by four major car parks as well as countless other easy parking opportunities. Milton car park is situated off the B829 out of Aberfoyle and is the starting point for the Lochan Ghleannain Loop. Another good car park location for other Loch Ard Forest rides is situated at Old Drymen Road a few miles to the south of Aberfoyle.

The Routes

A good base for rides in the Loch Ard Forest is the Milton Car Park situated off the B829, to the west of Aberfoyle. For an interesting and exciting (but easy) two hour circuit, try the 9 mile (14.5km) long Lochan Ghleannain Loop.

Leave the Milton Car Park heading west and follow the red waymarks. The trail leads around Lochan Ghleannain and then follows a long return route alongside Loch Ard. The riding is easy, the surroundings are unbelievable and, if you are lucky, the sun will shine.

Within the forest the original deciduous trees such as beech, oak, ash and alder are now far outnumbered by the forestry commission planting which is predominantly sitka spruce. This is now considered to be the most common tree in Britain, although it is a native of the North American continent. There are also large numbers of lodgepole pine, known as the native tree of "Bonnie Scotland" and hemlock, recognised by its elegant conical shape.

Nearby

The Queen Elizabeth Forest Park visitor centre will provide you with all the information that you are likely to need about the forest and the various waymarked routes. Within the centre there is an audio visual theatre for interpretative background information. This centre is well worth a visit. It is a great place to cool down on a hot day and there is a shop and a cafeteria as well as plenty of presentation boards and maps.

Ride 31

Aberfoyle to Inversnaid with Loch Katrine: Trossachs

A well-signed and waymarked route of forest and loch-side riding amongst the beautiful Trossachs Lochs.

Map: Landranger 1:50,000, Sheet numbers 56 and 57.

Distances: Aberfoyle return including Inversnaid visit (via Loch Katrine and Loch Venachar): 20 miles (32km); (via Park of Auchentroig): 27 miles (43km).

Waymarked: Yes. Good signposts and waymarks along the whole route.

Gradients: There are some ups and downs, nothing too demanding. The ride is perfectly manageable for the occasional cyclist. Remember to allow plenty of time and do not be too ambitious. Take your time and linger on the views.

Surface: All sorts, but mainly forestry tracks, all hard and well-drained.

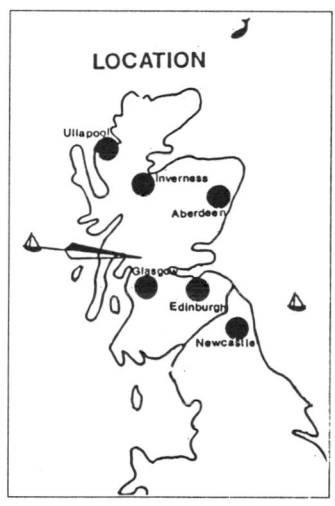

Future proposals: Constant maintenance.

Other cycle routes linking: Glasgow to Balloch; Aberfoyle to Balloch and Aberfoyle to Callander; Callander to Killin. Many other waymarked routes in the Queen Elizabeth Forest Park.

Bicycle hire: Aberfoyle.

Shops and Refreshments: Take a drink and a sandwich. The facilities are only in the towns and villages.

Introduction

This route should come with a warning concerning potential addiction and the possibility of overdosing on Scottish beauty. The grandeur of the Rob Roy country with its three-thousand-foot peaks combines with the soft magnificence of seven Lochs. Do not take it for granted. Take it slowly and soak up the surroundings and it will be good for your soul. Spend as much time as you can over the ride and absorb the atmosphere. Here is every conceivable facet of Trossach country, some harshness and rawness and much of the lush and colourful wildness that is Scotland at her finest.

Much of the route follows loch-side paths and there are numerous places to stop and enjoy the views. The surrounding peaks reach heights of around three thousand feet. Cruises can be joined at either end of Loch Katrine and at Inversnaid on the shores of Loch Lomond. There are interesting visitor centres at Aberfoyle, at Loch Katrine and at Loch Achray. Rob Roy's cave is situated near Inversnaid on the banks of Loch Lomond.

This ride deserves at least a full day and if you do have time, try going around the circuit twice, in different directions. You are guaranteed to see a great deal that you missed on your first circuit.

Main Access Points

The route can be joined at any point. There are numerous car parks around the Lochs and a good centre at Aberfoyle.

The Route

The route is well-waymarked and sign posted at regular intervals. Leave Aberfoyle either to the west or to the north as you please. Heading north you will soon encounter Loch Drunkie. Just beyond here, take the way-marked route to the east. This will guide you via very quiet back lanes and forest tracks past loch Achray to Loch Katrine, where you will go along the northern shore to the western tip before dropping down a short length of the southern shore and turning right. This will take you along the northern shore of Loch Arklet to Inversnaid and the banks of Loch Lomond. Look at the wonderful waterfall here.

To return to Aberfoyle, retrace your route along Loch Arklet and turn right through Loch Ard Forest. Pass Loch Chon and Loch Ard on their northern shores and you will arrive back in Aberfoyle.

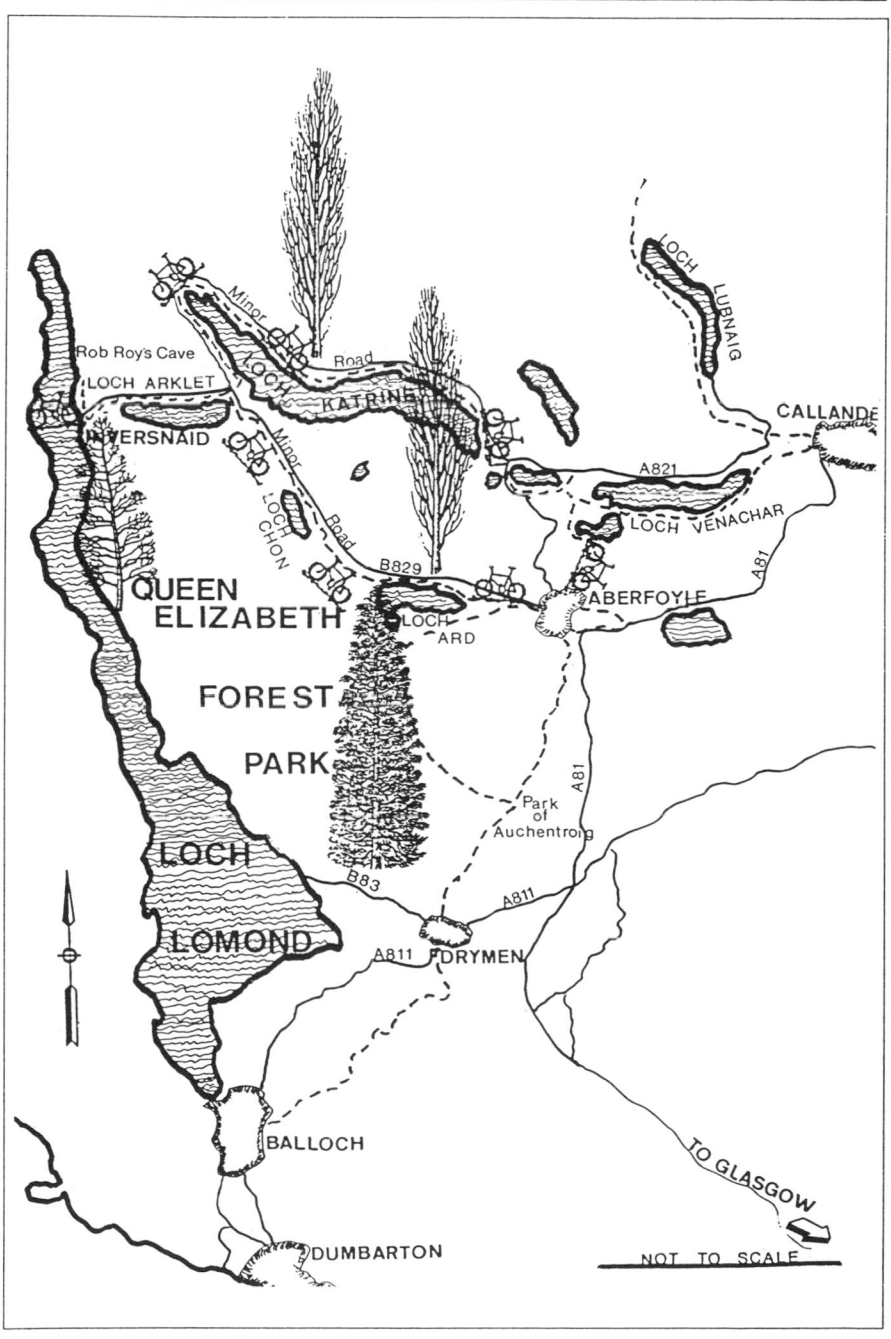

Peaceful waterside scenery at the visitor centre

Nearby

If you want to extend the route take the right turn after Loch Ard and follow the waterpipe access track through the forest. You can then return to Aberfoyle by turning right at the main meeting with the Glasgow to Killin Cycle Way.

At Stronachlachar, on the south-western shores of Loch Katrine and at Trossachs Pier in the east, near Loch Katrine Visitor Centre, you can join a cruise on the lovely old *SS Sir Walter Scott*. This old steam turbine-powered ship has plied the Loch since the turn of the century.

Ride 32

Glasgow to Loch Lomond Cycle Way

An off-road cycle way following rail paths, riverside paths and canal-side paths from Glasgow to Loch Lomond.

Maps: Landranger 1:50,000, Sheet numbers 56, 57 and 64.

Distances: 21 miles (33km); Return ride: 42 miles (66km).

Waymarked: Yes.

Gradients: Easy.

Surface: Good throughout. Solid, well-drained.

Future proposals: Various extensions to the route are proposed particularly linking the route to Callander and hence onto the Killin Cycleway.

Other cycle routes linking: The beginning of the Route in Glasgow is also the beginning of the cycle routes via Paisley to Irvine, Ardrossan and Greenock as well as the cycle route to Edinburgh and the commuter route to Cumbernauld.

Bicycle hire: Glasgow.

Shops and Refreshments: Numerous opportunities for refreshments.

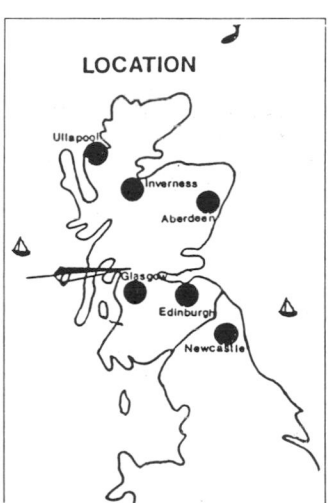

LOCATION

Introduction

The Glasgow to Loch Lomond cycle way runs for 21 glorious traffic-free miles (33km) from its beginnings just half a mile west of the bustling centre of Glasgow to the peace, tranquillity and magnificence of Loch Lomond's shores at Balloch. The cycle way was adapted during the mid- and late-1980s, finally opening as a through route in 1989. Since when it has been very well-used by cyclists of all shapes and sizes.

Some interesting features along the route include the Kelvin Hall Sports Centre and Transport Museum, which house a fine exhibition of old bicycles.

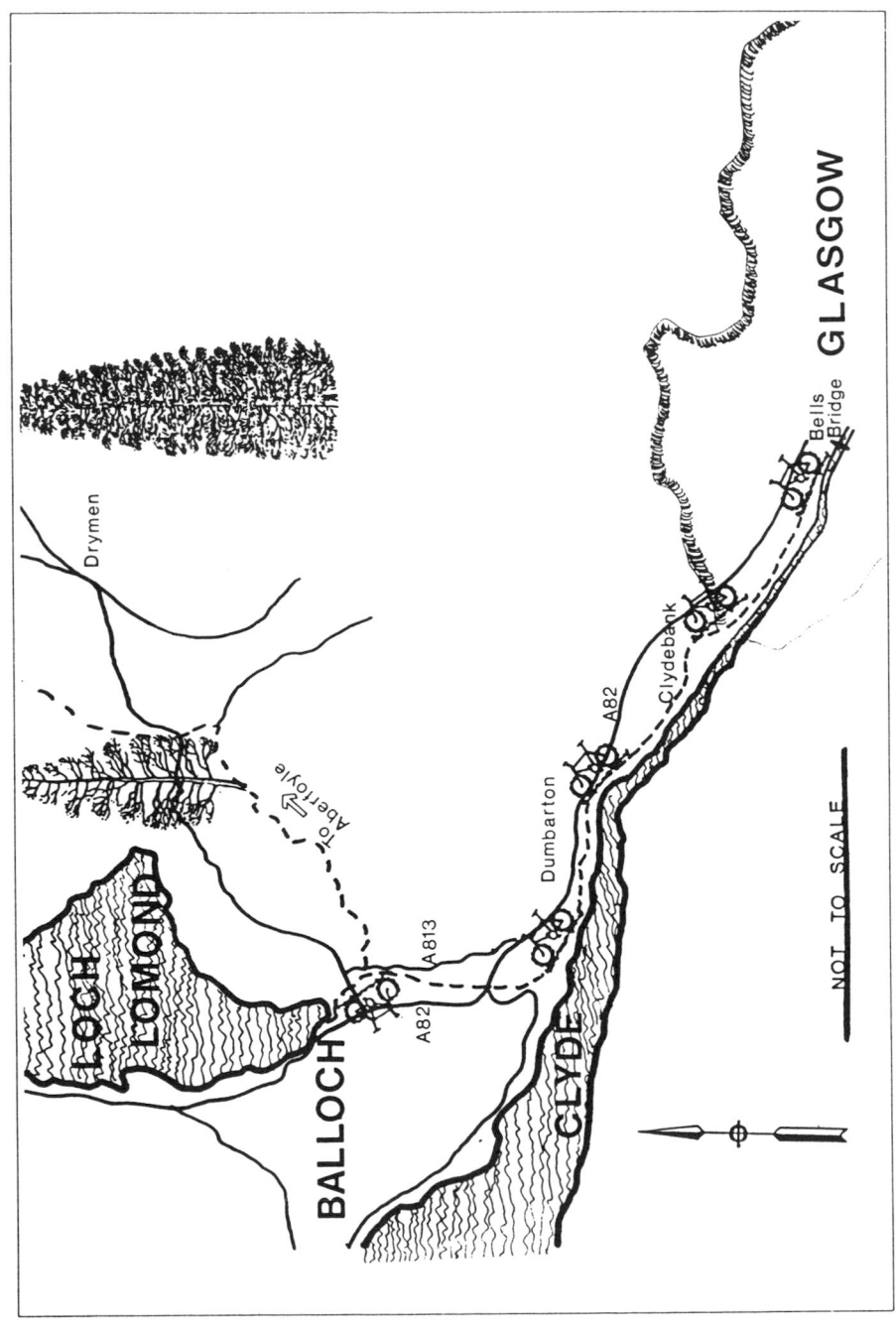

The Kelvin Grove Museum is basically an Art Gallery exhibiting some fine masterpieces. The 1971 Erskine Road Bridge would have the Victorian railway builders bemused. The main span is 1000 feet and the total span is 4334 feet. The designers claim that it can withstand winds of 130mph and its deck height at 180 feet above the river allows big ships to pass underneath.

The Scottish Maritime Museum at Dumbarton is a tribute to the times of the great ship builders. William Denny and Brothers carried out the finishing and fitting out of the Cutty Sark after it was built at Scott and Linton's Yard. The Cutty Sark is now on permanent display at Greenwich, London. William Denny's are also famed for the Denny Tank, a water tank specifically built for testing ships' design and seaworthiness.

Main Access Points

There are plenty of access points along the route. The Glasgow end is at Bell's Bridge, just by the Scottish Exhibition and Conference Centre, half a mile to the west of the city centre. This point is the confluence of this cycle way, the routes east to the Clyde Estuary and coast, and the routes west towards Edinburgh. At the Loch Lomond end of the cycle way the starting point is Balloch, at the tourist information centre.

Loch Lomond at Balloch

The Route

The route is very well-signed and waymarked, so that finding your way should not be a problem. From Glasgow, the cycle way heads off in a north-westerly direction with the River Clyde close on your left. Most of this section is actually on the disused track bed of a railway, the former Lanarkshire and Dumbartonshire Railway from Partick to Clydebank. You will pass the Clyde Tunnel and you may wish to cycle through it. Why? Why not? Perhaps to have a look at yourself from the other side!

Just past Yarrow's Shipyard and Yoker Sports Centre the Renfrew Ferry also crosses the Clyde. At Clydebank the cycle way joins the tow path of the Forth and Clyde canal and this takes you up to Bowling Basin where the canal meets the River. From here the route is on off-road pathways to Dumbarton where you are directed through the centre. After Dumbarton the cycle way heads up a riverside path to Loch Lomond, keeping the delightful River Leven on your right-hand side.

Nearby

Loch Lomond is the largest of the Scottish Lochs and in its own special way it is one of the most beautiful. It is surrounded by a gentler, greener landscape than the big northern Lochs and this softer atmosphere seems to make Loch Lomond less formidable, more welcoming. There are thirty islands in the Loch; it is 23 miles long and six miles wide in places. The maximum depth is an impressive six hundred and thirty feet. If you have not tried it before take the steamer trip, an excellent way to see the Loch.

Glasgow is the third city in Britain, in terms of population. It owes its growth to the industrial revolution and the heavy iron, steel and shipbuilding industries. The bleak slum problem that plagued the city for so many years is now very much a thing of the past, vast modern developments have been provided and the city is now something of a jewel in Scotland's social crown.

At Clydebank is the Clydebank District Museum which, amongst other exhibits, has a great collection of models of the great ships that were built in the once mighty shipyards. These include John Brown's Yard where the Queen Mary, the Queen Elizabeth and the Queen Elizabeth II were built. If you still have any energy left and fancy an exciting time on the flumes, try the Playdrome, a £7 million leisure centre.

Ride 33

Balloch to Aberfoyle (including Drymen and Queen Elizabeth Forest Park)

A well-signed and waymarked cycle route made up of a mix of quiet back roads and forest riding.

Maps: Landranger 1:50,000, Sheet numbers 56, 57 and 64.

Distance: Balloch to Aberfoyle - 20 miles (32km).

Waymarked: Yes. Good signposts and waymarks along the whole route for the Glasgow to Killin Cycleway.

Gradients: There are some ups and downs, nothing too demanding. The ride is perfectly manageable for the occasional cyclist, remember to allow plenty of time and do not be too ambitious. Take your time and enjoy your surroundings.

Surface: Tarmac and some stone. All hard and well-drained.

Future proposals: To bypass the road section.

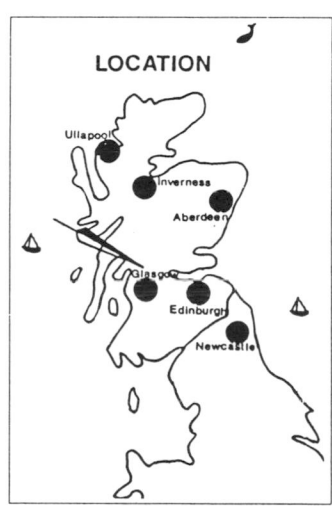

LOCATION

Other cycle routes linking: Aberfoyle-Loch Lomond (Inversnaid) Circuit; Glasgow to Balloch; Pass of Leny and Glen Ogle

Bicycle hire: Aberfoyle.

Shops and Refreshments: Take a drink and a sandwich. The facilities are only in the towns and villages.

Warnings: The "A" road section, where higher traffic density is likely to be encountered is from Croftamie to Drymen on the A809 and the A811. Thankfully, this is only a short section of the otherwise virtually traffic-free route.

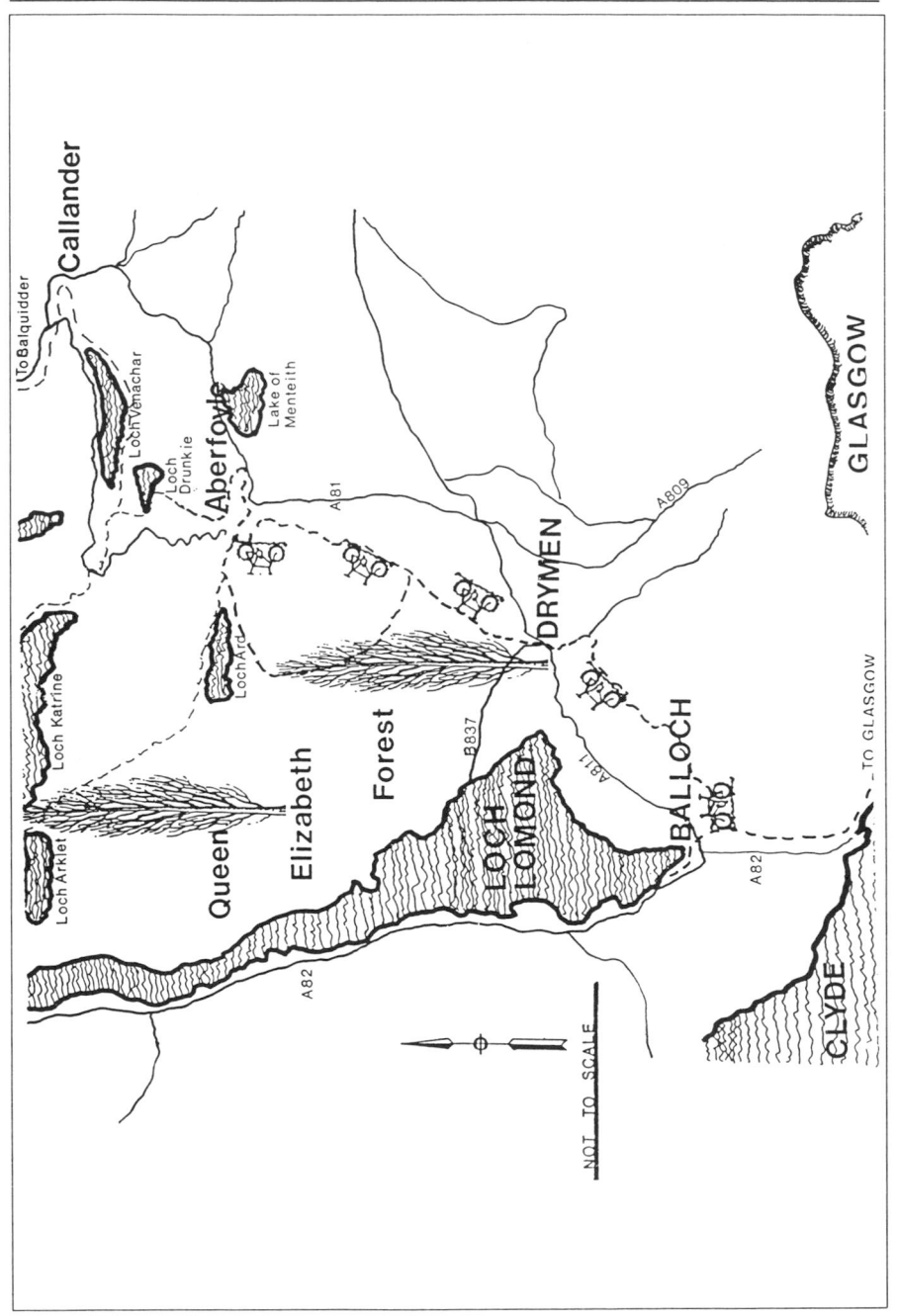

Introduction

The ride from Balloch to Aberfoyle utilises the waymarked Glasgow to Killin Cycle Way route which is virtually traffic-free except for two short "A" road sections. The ride takes you from the southern part of Loch Lomond, on to Drymen and through the edge of Loch Ard Forest to Aberfoyle. If you want to extend the ride, there is a choice of directions from Drymen. You can head north over the Menteith Hills and then along the beautiful southern shore of Loch Venachar or east through the Queen Elizabeth Forest Park and onto Loch Katrine and Loch Arklet.

The danger with this ride is the possibility of overdosing on the sheer magnificence of the surroundings and taking the extraordinary landscapes for granted. Do not do that but spend a little time over the ride and take in as much as you can absorb. This is some of the finest country in Scotland with a hint of softness, a hint of wildness and a million memories to savour on those dark winter nights.

The route has to be experienced to appreciate fully the extent of the scenic delights. Each individual will make their own interpretations and recall their own personal favourite spots. Rest assured that you are guaranteed some substantial return for your efforts. There are so many highlights of the route it is best to allow for plenty of stops. A few places that nobody should miss are the delightful village of Drymen, the busy tourist centre of Aberfoyle and the Park of Auchentroig. There are many many more fantastic sights so get on your bike and see for yourself.

Main Access Points

The route can be joined at numerous points; these are the main centres *en route*: 1. **Balloch.** By the tourist information centre pick up the signposts to the west after about half a mile. 2. In the village of **Drymen**, the route is easily found from the pretty village square. 3. Clearly marked in all directions from **Aberfoyle**. Head out west from here to gain access to Loch Ard, Loch Chon and Loch Arklet down to the edge of Loch Lomond. Head north or west for the loop return trip via Loch Katrine.

The Route

The route is well-waymarked and sign-posted at regular intervals. After leaving Balloch, the signposts will guide you via very quiet back lanes to Croftanie, where there is a short main road hop to the delightful village of Drymen. From here, the route reverts to back lanes and then forest towards Aberfoyle. Your first choice of direction comes at the Park of Auchentroig, where you can continue straight on to Aberfoyle or turn left deeper into the forest, to meet up with the Loch Ard trail coming west out of Aberfoyle.

If you want to extend the ride north at Aberfoyle, carry straight on through the town and upon reaching Braeval turn right and continue on your way via the southern shore of Loch Venachar to Callander. Be warned though, you will have a climb or two ahead.

Nearby

Call in at the Queen Elizabeth Forest Park Visitor Centre just outside Aberfoyle and learn all about forestry. There is more to it than meets the eye. At Callander is the Rob Roy and Trossachs Visitor Centre. Here you will find out about the trials and tribulations of Rob Roy Macgregor. There is a sight and sound experience exhibition here and all sorts of unusual souvenirs.

North of Drymen

Ride 34

Callander to Balquhidder through The Pass of Leny: North Central

A well-signed and waymarked cycle route comprising a mix of quiet back roads and a magnificent loch-side railway path.

Map: Landranger 1:50,000, Sheet number 57.

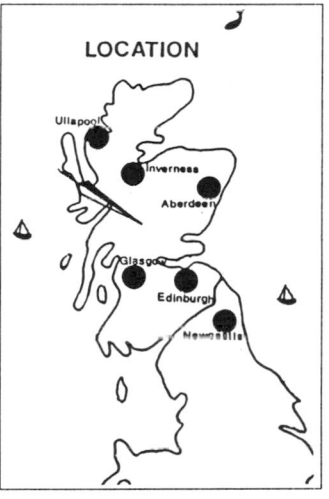

LOCATION

Distance: Callander/Balquhidder/Callander: 24 miles (38½km).

Waymarked: Yes. Good signposts and waymarks along the whole route.

Gradients: There are some ups and downs, nothing too demanding. The ride is perfectly manageable for the occasional cyclist. Remember to allow plenty of time and do not be too ambitious. Take your time and enjoy your surroundings.

Surface: Tarmac and consolidated stone. All hard and well-drained.

Future proposals: Constant maintenance programme.

Other cycle routes linking: Callander to Balloch and then on to Glasgow. For the fit sports cyclist, this ride can be extended north, through Glen Ogle to Killin, following the route of the Glasgow to Killin cycle way and then east along quiet lanes and tracks that run down the southern shore of Loch Tay.

Bicycle hire: Glasgow.

Shops and Refreshments: The facilities are only in the towns and villages.

Warning: If you decide to proceed to Killin, there is an "A" road section where higher traffic densities are likely to be encountered. It is at Kingshouse to Killin on the A84, the A85 and the A827. This is only a short section of the otherwise virtually traffic-free route. Do not rely on finding a shop or a pub around the next corner. Take some sandwiches and drinks and you will have no trouble finding a delightful place to eat.

Introduction

The ride from Callander to Balquhidder utilises a waymarked railway path which is virtually traffic-free, except for a short back road section, just entering Balquhidder. The ride takes you from Callander at the eastern tip of Loch Venachar through the Pass of Leny around the breathtakingly attractive Loch Lubnaig and then on up the river valley to Balquhidder.

The Pass of Leny is dominated by the imposing rocky flanks of Ben Ledi and Ben Vane, rising to heights of nearly 3000 feet (914 metres) to the west and Ben Each and Stuc a'Chroin, which rises to over 3000 feet (914 metres), in the east. The route follows the bending western shores of Loch Lubnaig along the old track bed of the Callander to Crainlarich section of the Caledonian Railway. At the head of the Pass is the charmingly beautiful village of Balquhidder and Rob Roy's Grave.

Along the way, you will see waterfalls, the magnificence of the Loch, the imposing mountains and more wild flowers and birds than most people see in ten years. The air is clean, the noise level is low (and what you can hear is natural), the riding is on a good surface with easy gradients and the views are unbelievable. If you do not enjoy this ride, you should sell your bicycle.

On the railway path

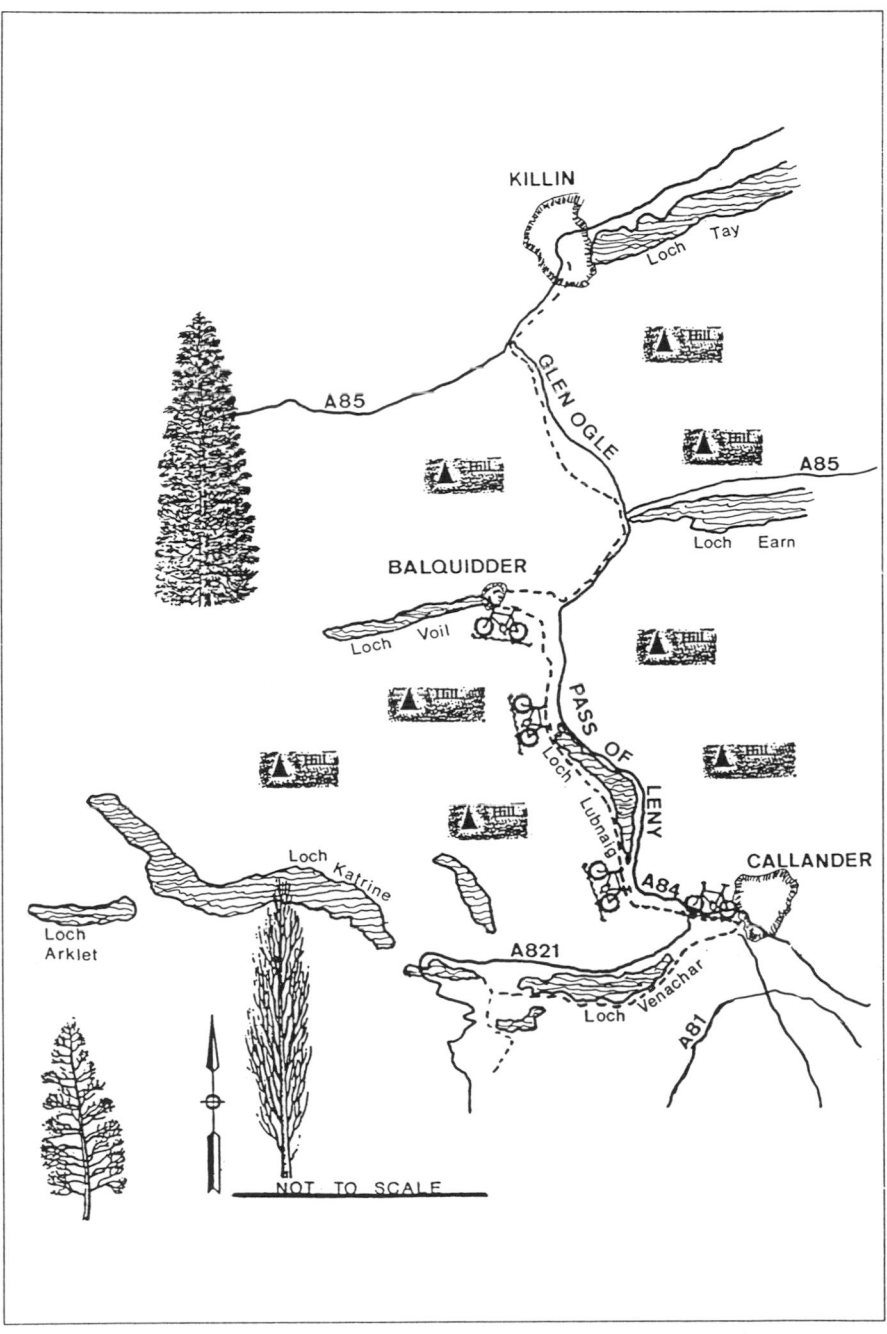

Main Access Points

The route can be joined at many points. The main centres are Callander and Balquhidder:

The Route

The route is well-waymarked and sign-posted at regular intervals. After leaving Callander, the signposts will guide you past the impressive Falls of Leny and on into the pass on the railway track bed. The last little section into Balquhidder is on quiet back roads.

If you feel like continuing to Killin, you should head east towards the main A84. The short main road section up to Lochearnhead is quite pleasant and after the village the signs will encourage you to continue through Glen Ogle and straight on to Killin. Glen Ogle is not as easy as the section that you have just done, but is not a route that should instill undue fear or trepidation.

Nearby

If you want to extend the route beyond Killin take the quiet roads on the southern shore of Loch Tay and the route through to Aberfeldy and Pitlochry is manageable. Once again, the surroundings are superb although the scenery softens up as you head east. If your calling is towards the west, take the Craignavie/Auchlyne route out of Killin before joining the main road. However, this route is not, by any stretch of the imagination, traffic-free.

Ride 35

Glenbranter to Benmore Younger Botanic Gardens on the Cowal Peninsula

A glorious eighteen-mile loch-side forest return ride.

Map: Landranger 1:50,000, Sheet number 56.

Distance: 18 miles (29km).

Waymarked: Green.

Gradients: Minimal.

Surface: Good solid, stony and well-drained forest tracks and roads.

Future proposals: N/A

Other cycle routes linking: There are other way-marked cycle trails in Argyll Forest Park.

Bicycle hire: Glasgow.

Shops and Refreshments: Take a sandwich and a drink.

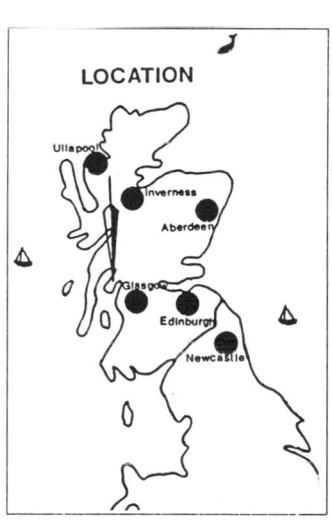

LOCATION

Introduction

The Argyll Forest Park occupies a large area of the beautiful Cowal Peninsula. To get there from the Glasgow area, take the ferry from Gourock to Dunoon. There is so much to see on Cowal that it is worth allowing plenty of time for your trip.

The route takes you on a fairly level ride through the edge of the forest, on the western banks of Loch Eck. There are numerous picnic places or quiet clearings to just relax for a while. This is truly stunning landscape, so make the best of it whilst you are here.

Loch Eck is cut deep into a narrow valley and surrounded by forest on all

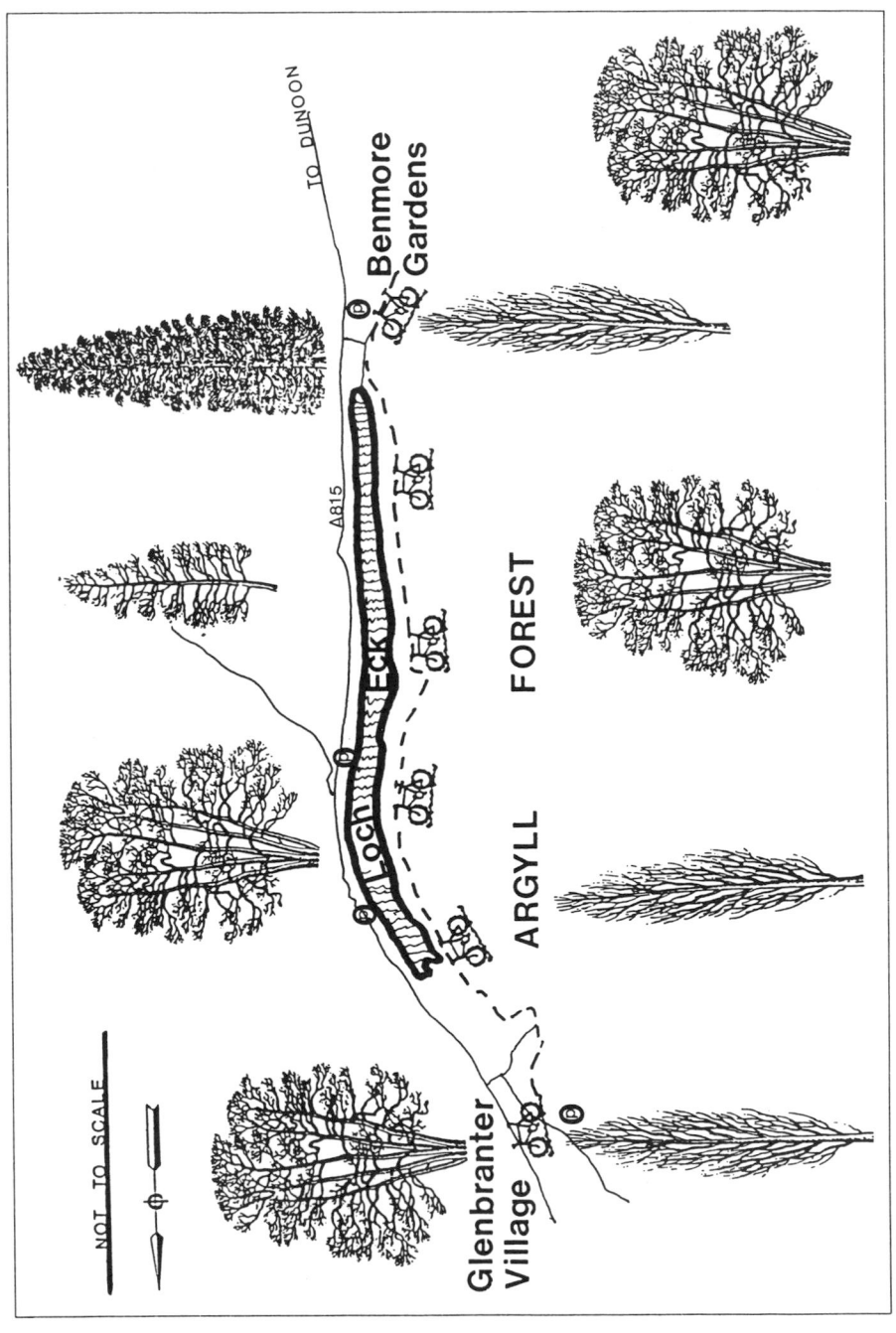

sides. If the weather is on the blustery side, this is normally a nice sheltered ride and if the weather is warm, there is plenty of shade cover. Do not rush the trip but stop occasionally to look at the beauty and listen to the silence; it is a rare commodity.

Loch Eck (photo courtesy of the Bute & Cowal Tourist Board)

Main Access Points

Start at either end of the ride.

To find Glenbranter village car park go three miles to the south of Strachur on the A815 and turn right over the River Cur. It was here that the first plantings of the Argyll Forest Park were made in 1921, on land leased from the famous musician Sir Henry Lauder.

To find the Younger Botanic Gardens car park, drive out of Dunoon on the A885, later turning left onto the A815. The Gardens are off a side road on the left.

The Route

Leave Glenbranter village car park by turning right and following the roads along the green waymarked trail. This will lead you to the glorious loch-side path. Follow this for eight miles and you will find Benmore Gardens, just south of the end of the Loch. Retrace your route to return.

Nearby

The stunningly wonderful Benmore Younger Botanic Gardens at the southern end of the ride are worth a visit on their own merit. Planted by a James Duncan over a ten year period between 1870 and 1880, the gardens passed into the ownership of the Younger brewery family (hence the name) and in 1928 were gifted to the nation. The central feature of the gardens is a grand grassy avenue of Californian redwoods. Rhododendrons are profuse, there are ponds, enormous scots pine trees and rolling parkland. This is a wonderful place to be on a fine sunny summer's day.

Dunoon is the biggest town on the Cowal Peninsula and boasts a great deal of fine Georgian and Edwardian architecture. There is an excellent example of a typical Edwardian promenade with superb vistas and sea air, for an after dinner stroll.

Ride 36

The Crinan Canal at the Neck of Kintyre: Argyll

An 18 mile (29km) return trip ride along the revitalised and scenic towpaths of the old Crinan Canal.

Map: Landranger 1:50,000, Sheet number 55.

Distance: 18 miles (29km)

Waymarked: Follow the towpath.

Gradients: None, except lock rises.

Surface: Solid well-drained tarmac, ash, clinker and stone. There are some sections that are still potentially muddy so this ride is best tackled after a dry spell.

Future proposals: Constant improvement of the towpath.

Other cycle routes linking: N/A.

Bicycle hire: Ardrishaig.

Shops and Refreshments: Limited.

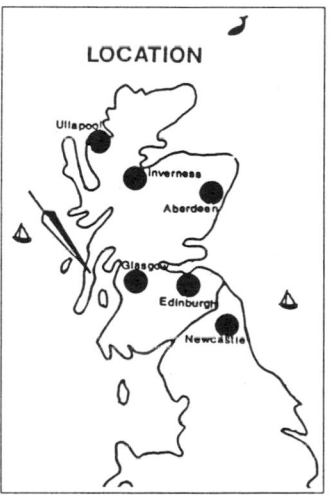

Introduction

The Canal was constructed in an eight year period between 1793 and 1801. It was cut to join Ardrishaig, tucked away on the shores of Loch Gilp in the south-east, to Crinan, nestling in a corner of Crinan Loch in the north-west. From Crinan Loch, boats can access the Sound of Jura and the open sea beyond. From Ardrishaig and Loch Gilp, boats can access Loch Fyne. This drastically cuts the northern sea route to Inveraray and the chain of communications to the maze of Lochs in the east. The nine-mile Crinan Canal cut over 120 miles off the sea route around the Mull of Kintyre.

Yachts, fishing craft and small commercial coaster ships still use the canal

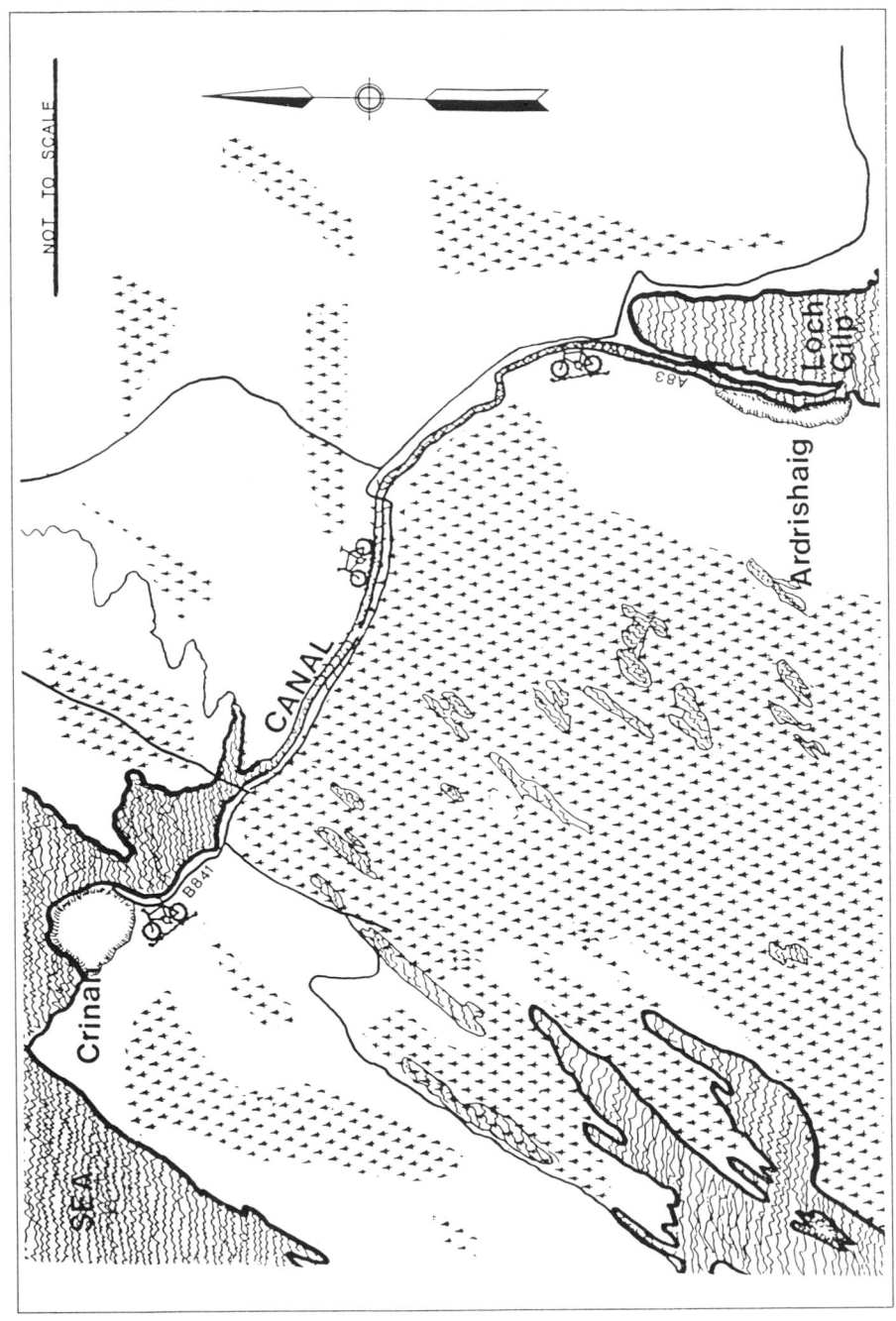

today and the economic arguments are still just as relevant and valid as they were in 1793. The chief engineer involved in the construction was Sir John Rennie. He enlisted help from another famous engineer of the time, Thomas Telford, who is sometimes incorrectly credited with the canal's entire construction.

Shelter from the stormy sea at the canal terminus
(photo courtesy of British Waterways, Crinan)

The sea lock, in Ardrishaig's sheltered harbour, is the first of eight locks to take the canal up to its summit level. A heather and highland landscape is the backdrop for a delightful ride to the west. This summit is a short mile in length, before you commence the decent down the first of seven locks to sea level at Loch Crinan. This western part is a harsher, rockier, landscape.

Main Access Points
Start at either end. You will have no parking problems and you will easily find the canal.

The Route

The route is self explanatory; just follow the towpath and return as you came. There are some very good views of the Western Isles as you progress towards the pretty little harbour at Crinan.

Nearby

Take time to stop at some of the locks, particularly if they are in use. It is interesting to observe some of the different attitudes and ideas of the boat crews.

Crinan itself is a bustling yachting centre and a delightful place to relax for a while. It is overlooked by Duntrune Castle, an early 11th century defensive structure, one of the oldest in Scotland and still inhabited today. Four miles away to the south-east is the ruin of Dunadd Hill Fort, reputed to be the capital of "Dalriada", the Scottish Kingdom.

There is a lovely picturesque stone harbour at Ardrishaig.

Ride 37

Craigvinean Forest and The Hermitage, Tay Forest Park

A fairly energetic but very rewarding 11½ mile (18km) circuit ride in the forest and a visit to The Hermitage.

Map: Landranger 1:50,000, Sheet number 52.

Distance: 11½ miles (18km) in total.

Waymarked: Follow the blue waymarks.

Gradients: Moderate. One short steep section and some undulating sections.

Surface: Solid well-drained forest tracks and roads.

Future proposals: N/A

Other cycle routes linking: There is a shorter RED waymarked route which largely follows the BLUE route but takes a short cut to miss out a loop.

Bicycle hire: Dundee. Dunkeld.

Shops and Refreshments: None. Take a sandwich and a drink.

Warning: Be careful on loose surfaces particularly on descents.

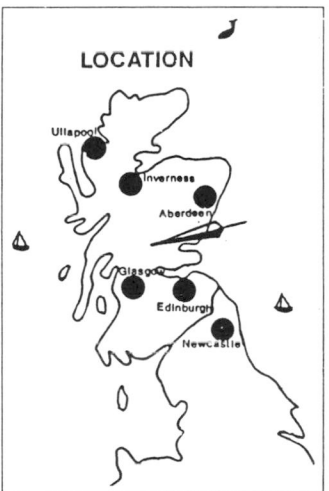

Introduction

The Tay Forest Park offers waymarked cycle trails in Drummond Hill Forest and in Craigvinean forest. Craigvinean Forest has been described as one of the most historic Scottish woodlands and has modern origins dating back to 1759 when James, the second Duke of Atholl, was the first landowner to introduce the science that we refer to today as forestry. He was the first to plant large areas of conifers, initially on Craigvinean Hill. The Forest now

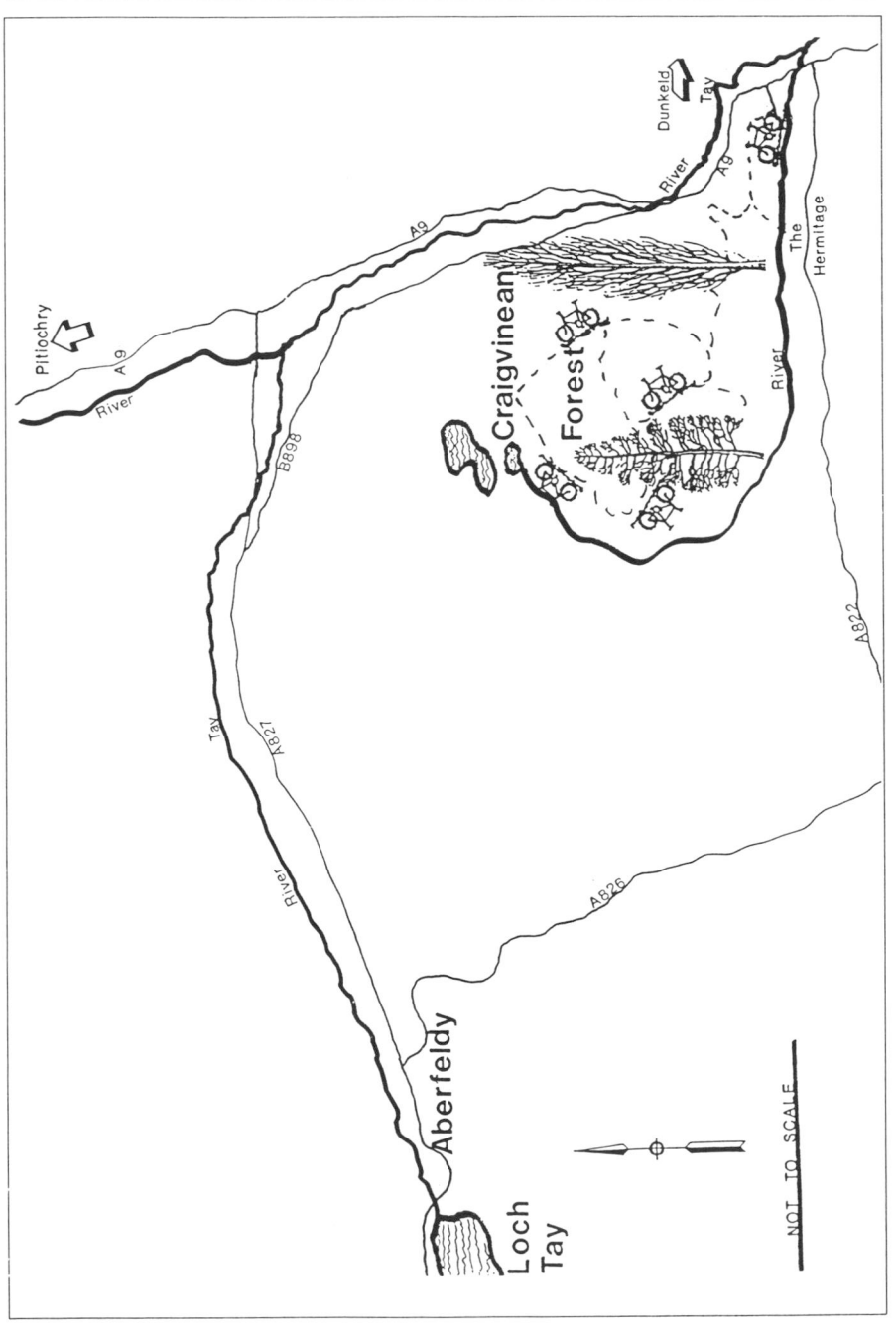

extends to over 2000 hectares (4950 acres) and the rest of the Scottish conifer forests are directly attributable to the commercial success of Craigvinean.

The forest is not entirely conifer for large areas of deciduous broad leaf trees are planted on the lower, less exposed slopes. Wildlife in the forest is diverse, including clumsy capercaillie, furry red squirrel and shy roe deer. Look up and you should see some magnificent birds of prey.

There is an excellent trail laid through the forest which is divided into two waymarked routes, one just a shorter version of the other. A great diversion is the National Trust Folly situated on the edge of the forest.

This is the way to The Hermitage

Main Access Points

The ride begins from the Craigvinean Forest Car Park. This car park is situated off the A9 south of Pitlochry and just north of Dunkeld.

The Route

The Blue route is clearly marked from the main Craigvinean Forest Car Park. There is a steep section of track about one mile into the trail which you may wish to walk; it is only about 300 metres in length. Shortly after this section you will be able to choose between the blue and red routes. The blue route is a bit longer, no more difficult,and worth the extra effort. The waymarks will return you to the car park.

The Hermitage is sign-posted just up the trail from the car park. You may be well-advised to leave your bicycle behind for this diversion.

Nearby

The Hermitage is a beautifully situated folly, in the form of a viewing house over the lush wooded gorge of the River Braan. The Hermitage, which is also known as Ossian's Hall, sits high on a rocky cliff and has an open railed gallery from which visitors can enjoy a panoramic vista over the rocky waterfalls. All this is set in rich green woodland which boasts a splendour of mixed conifer and deciduous trees and especially feature some wonderfully impressive Douglas Fir trees. Further along the gorge is a lovely little bridge, a delightful walk and Ossian's Cave.

The Hermitage was built in 1758 and gifted to the National Trust for Scotland by the wish of the 8th Duke of Atholl, presented by his widow Katharine, Duchess of Atholl in 1944. It was restored once in 1952 and again in 1986. It is well worth a diversion from the ride.

Ride 38

Glen Tilt: Blair Atholl to Forest Lodge

A ride along one of the great "mounths" on a riverside track. Follow the route taken by Queen Victoria. (She did not go by bicycle!)

Map: Landranger 1:50,000, Sheet number 43.

Distance: 7 miles (11km); Return trip: 14 miles (22km); Falls of Tarf: 15 miles (23½km).

Waymarked: Signposts by the Scottish Rights of Way Society. "Glen Tilt."

Gradients: A steep climb out of Blair Atholl. An undulating route.

Surface: Riverside track and tarmac roads.

Future proposals: N/A.

Other cycle routes linking: N/A.

Bicycle hire: Blair Atholl.

Shops and Refreshments: None beyond Blair Atholl.

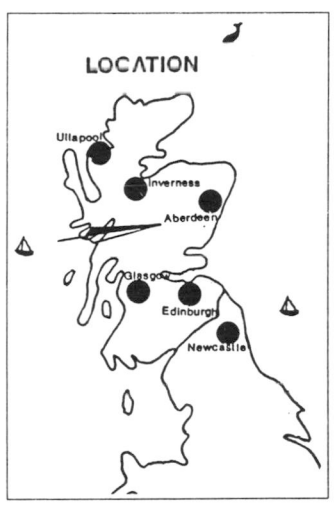

Warning: Do not rely on finding a shop or a pub around the next corner Glen Tilt is wild country. Take some sandwiches and drinks and you will have no trouble finding a nice riverside picnic spot.

Make sure that you have plenty of bad weather gear if you have any doubts about the weather and if you are travelling alone or in small groups, tell someone where you are heading and when you expect to return.

Introduction

Blair Atholl is a pretty village situated on the River Garry amidst the beauty of some of the finest Highland valley scenery. The Duke of Atholl built Blair castle in 1269, choosing this point because it was the natural meeting point of several Glens. A local generic term for these Glens is "The Mounths". This is used to describe the routes that link up the various valley settlements, via the valleys that weave between the great granite humps of the Atholl Highland Range.

In October 1861, Queen Victoria travelled up Glen Tilt, two pipers playing all the time ahead of her entourage. The Queen was said to have described the pipers and the journey: "The pipers had a most cheerful effect. The wild strains sounded so softly amid these noble hills; and our caravan winding along, our people and the Duke's all in kilts, and the ponies, made altogether a most picturesque scene."

In 1847 the Scottish Rights of Way Society won an historic legal battle to affirm access through Glen Tilt, a case that formed an important precedent. This had resulted from attempts by the Duke of Atholl to close the Glen to the public. He had wanted to keep it to himself for deer hunting. Some of his ghillies had tried to prevent a certain Professor Hutton-Balfour (an Edinburgh University Botany Professor) from using the route. The Professor's famous victory is celebrated in the lines of "The Ballad of Glen Tilt".

> *Balfour he had a mind as weel*
> *As ony Duke could hae, man,*
> *Quo' he, "Ther's ne'er a kilted chiel*
> *Shall drive us back this day, man.*
> *Its justice and its public richt,*
> *We'll pass Glen Tilt afore the nicht,*
> *For Dukes shall we*
> *Care a'e bawbee?*
> *The road's as free*
> *To you and me*
> *As to his Grace himself, man.*

This is a delightful ride in good weather conditions but can be hard in wet or particularly windy weather. There is a steep climb out of the valley if you start from Blair Atholl, but this will translate to a glorious freewheel on your return. (A climb is always best dealt with at the beginning of the ride.)

Main Access Points
Blair Atholl. Take the road heading north out of the village sign posted to Glen Tilt.

The Route
Leave Blair Atholl via the minor public road signed "Glen Tilt". There is a fairly steep on-road climb before the ride levels off into the Glen itself. The route follows the easily defined track along the lovely banks of the busy

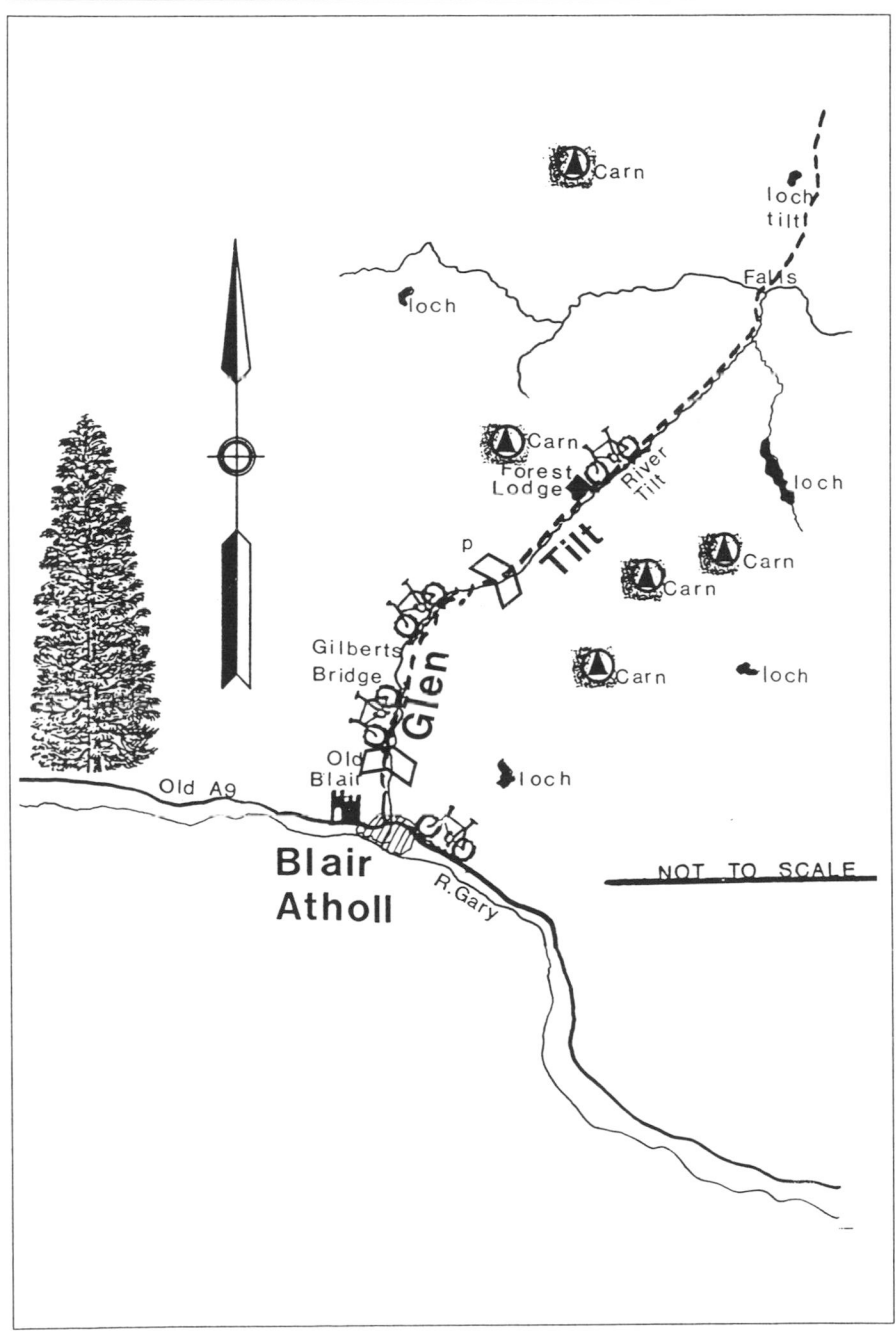

River Tilt, crossing it at Croftmore and Marble Lodge. Although the suggested route ends at Forest Lodge, it is possible to continue to the Falls of Tarf (or further if you wish). Beyond Forest Lodge, the going is harder than the first section, but the Falls of Tarf are a magnificent sight. Return by the same route and enjoy the wind in your face on the lovely freewheel back into Blair Atholl.

Nearby

Blair Castle was originally built by the Duke of Atholl in 1269. Today, it is a fine mix of stately home and 13th century defences. It is the mustering ground for the Atholl Highlanders Army who are the only private army still legally in existence in Great Britain today. This is a result of a decree by Queen Victoria in a moment of romantic weakness.

The Castle has withstood many Jacobite uprisings and has a good range of artefacts in its museum including some very impressive suits of armour. It also boasts a most interesting room of tapestries. The Castle is open to the public at times that are variable throughout the year. Details should be checked with the tourist office before visiting.

Ride 39

Glen Tarbert and Loch Sunart: North-West Scotland

Glen Tarbert, "The Road to Sunart and Beyond". Paradise on two wheels? This is a ride on public roads offering virtually traffic-free riding conditions.

Map: Landranger 1:50,000, Sheet numbers 40, 41 and 49.

Distance: Corran Ferry To Strontian, 14 miles (22½km); Strontian to Polloch, 9 miles (14½km); Strontian to Acharacle, 12 miles (19½km); Full return ride from Corran Ferry: 70 miles (112½km).

Waymarked: Not as such. Follow the A861 and either continue through Strontian, past the glorious Loch Sunart and onto Acharacle, or take the very quiet public road north out of Strontian and follow it to Polloch and Loch Shiel.

Gradients: The route is undulating but there is nothing that should cause any great problems.

Surface: Tarmac.

Future proposals: N/A

Other cycle routes linking: N/A

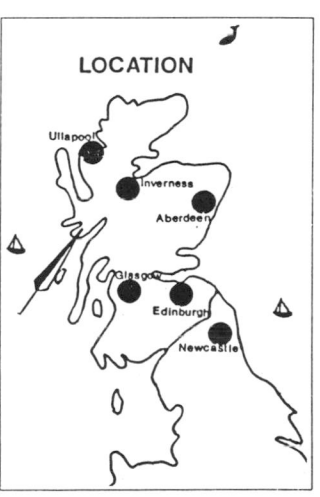

LOCATION

Bicycle hire: Fort William.

Shops and Refreshments: Limited apart from village facilities. Take a picnic.

Warnings: Winds - if you are planning a one-way trip, take advantage of the prevailing winds which are most likely to be from the south. Much of this route is on "A" roads but the traffic between ferries is extremely light. Often a bunch of vehicles will arrive and pass you all seemingly together after which it may be up to half an hour before you see another car. This is because the ferry at Corran spits out its load and then takes half an hour or so before it returns with another batch. Because of the peace and quiet of the area, you will hear traffic some distance away and if you prefer, you can dismount until it has passed. Whatever you decide, do not be put off this route by the fact that it uses public roads, as it is a wonderful ride.

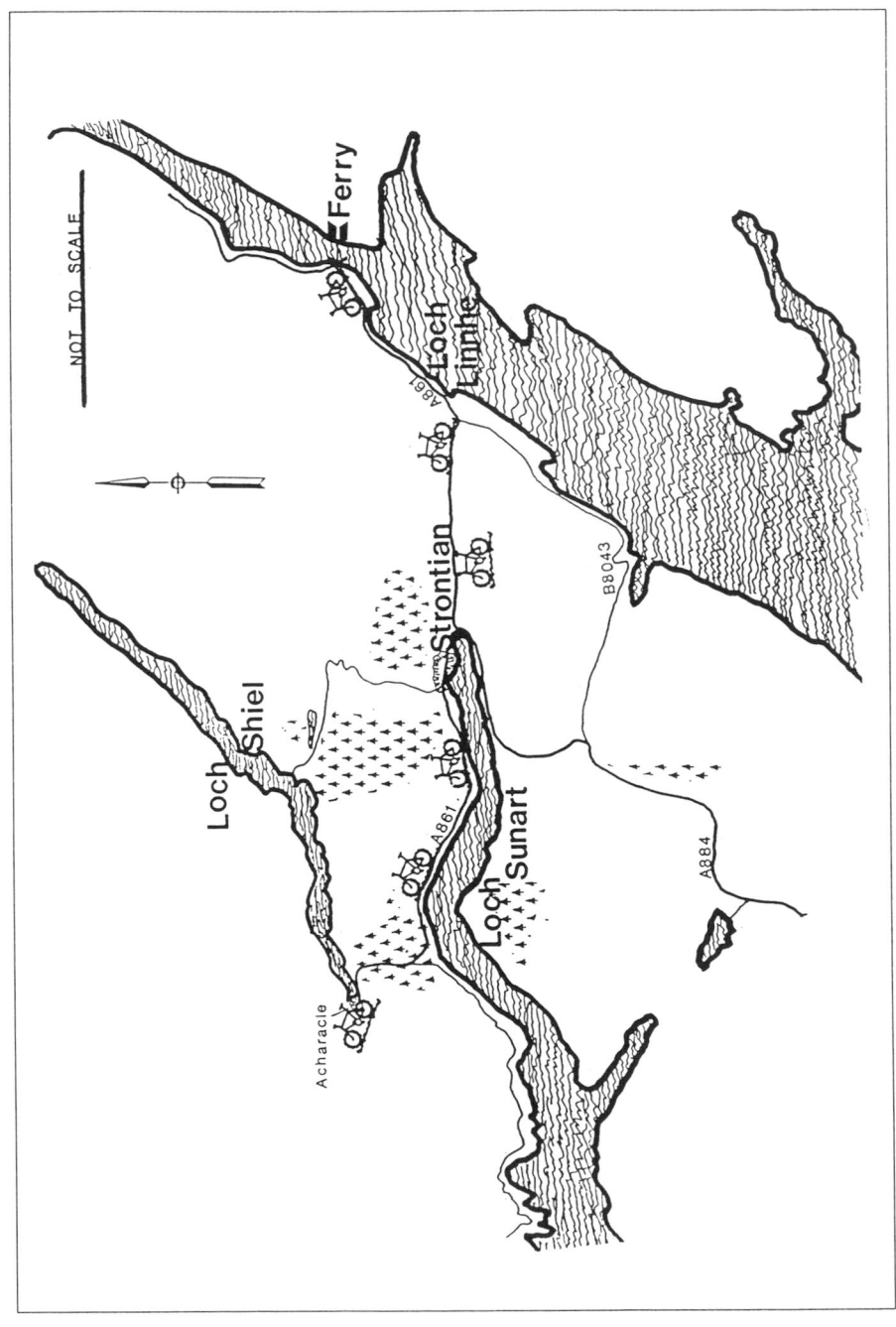

Introduction

Glen Tarbert, "the Road to Sunart and Beyond" is the A861 from the Corran Ferry to Acharacle. The "Beyond" is the public road from Strontian village to Polloch and Loch Shiel. Although the ride is on a public road, the traffic is very light and the riding is very easy, apart from some minor climbs.

This is a ride which can easily be divided into two or three sections to suit your time schedule and energy reserves. If you only want a short ride it would be sensible to base your starting point at Strontian village. The surroundings are truly magnificent and because of difficult access the area is not crowded either in terms of people or traffic. There can surely be few better areas to be riding a bicycle.

Main Access Points

Leave your car near the Ferry slip, off the A82, south of Fort William and take advantage of the "FREE for pedestrians and cyclists offer" on the ferry. Turn left off the ferry and a leisurely ride will get you to Strontian in about an hour and a half.

The Route

The Corran Ferry, south of Fort William, is operated by Caledonian MacBrayne Ltd and offers a free transit to pedestrians and cyclists. When you come off the ferry, turn left and follow the bay around along the western shore of Loch Linnhe. At the junction with the B8043, follow the A861 towards Strontian and Sunart. If you decide to turn left onto the B8043 and follow the road down Loch Linnhe, this is initially a most beautiful ride but to get to Loch Sunart via the A884 you will be involved in some serious climbing.

At Strontian village, continue along the A861 and enjoy the magnificent loch-side ride to Salen before turning north onto the short section to Acharacle on the western tip of Loch Shiel.

In order to get to the central area of Loch Shiel, past Polloch, return to Strontian and take the minor public road north out of the village. Be warned, this minor road does include some climbing.

Nearby

Strontian was made famous by a Penzance-born Cornishman, Sir Humphry Davy. In 1808 he discovered the element Strontium (named by him after the village) in the old mines behind the village. Strontium is a reactive metal which is best known for its use in fireworks. When mixed with water it imparts a bright red flame. In a less-desirable form the isotope Strontium 90 is only produced as a by-product of nuclear reactions. The high energy beta-rays emitted from this isotope have all sorts of nasty side effects but unless there has recently been a nuclear explosion in the area, you will have nothing to worry about!

1808 was a good year for Sir Humphry. In 1807 he had to be satisfied with discovering only one element, Potassium. 1808 brought a bumper crop, because as well as discovering Strontium, he also discovered Sodium, Calcium, Barium and Magnesium.

Ride 40

The Great Glen and Caledonian Canal Cycle Ride. Part 1: Fort William to Laggan

An easy canal-side and loch-side ride through
The Great Glen.

Maps: Landranger 1:50,000, Sheet numbers 41 and 34.

Distance: Fort William to Laggan, 23 miles (39km); Fort William to Laggan return, 46 miles (78km).

Waymarked: Follow the directions.

Gradients: All of this section is fairly easy going. Be warned that if you decided to continue up the Glen, the going generally gets harder as you go further north.

Surface: Variable. Road/ forest road/ towpath. All fairly solid and well-drained but watch the towpaths after rain.

Future proposals: Plans are being prepared to complete the route, through to Inverness. At present the Great Glen Route after Drumnadrochit is entirely an on road and heavy traffic situation.

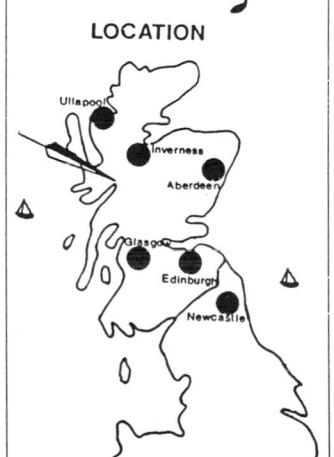

LOCATION

Other cycle routes linking: Forest routes in the Glen.

Bicycle hire: Fort William.

Shops and Refreshments: Limited, apart from village facilities. Take a picnic.

Winds: If you are planning a one-way trip, take advantage of the prevailing winds which are most likely to be from the south.

Introduction

Unarguably some of the most dramatic and ruggedly beautiful scenery in Europe, the Great Glen is the huge geological fault line depression running north-easterly from Fort William to Inverness. Within the Glen are Loch

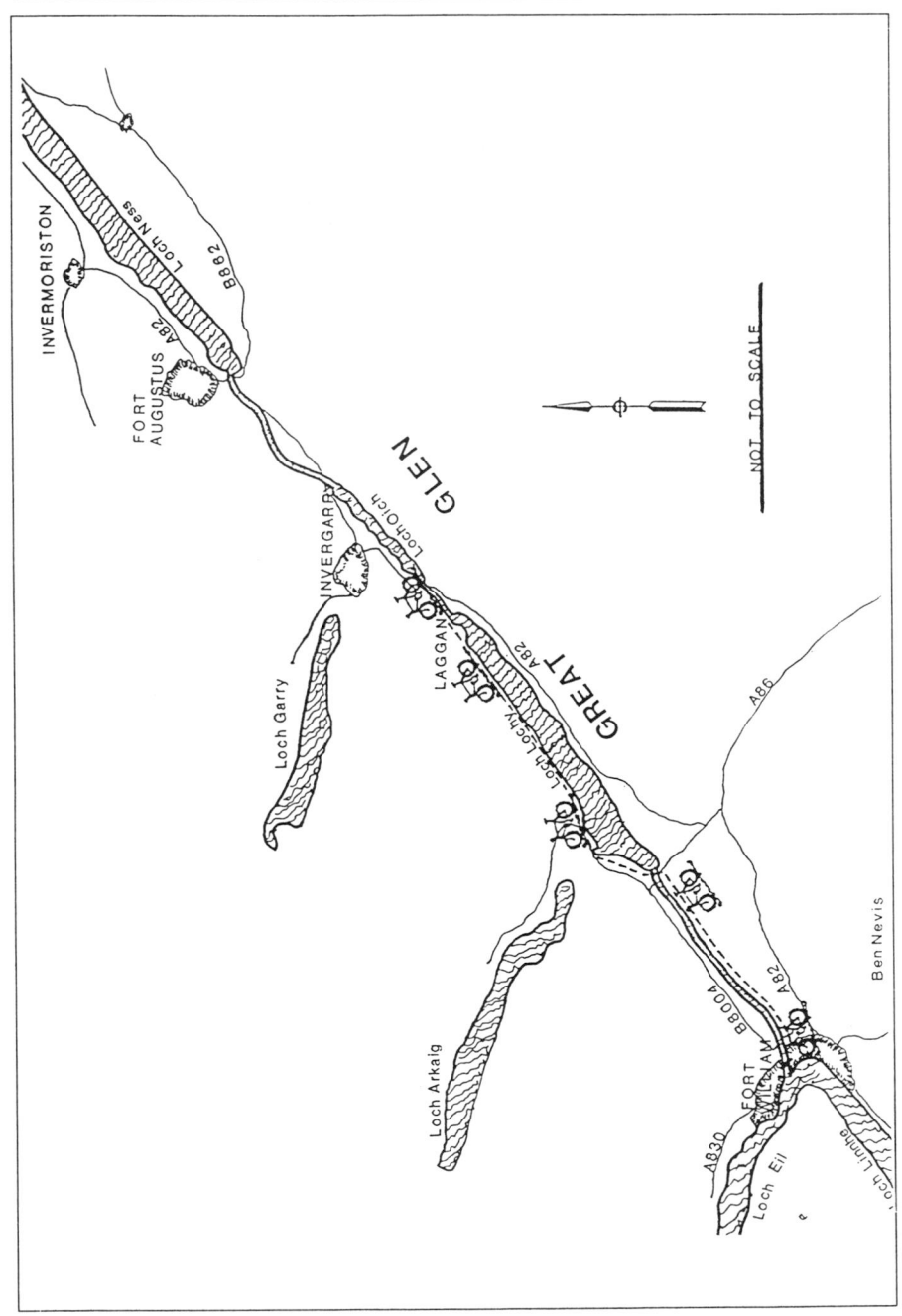

Lochy, Loch Oich and Loch Ness. The Glen is approached at the south-westerly end by Loch Linnhe and at the north-easterly end via the Caledonian Canal from the Moray Firth and Beauly Firth. This section covers the top end of Loch Linnhe to the top end of Loch Lochy.

Along the towpath to Fort William

This ride forms just one part of the Great Glen Cycle Route but, at this time, the extreme north-east of the Glen does not have any proper facility for cyclists, who have to take their chances on the very busy A82 Trunk Road. This part of the route, from Fort William up to Laggan, at the top of Loch Lochy, is almost entirely off-road or on very quiet back lanes, following a mixture of roadside cycle track, canal towpath, forest road and single track tarmac road. This is the easiest section and unless you are intending to route through the whole Glen, 23 miles (37km), it is sufficient for a very pleasant day's return riding which could be easily extended into a more major expedition by incorporating some of the multitude of forest trails within the Glen. Alternatively, if you just want a very easy trip as a taster of the Great Glen, base yourself at Clunes and ride either alongside Loch Lochy for a short way or down the canal towards Fort William, returning when you feel that you've had enough.

There is a good variation of riding, a fascinating amount of interest and unbelievable views in any direction that you care to gaze. If you are lucky, you could see a red deer or a golden eagle on the steep mountain sides all around the Glen, which include the mighty Ben Nevis towering above Fort William. The flight of 8 locks at Banavie are known as "Neptune's Staircase" and are well worth studying. They are a fine example of the expansive and innovative imagination and genius of Thomas Telford. The canal was built over a period of nineteen years from 1803 to the eventual opening in 1822. What a magnificent achievement for the era!

Neptune's Staircase

Main Access Points

At the canal swing bridge at Banavie on the A82(T) just outside Fort William or at any point along the route. There are plenty of signs on the surrounding roads.

The Route

Head north out of Fort William on the A82(T). At the canal swing bridge at Banavie, take the right-hand towpath. At Gairlochy, turn left over the bridge and follow the B8005 into Clunes. Keep Loch Lochy on your right and follow the forest roads towards Laggan.

Nearby

Inverness and Fort William are the major towns in the area. Both offer much fascination and an abundance of interest. In order to discover all about them, use the local tourist information offices

Ben Nevis is 4418 feet (1350 metres) high, the highest mountain in the UK. If you fancy a walk to the top start 2½ miles (4km) from Fort William, at Achintree Farm, on the eastern bank of the River Nevis. Here is a track which winds five miles to the summit (on foot). Unbelievably, in 1911, somebody drove a car to the top by this route. A notice in the tourist office warns people to take great care when climbing up the precipitous cliffs of the northern flank. I wonder how many casual tourists have benefited by that good advice. I certainly didn't attempt to climb the northern flanks!

Ride 41

The Great Glen and Caledonian Canal Cycle Ride. Part II: Laggan to Invermoriston

Riding in the Great Glen with magnificent panoramic vistas.

Map: Landranger 1:50,000, Sheet number 34.

Distance: Laggan to Invermoriston, 19½ miles (31km); Laggan to Fort Augustus, 11 miles (17½km); Fort Augustus to Invermoriston, 8½ miles (13½km); Laggan to Invermoriston return, 39 miles (62km).

Waymarked: Follow the directions.

Gradients: There is a mild climb from Laggan to the Craig Liath Forest Road followed by a tarmac descent into Mandally. A purpose built climb out of Glengarry is eventually followed by a descent into Loch Oich. Throughout the route there is constant undulation. Do not be put off by the climbs, because they are not too bad and the views are worth every bead of sweat.

Surface: Variable. Road/ Forest road/ Towpath. All fairly solid and well-drained but watch the towpaths after rain.

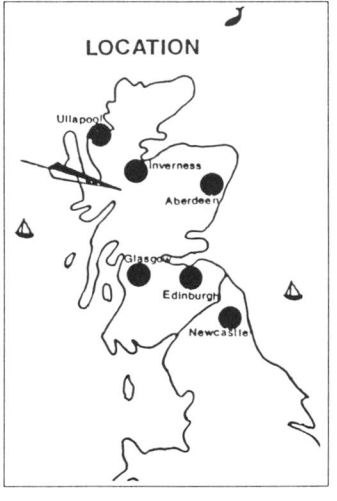

LOCATION

Future proposals: Plans are being prepared to complete the route, through to Inverness. The route presently terminates at Drumnadrochit.

Other cycle routes linking: Forest routes in the Glen.

Bicycle hire: Fort William and Inverness.

Shops and Refreshments: Plenty of opportunities along the route.

Winds: If you are planning a one-way trip, take advantage of the prevailing winds which are most likely to be from the south.

Introduction

This part of the Great Glen route, from Lagan up to Invermoriston, a quarter of the way up Loch Ness, is mainly off-road, following a mixture of forest road, winding single track tarmac road and cycle path. This is the second easiest section after the Fort William to Laggan ride. It is 19½ miles (31km) in length and includes some of the finest views of Loch Ness.

At this time, the extreme north-east of the Glen does not have any proper facility for cyclists, who have to take their chances on the very busy Trunk Road. If you have already cycled up from Fort William, you will have appreciated the sheer grandeur of the scenery with Ben Nevis as the massive backdrop.

In good weather, this is some of the finest cycling that is available anywhere. The Caledonian Canal is of great interest to industrial archeologists. There is no doubt that it would be used commercially today if the sheer size of our merchant vessels had not outgrown it. The only real users of the canal these days are pleasure craft. Do not forget to look out for the monster in Loch Ness and take a camera. Perhaps you can get the photograph that will finally quash all those old sceptics.

Main Access Points

The route can be accessed at any point along the way, but the main access points are at Laggan, Fort Augustus, Allt na Criche car park and picnic area and Invermoriston.

The Route

To get into Laggan from the south, follow the cycle path to avoid the A82(T). Join the Craig Liath Forest road which climbs up to give great views over Loch Oich, Invergarry Castle and beyond, up the Glen.

Enjoy the descent to Mandally where you will join a tarmac road. Here you should go east for a third of a mile (½km) before turning left at the A82(T) to cross the River Garry. Turn left onto the A87 and rejoin the cycle route past the hotel. Climb out of Glengarry on the purpose built track and then follow the forest road to Oich Bridge. A short stretch following the A82(T) will take you to the Caledonian Canal towpath and onto Fort Augustus. Here you must follow the A82(T) for 1½ miles (2½km) before getting back into the forest at the Allt na Criche car park and picnic area. From here, just stick to the forest and you will arrive at Invermoriston. On the way, look at the size of those douglas firs!

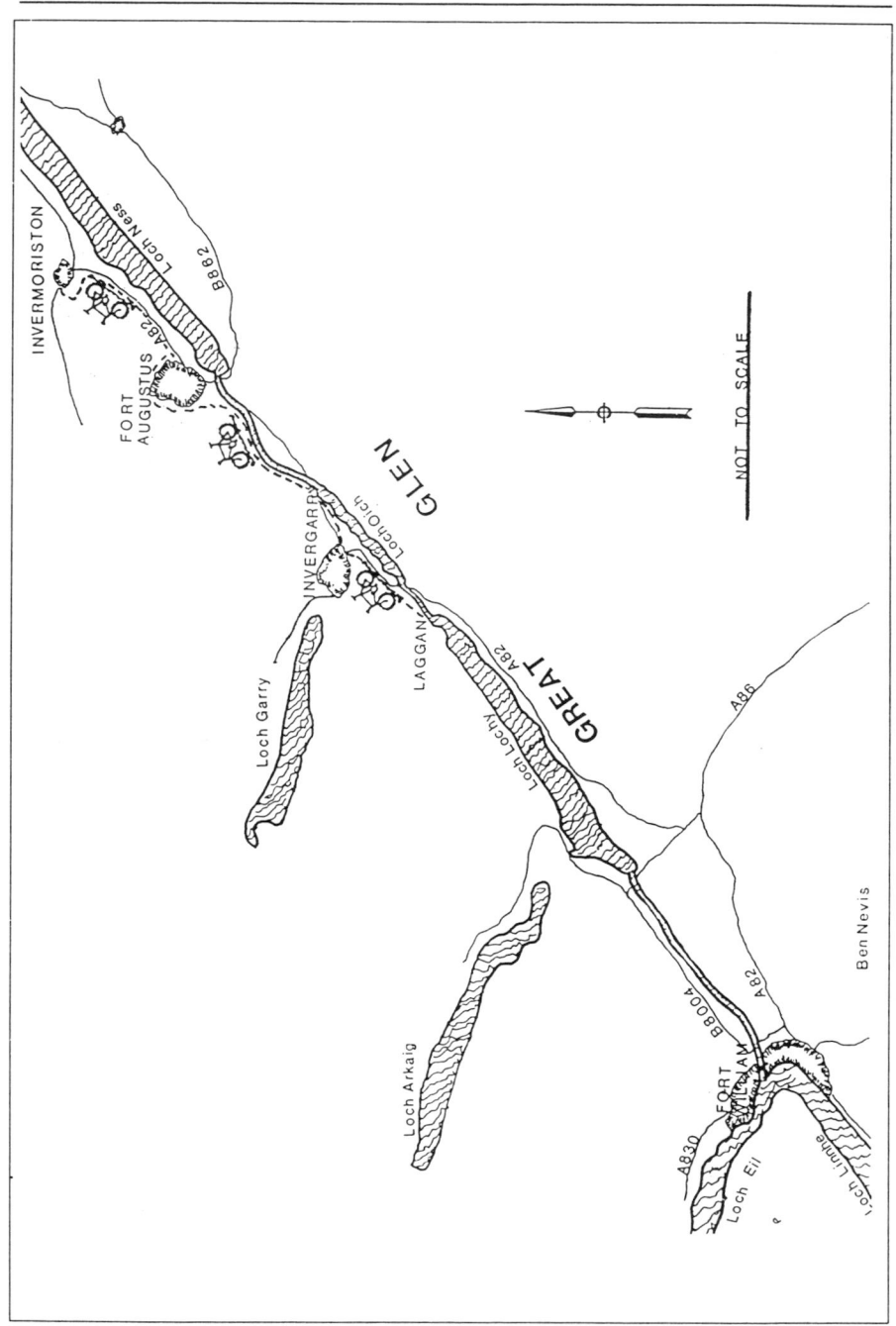

Nearby

Loch Ness is Scotland's largest inland Loch with a length of over 24 miles, depths averaging 400 feet (122 metres) with more than 1000 feet (305 metres) in places. The waters are dark from the peat soils discharged from the many streams and although the loch never freezes, the temperature has never been above 6C (42F), which is the ideal mark for warty, slimy monsters.

If you believe that there is not a monster, ask yourself why there have been so many reports, similar in detail to those from monster observers around Loch Ness. The reports have come not only from here but also from other big lakes in the world, as far afield as Norway, Ireland and British Columbia.

Ride 42

Leanachan Forest, Ben Nevis range: The Great Glen

A Forest Ride at the foot of Ben Nevis. Magnificent views of the Great Glen.

Map: Landranger 1:50,000, Sheet number 41.

Distance: 25 miles (40km) in total.

Waymarked: The easier trails are marked with reassurance waymarks. This is a working forest and the latest information should be checked at the Forest Office before starting out.

Gradients: Although these trails are at the base of Ben Nevis, they do not present difficult gradient problems.

Surface: Good forestry road. Solid, stony and well-drained.

Future proposals: N/A

Other cycle routes linking: N/A

Bicycle hire: Fort William.

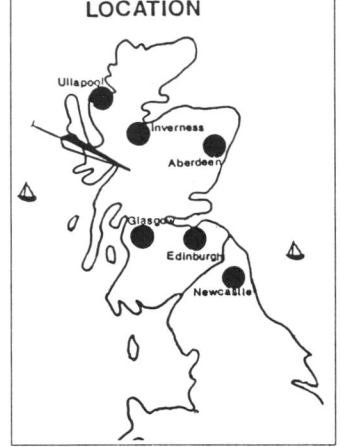

LOCATION

Shops and Refreshments: None in the forest.

Warning: The mist can fall off the mountain fairly quickly. Remember to stick to the forest road and if in serious doubt, down hill is good news. You will eventually find a road. Do not rely on finding a shop or a pub around the next corner, especially if you venture into the forest. Take some sandwiches and drinks and you will have no trouble finding a panoramic spot to stop for a picnic.

Introduction

Leanachan Forest covers a vast area of 3050 hectares (7500 acres) on the base slopes of the Nevis Range. Most of the forest is planted with tall conifers, but the scene is broken by ribbons of rich broad leaf trees alongside the multitude of streams and watercourses. These give depth and feel to the forest.

The Ben Nevis Massif dominates these foot slopes and even amongst the tallest conifers, you are always aware of its mighty presence. The internal and external fences and gates in the forest are fitted with special bicycle flaps and the official cycling trails are well-waymarked.

While you are in the forest, keep a careful eye open for a glimpse of a red deer; there are plenty here. They will appear, sometimes quite close by and as quickly as you can turn round to your companions and say "Look at that!" the deer will have mysteriously disappeared without trace, leaving you with a dubious reputation for seeing things that are not there. Best to say nothing and let your companions find their own deer. Overhead, you will have no problem seeing the magnificent buzzards, circling over some poor unsuspecting vole, or herons waiting to spot a lazy fish. If you have plenty of patience (and binoculars) you may even see an eagle patrolling the higher slopes of Ben Nevis.

Main Access Points

The Forest Office is approached from the A82 at Torlundy, crossing over the railway just to the north of Fort William. Information may be obtained here.

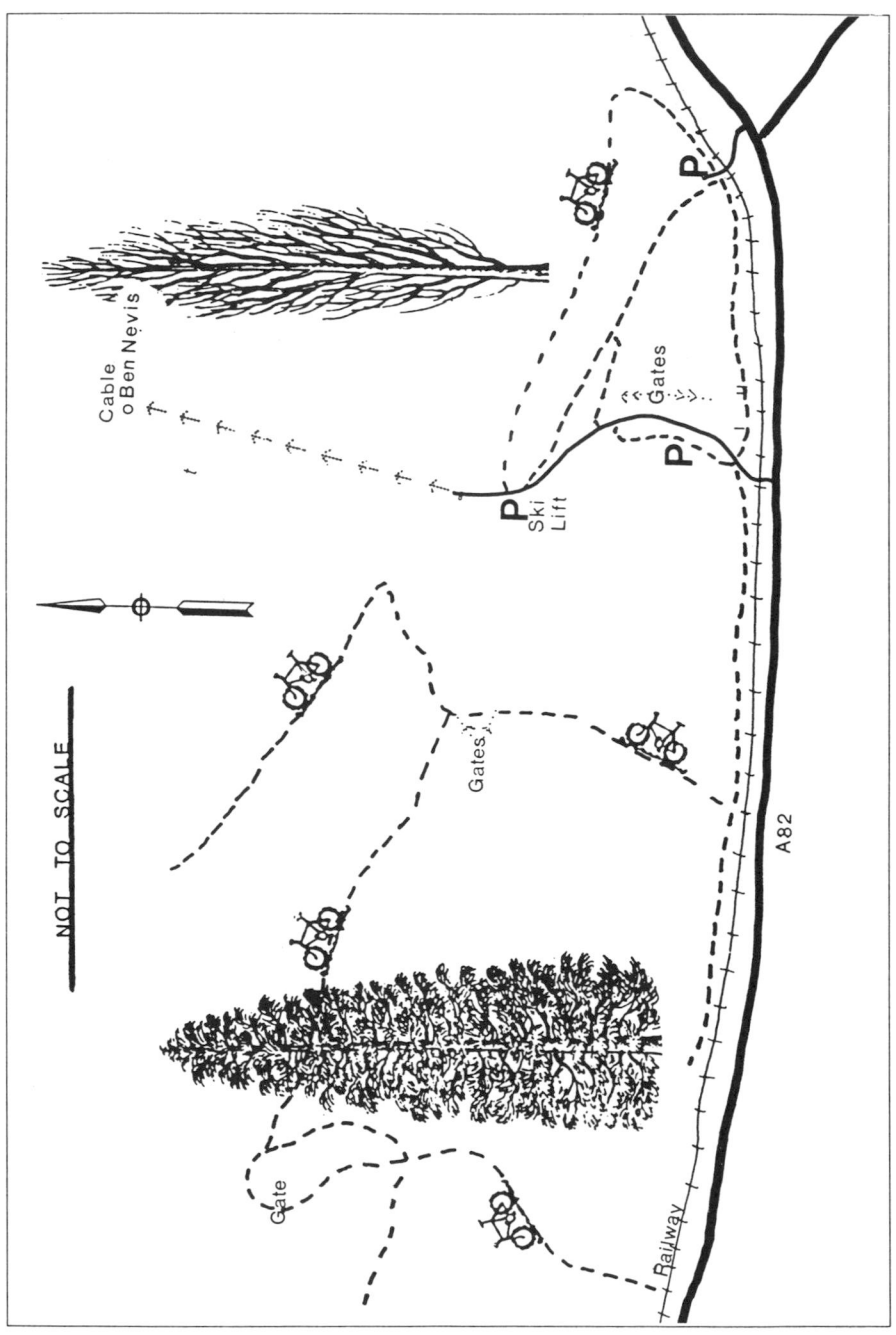

A bicycle made for two, under the Ben Nevis cable car (photo by Alex Gillespie)

Another good place to start your ride is from one of the big Car Parking Lay-bys situated on the access road to the Aonach Mor Ski Facility. This again is found just off the A82, a little further north out of Fort William.

The Route

Leanachan forest is dominated by the massive presence of Ben Nevis. The great range of waymarked trails all have an aura of this gigantic massif and they enjoy the magnificent panorama of the Great Glen. The rides traverse the foot slopes of the range below the highest mountain in Great Britain. The easier trails tend to follow the runs of rivers and streams so there is always a plethora of beauty all around.

Nearby

Ben Nevis towers to a height of over 4,400 feet (1341 metres) above sea level. At the lay by just off the A82, you are just about 400 feet (122 metres) above sea level. This means that you are looking up at 4000 feet (1219 metres) of solid rock.

Fort William takes its name from the original earth and wattle fort that was built in 1655 by General Monk, the 1st Duke of Albemarle. After being rebuilt in 1690, the Fort withstood many attacks and was garrisoned until 1855.

Call into the West Highland Museum in Fort William and you can see the famous secret picture of Bonnie Prince Charlie. It can only be recognised if it is reflected onto the curved mirrored surface of a cylinder.

Ride 43

Black Hall Forest, Banchory: North-East Scotland

A delightful ride from Banchory across the great salmon runs of The Dee and into the depth of the forest.

Maps: Landranger 1:50,000, Sheet numbers 37 and 38.

Distance: 12½ miles (20km).

Waymarked: First follow the Blackhall Road from Banchory, join the red waymarked trail which will then lead you to a white waymarked loop. After completing the loop, return as you came.

Gradients: Easy throughout.

Surface: Forest Roads and tracks. Well-drained and solid.

Future proposals: N/A

Other cycle routes linking: N/A

Bicycle hire: Aberdeen.

Shops and Refreshments: None in the forest.

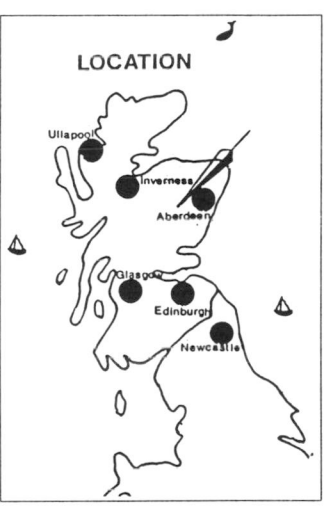

Introduction

Black Hall Forest is situated on the southern banks of the River Dee, just to the west of the lovely town of Banchory, noted for the Dee Lavender Water Company, which produces the lavender water from locally grown plants. To the east of Banchory is the "Brig o' Feugh". This is an eighteenth century bridge with an observation platform, from which you can watch the salmon as they jump up the bustling river.

The forest and the adjoining Scolty Woodland Park have a mature and diverse selection of trees and offer superb level trails ideal for family cycling.

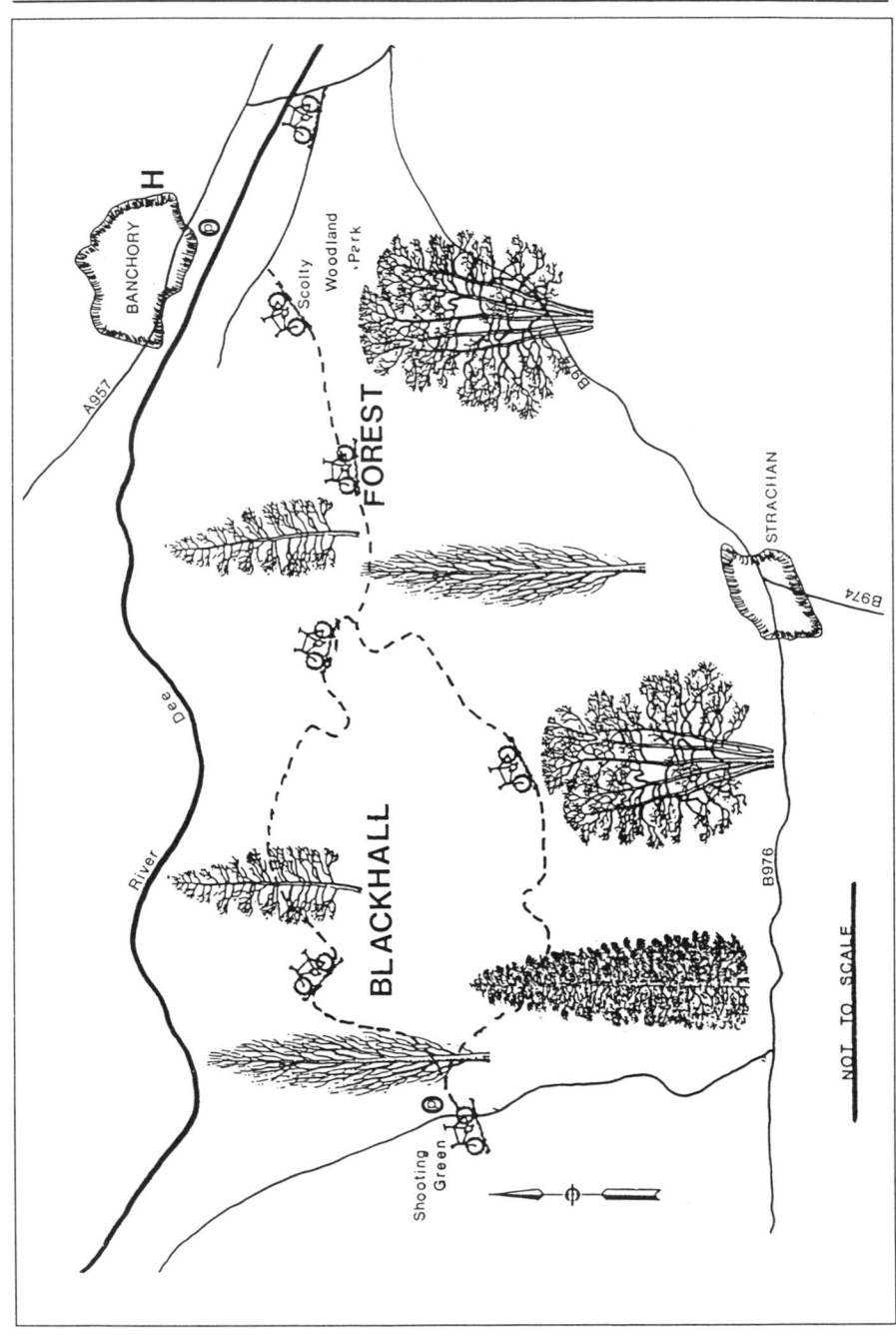

There are plenty of excellent picnic areas in the forest as well as sunny glades to sit and relax when you decide on a break from the riding.

If you prefer, go to Shooting Green Car Park a few miles to the west of Banchory and start the ride from there, perhaps stopping to look around Banchory before returning on the other side of a circular loop.

Main Access Points

Leave your helicopter on one of the helipads in Banchory (if you arrive by car there is a car park). Leave Banchory by crossing the B974 Dee Bridge and turn right onto the Blackhall Road, south of the River Dee. Follow this road and access the forest on the edge of Scolty Woodland Park.

Alternatively start from Shooting Green Car Park. To find this, leave Banchory across the Dee Bridge on the B974 and continue to the village of Strachan, turning right onto the B976. Turn right off the B976 about 3½ miles (5½km) west of Strachan. The car park can be found along this road on the right-hand side. There are a few basic facilities at the car park including a WC.

Sun and shade in the trees

The Route

Leave Banchory on the quiet B974, taking the bridge crossing of the River Dee. The Dee and the River Don, slightly further north, are two of the finest salmon rivers in Scotland. Turn right down Blackhall Road and follow it past the beautiful deciduous woodlands until, on your left, you will find the access point to the red waymarked route into the forest.

The red route will take you to the white route which forms a loop to return you on your original track.

Nearby

Banchory has found a niche as a major commuter town for Aberdeen. It is also widely used as *the* place to entertain corporate guests (Dallas Style). Salmon rods on the Dee are numerous and readily available, at a price. The expensive hotels offer an international standard of cuisine although the prices for rooms and suites are somewhat higher than the Y.H.A. However, most of them do have helipads, a facility rarely offered by the Y.H.A.

There are plenty of interesting shops in Banchory and even if you are not buying, it is quite pleasant to wander round the town.

Ride 44

Drumtochty and Fetteresso Forests: North-East Scotland

34 miles (55km) of great forest riding, through two forests, all on well-surfaced forest roads.

Map: Landranger 1:50,000, Sheet number 45.

Distance: 34 miles (55km) in total.

Waymarked: For the through route from Drumtochty Glen to Fetteresso follow the white waymarks and fork either left or right onto the yellow loop. This will take you right through to the A957 "Slug Road".

An alternative route: From Swanley in Fetteresso Forest follows a **different** white waymarked route which joins a blue waymarked return loop.

A red link loop joins these two systems but the going on this red section is slightly harder than either of the other sections

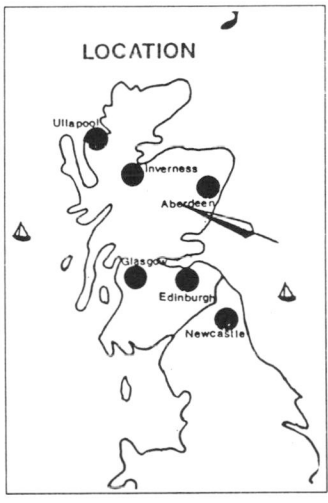

Gradients: Generally moderate. There is a climb out of Drumtochty Glen and various slight climbs along this white route into Fetteresso. The red link route is the hardest going. Don't be put off by these climbs as they only form a very small part of a basically level system of forest roads.

Surface: Good forestry roads. Solid and well-drained.

Future proposals: N/A.

Other cycle routes linking: N/A.

Bicycle hire: Aberdeen.

Shops and Refreshments: None in the forest.

Introduction

The two forests of Drumtochty and Fetteresso are both well into their second rotations, so offer a delightful mix of maturity and species. The Cowie Water River in Fetteresso and the Bervie Water in Drumtochty cut lush paths through the trees and are crossed and re-crossed on several occasions by the routes.

Either enjoy a ride in one forest (Fetteresso is the best choice for this) or try the link between the two. This is about 15 to 18 miles (24 to 29km), depending on which exact route you choose and, although it is slightly more challenging than the simpler Fetteresso rides, it will give you a great deal of enjoyment and satisfaction.

While you are in the area why not have a look at Dunnottar Castle which is about 1½ miles (2½km) south of Stonehaven. It occupies a spectacular position on a promontory reached by a precipitous path. Its main claim to fame was that it was the last castle to hold out against Cromwell's onslaught before eventually falling in 1652 after eight months of siege.

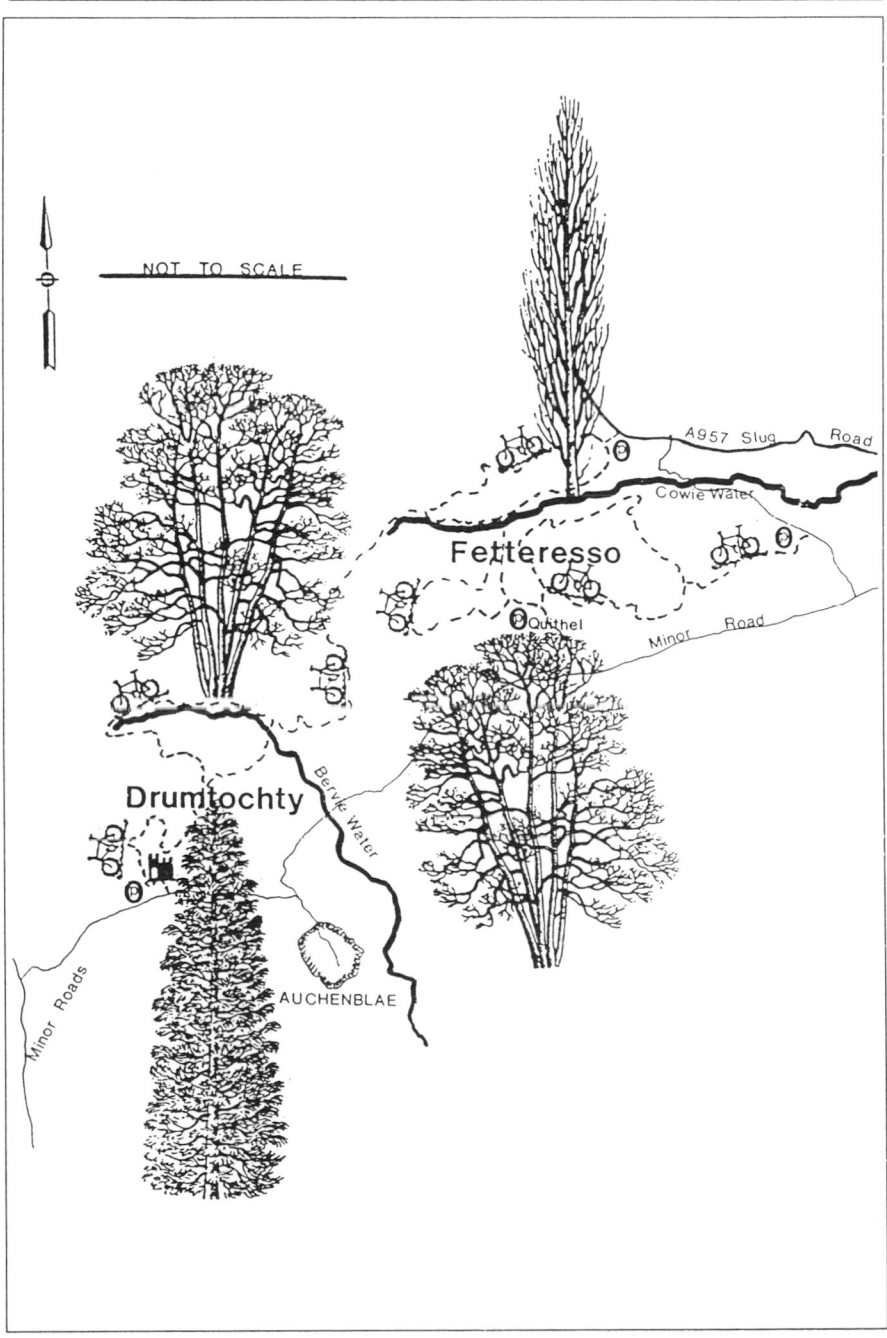

Main Access Points

There are four car parks.

1. At Drumtochty Glen. Take the B974 south from Banchory and after about 10 miles (16km) look out for the signs on the left to Drumtochty forest. The car park is situated a couple of miles along this quiet public road.

2. North of Quithel in the Brae of Glenbervie. Leave Stonehaven on the minor public road through Tewel. Turn right into the forest at the signposts near Tannachie. This car park links into the blue and red waymarked routes.

3. At Swanley. Leave Stonehaven on the A957 "Slug Road" and take the left turn towards Mergie. The car park is off this road and links into the northern white waymarks.

4. Off the A957 "Slug Road" just over 5 miles (8km) west of Stonehaven. This car park links into the yellow route.

The Route

There are several routes in the Fetteresso and Drumtochty forests and none of them are too strenuous for the average rider. The yellow and blue routes are particularly suitable for family groups.

A most enjoyable and satisfying ride is the through route, linking the Fetteresso and Drumtochty forests. There are a few climbs, nothing too great, and the surfaces are all good. If you allow plenty of time this is a suitable family ride.

Leave the Drumtochty Glen car park in a northerly direction following the white waymarks. There is a climb in this initial part of the ride. The route takes you deep into the forest where a loop can take you either way. Try going out one-way and returning on the other side later on.

Eventually you will meet the yellow waymarks. Go left or right, it will lead to the same destination on the A957 "Slug Road." Return via the same route but use the opposite sides of the two loops.

Nearby

Stonehaven is a popular, if somewhat sedentary, holiday town. The beach is shingle as opposed to sand and the harbour is an interesting mix of pleasure and commercial craft. One of the most famous citizens of Stonehaven was William Thomson (1822- 1873). In his comparatively short life he invented the pneumatic tyre, the dry ships dock and the fountain pen. Every June a veteran car rally is held in his memory.

Ride 45

Formartine and Buchan Way. North of Aberdeen

A pleasant 12 mile (19½km) ride along a pretty recreational railway path north of Aberdeen.

Maps: Landranger 1:50,000, Sheet numbers 38 and a tiny sliver of 39.

Distance: Parkhill to Ellon, 12 miles (19½km); Return ride, 24 miles (39km).

Waymarked: Yes. The route is easy to follow.

Gradients: Minimal.

Surface: Level, well-drained and solid.

Future proposals: A policy of ongoing and constant improvements. Subject to the normal economic constraints of these projects, the intention is that the route will eventually continue north from Ellon to Maud, from where it will link to Peterhead on the west coast and Fraserburgh on the north coast.

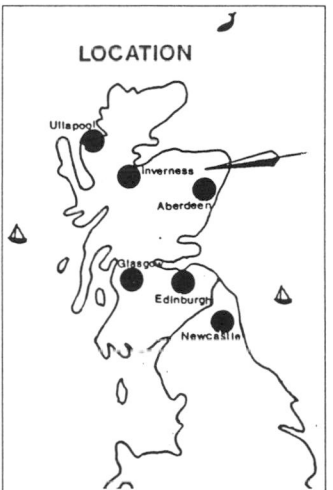

LOCATION

Other cycle routes linking: See future proposals. It is possible to continue beyond Ellon and the going is generally quite acceptable. Beware of a few areas of loose surface and generally overgrown vegetation.

Bicycle hire: Aberdeen.

Shops and Refreshments: There are watering holes in various places near the route but it is a fairly rural ride. Take a sandwich and a drink.

Introduction

The Great North of Scotland Railway Company, the builders of the Formartine and Buchan Line opened the first section for business in 1861. The ride from Parkhill to Ellon forms about half of this earliest section, which ran up as far as Old Deer. The later sections linking Fraserburgh and Peterhead were opened over the following four year period, until, on the

24th April 1865, the whole line was officially declared open. It was formerly named the "Formartine and Buchan Railway."

The company amalgamated with the giant London and North Eastern Railway Company in 1923 and became part of British rail under the 1948 nationalisation. In 1963, the railway's days were numbered under the Beeching cuts and the last passengers were carried in 1965. The railway closed down for good in 1979 having struggled on with a limited freight service for the intervening few years.

Formartine and Buchan Railway path

The railway track bed was acquired by the local authority and ongoing works are revitalising it as a recreational route. As if history is repeating, the first section to open is again this section just north of Aberdeen.

Main Access Points
1. Parkhill. (Off the A947 north of Dyce by the disused rail bridge)

2. Newmachar. (Off the B979)

3. Udny Station.

4. Logierieve. (B9000).

5. Ellon.

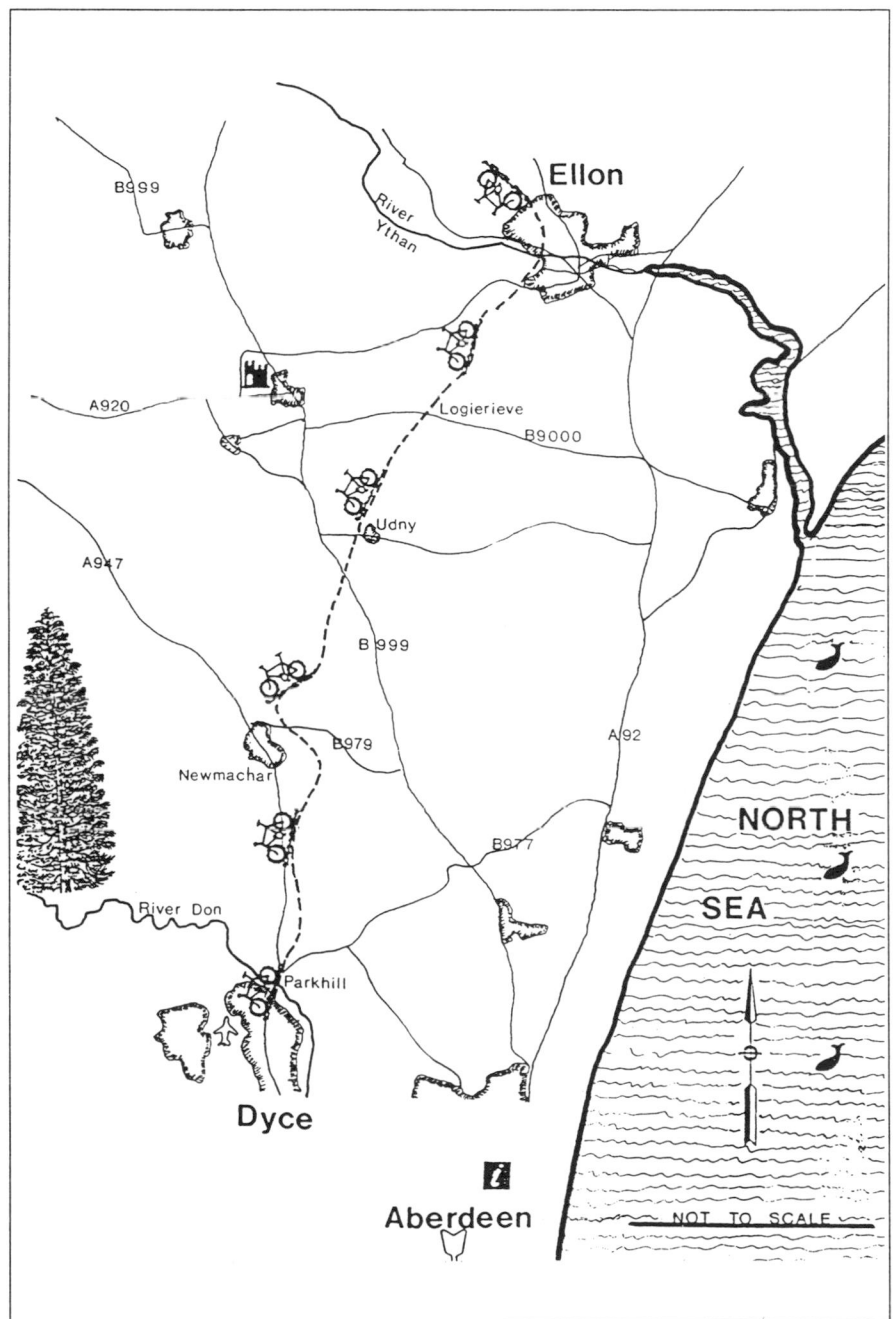

The Route

The route is along a linear railway path and is easy to follow. From Parkhill, the route heads north leaving the A947 to the west. It draws close to Newmachar in deep cuttings and crosses the B979 before setting out into open countryside again. Here, at the summit level of the railway, there are superb views of the Donside and Deeside mountains.

After passing Udny Station, the surroundings are open farmland to Logier-ieve and then cuttings before crossing the viaduct over the Ythan valley to the edge of Ellon.

If you decide to continue further, the way is clear through to Mintlaw and beyond to Fraserburgh and Peterhead, but certain patches of the surface are hard going and ongoing work may sometimes block your way forward.

Nearby

Although Aberdeen has roots in Roman times and has numerous relics of the middle ages, the modern city has experienced its most dramatic growth since the turn of the 19th century. The busy harbour is situated at the mouth of the River Dee and services commercial traffic, fishing fleets and most recently, in a very big way, the North Sea Oil Fields.

The result is a strange brew of ancient Scottish Heritage mixing with modern Scottish commerce, modern Scottish administration and worldly international concerns, complete with their helicopters, credit cards and expense accounts.

Sights worth visiting in Aberdeen are many and varied but do see the harbour where there is always something going on and the Union Terrace Gardens which are famed for the display of 100,000 roses. They are quite a sight in full bloom.

Ride 46

Glen Sgiach & Torrachilty Forest, Easter Ross: North Scotland

A fine 16 mile (26km) forest ride in the backdrop of the 3,433 foot (1050 metre) Ben Wyvis. Following the stony torrent and waterfalls of the Black Water River.

Maps: Landranger 1:50,000, Sheet numbers 25 and 26.

Distance: The Glen Sgiach route: 16 miles (26km).

Waymarked: Blue Cycling Markers.

Gradients: Pleasantly Manageable.

Surface: Solid and well-drained forest roads.

Future proposals: None.

Other cycle routes linking: None.

Bicycle hire: Inverness.

Shops and Refreshments: Take a picnic and a drink.

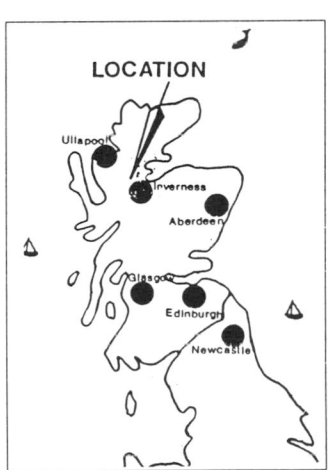

LOCATION

Introduction

Torrachilty Forest is situated around the south-western tip of the Cromarty Firth, in the Easter Ross area of northern Scotland, about 15 miles (24km) north-west of Inverness. Torrachilty lies in the backdrop of Ben Wyvis, the 3,433 foot (1050 metre) mountain, located to the north of the forest. The A835 trunk road runs through the south and western parts of the forest and Loch Garve forms a major feature in the area.

The Blackwater River tumbles and splashes its merry way down the valley and forms a major feature of the Glen Sgiach Route. The cycling is most pleasant, the gradients are acceptably mild and the surface is solid and well-drained forestry road. There are superb views at many locations along

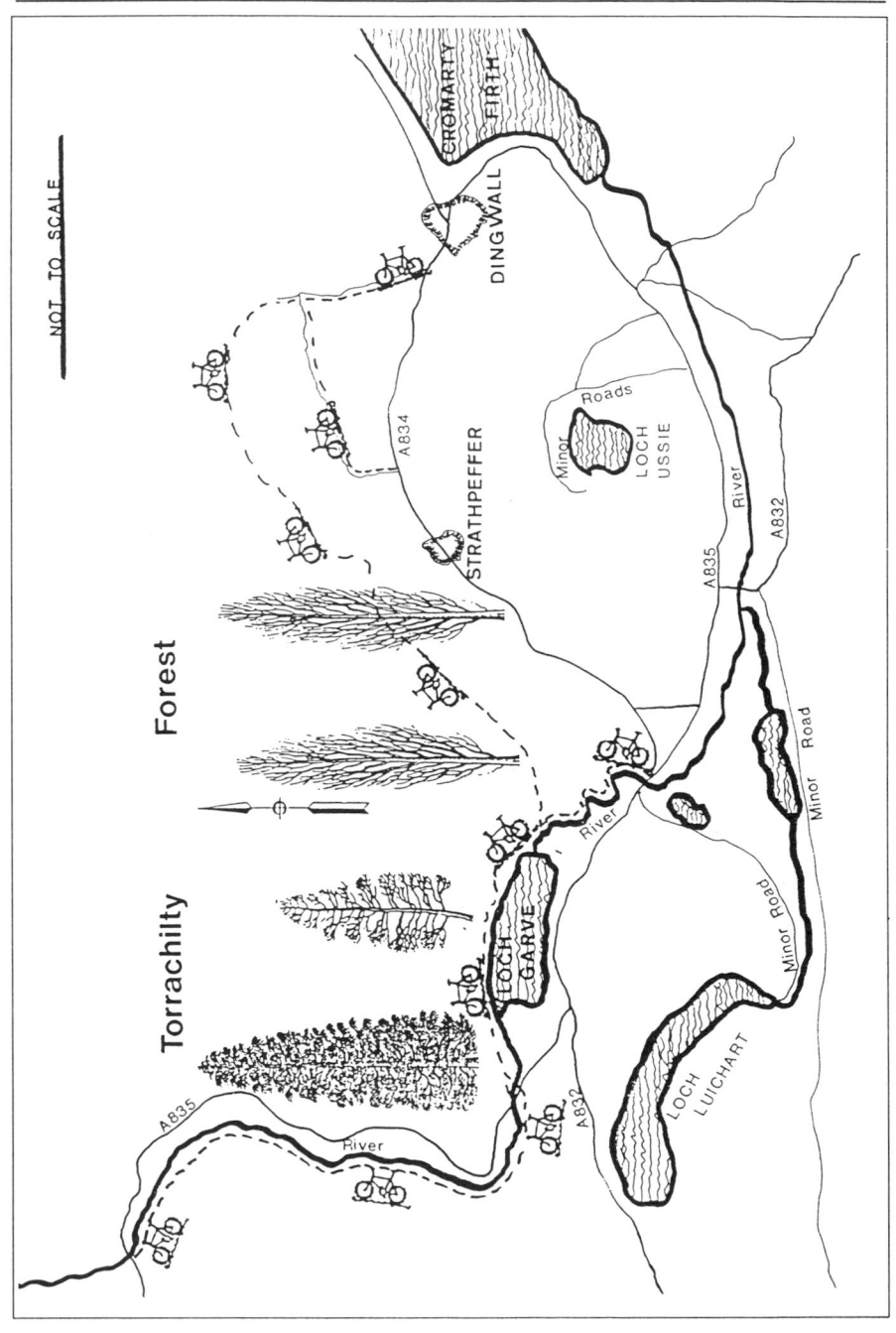

In the forest

the route, so a camera and binoculars will be well worth taking along. A very pleasant picnic area lies around Loch Garve.

Amongst the wealth of wildlife in the forest you may be lucky enough to see some capercaillie. These grey-black ground nesting birds will go croaking across your path in a most undignified manner, trying to fool you into thinking that they are turkeys. Capercaillie are not turkeys, but are an oft ignored wild bird species, which, in the UK, are presently only found in the Highlands of Scotland

Main Access Points

Although the route is designated to start at Contin Car Park, it can also be accessed from Loch Garve and from various points on the A835 by finding the blue cycling waymarks in the forest.

The Route

The Glen Sgiach Route is waymarked with BLUE markers and starts at the Contin Car Park near the eastern junction of the A835 and the A834. The route is easy to follow, but if you do get lost, remember to keep on the low ground and broadly stay with the river. You will soon find your position.

Nearby

Dingwall is the nearest town, a charming quiet settlement on the Cromarty Firth coast, with a population of just 5000 and somewhat forgotten by the rest of the world, since being bypassed by the main traffic routes. The Munros are major land holders in this area and some of their lands are held on "Snowball Rent". One of the legal requirements of their tenure is that they supply a mid-summer snowball, on demand, to their overlords. If the condition was ever applied, which is unlikely, it should be possible to find some snow among the Northern Corries on Ben Wyvis at any time of the year. If you doubt this, feel free to nip up and check my claim at any time.

The 16th Century Castle Leod, north of Strathpeffer, is the home of the Earl of Cromarty and the venue for the annual Strathpeffer Highland Games which are held in the wooded castle grounds every August.

Strathpeffer was an active spa town in the 18th and 19th Century and much of the Bavarian style and Germanic architecture was in deference to the popularity of the Bavarian Spas at that time. The peak of the Spa's activity was when the Highland Railway opened a branch line to Strathpeffer in 1885. The resultant boom in tourism is said by some to have been the Spa's downfall.

Ride 47

Black Isle Forest, Military Road: North Scotland

A 10 mile waymarked cycle route in the Black Isle Forest enjoying great panoramic views of the Cromarty and Moray Firths.

Maps: Landranger 1:50,000, Sheet numbers 21,26 and 27.

Distance: The Military Road, 10 miles (16km); with typical access road diversion: 16 miles (26km)

Waymarked: Red waymarks and Military Road signs.

Gradients: Manageable.

Surface: Solid forestry roads, well-drained.

Future proposals: N/A

Other cycle routes linking: N/A

Bicycle hire: Inverness.

Shops and Refreshments: None. Take a sandwich and a drink.

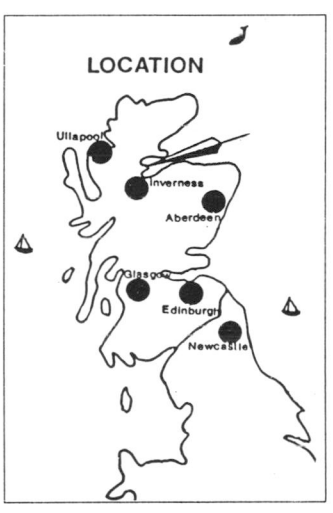

Introduction

Black Isle Forest covers some 5000 hectares (12,350 Acres) of the Black Isle Peninsula. The predominant planting is of scots pine and the whole forest is well into its second rotation. The scots pine is Britain's only native pine tree and it looks mighty impressive, some growing to heights of over 130 feet. The trees can easily be recognised by the characteristic upper bark, which is cracked into small, smooth plates and rusty brown to orange in colour.

Black Isle is not an island and it is not black. It has no particular industry

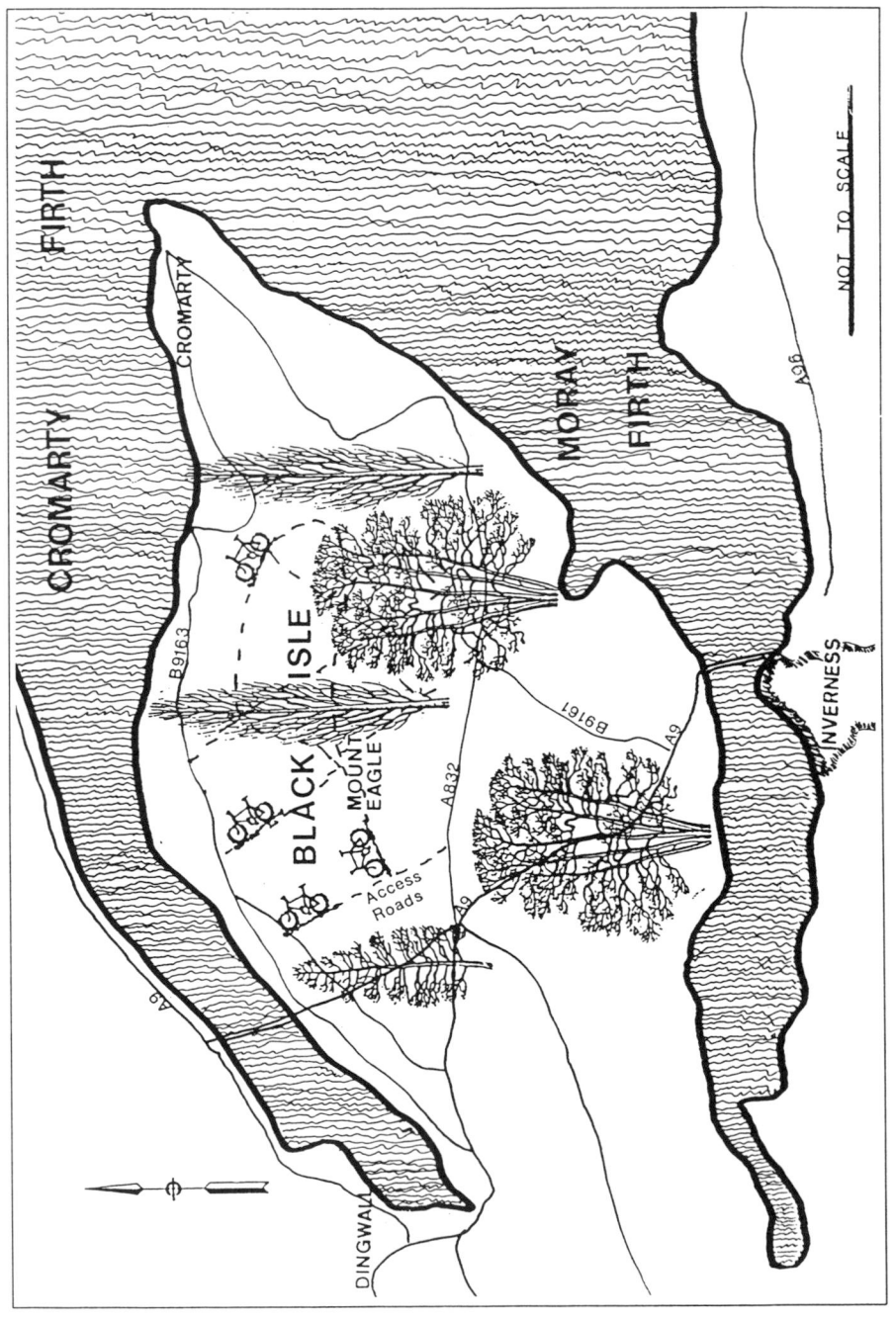

although its name might suggest this if you stem from the English Midlands. It gets its name from the fact that it is rarely white from snow, unlike the higher ground to the west and north. Black Isle is mainly farmland and forestry with just the the occasional boggy oak wood to give some hint of an impression of the ancient woodlands that once dominated the area.

At the eastern tip of Black Isle is the town of Cromarty, guarding the entrance to the vast natural safe harbour of the Cromarty Firth. The British Fleets were entrusted to these waters off and on during both world wars.

Main Access Points

The Military Road is waymarked throughout its route and is crossed by roads in several places. A good place to start is at the south end by Mount Eagle Mast. The mast will be in view for a lot of the route (apart from when trees obscure the view)

Through a clearing

The Route

Start at the south end of the Military Road. Parking is available adjacent to the Mount Eagle Mast, just off the road that runs between Munlochy and Culbokie. The Military Road is waymarked and signed. The main feature is always the forest which has a good range of old and young trees. As an alternative to the Military Road, the few tarmac public roads that criss cross the forest are very quiet and offer some lovely cycling, breaking in and out of the tree line into peaceful grazing meadows and clearings.

Nearby

Clootie Well is a spring whose waters are said to have magic healing properties. Drink from the spring, and afterwards take a piece of cloth, a handkerchief or any other piece of redundant clothing and hang it on the surrounding bushes. This will bring you great fortune. A church stood on the site, until the powerful clergy of the day had it demolished in the 18th Century. This was an attempt to put a stop to the superstitions which abounded around the mysterious magic of the Clootie Well water.

In Cromarty, you will find Hugh Miller's Cottage (circa 1711), which is now entrusted to the National Trust for Scotland. An exhibition and video programme celebrate his life's work as a stonemason, an eminent geologist, an editor and a writer.

Ride 48

Inverlael Forest & Loch Broom, near Ullapool. North Scotland

Inverlael Forest Riverside Ride is a delightfully easy ride, in a magnificent riverside setting with spectacular views down Loch Broom.

Map: Landranger 1:50,000, Sheet number 20.

Distance: Riverside route, 4 miles (6½km); Upper Glen route, 8 miles (13km).

Waymarked: Riverside Route marked PURPLE.

Upper Glen Route marked RED. (Includes road section)

Gradients: The Riverside Route enjoys easy gradients.

Surface: The Riverside Route is entirely on well made up, solid and well-drained forest roads.

Future proposals: N/A

Other cycle routes linking: N/A

Bicycle hire: Inverness.

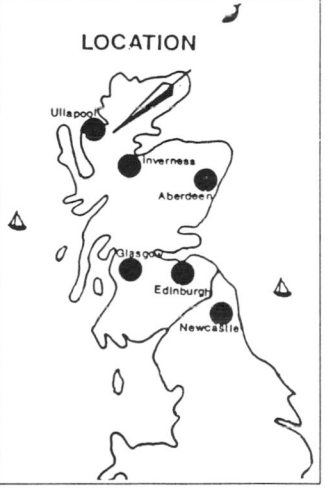

Shops and Refreshments: Take something with you.

Introduction

Inverlael Forest is situated at the oft forgotten end of Loch Broom, where the wild Coigach district spreads out to the east. Here we are on the same line of latitude as Siberia but due to the caress of warm Atlantic currents, sub-tropical plants and gardens thrive in sheltered valleys. There are two Loch Brooms adjacent to each other, the more westerly one being known as Little Loch Broom.

The ride in Inverlael Forest is the Purple Riverside Route, following the fast rushing River Lael as it tumbles down its last few miles to pay its dues to Loch Broom. This beautiful route boasts a fantastic variety of colourful trees

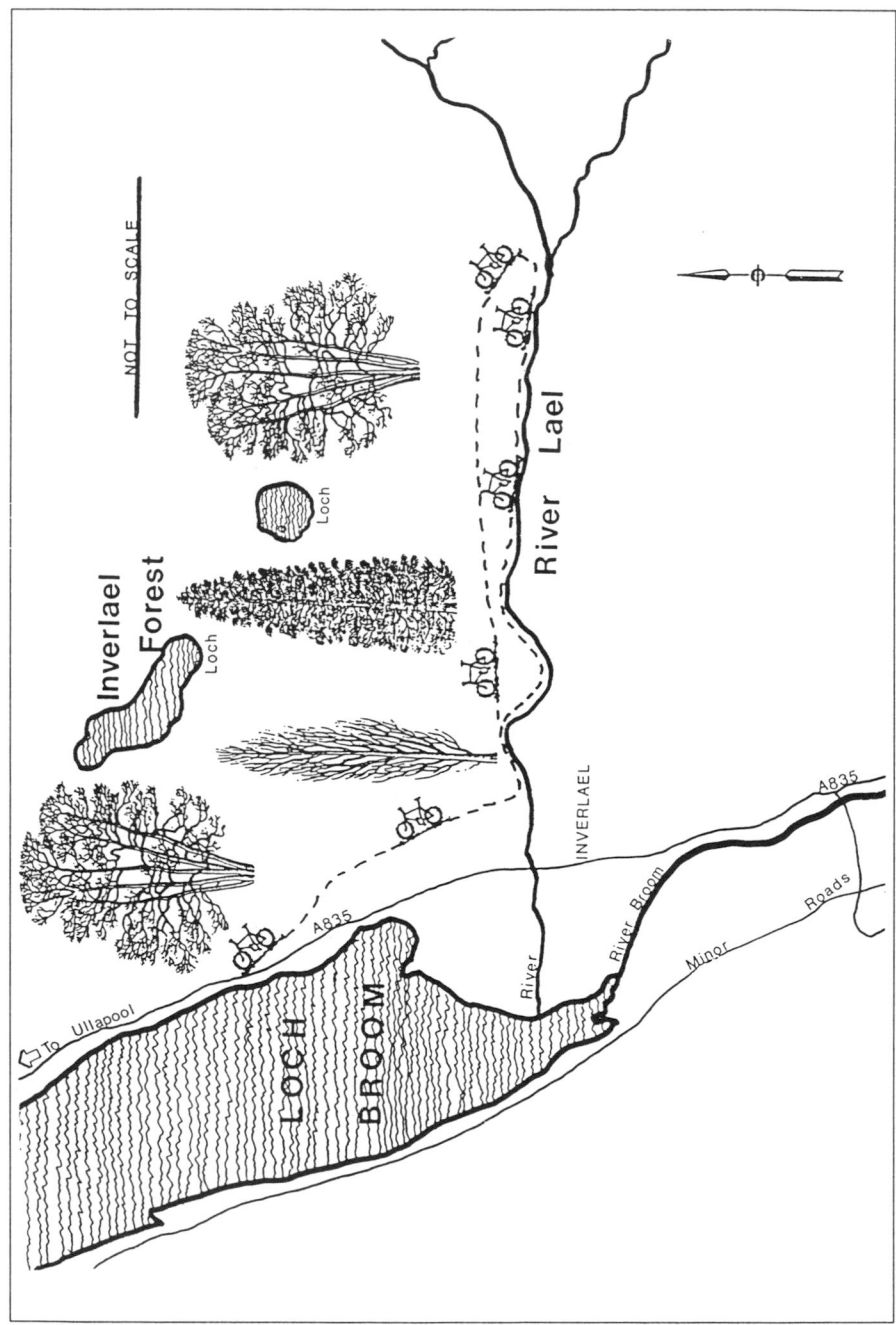

and plants in all shapes and sizes. When the sun is setting in the western sky, some of the light and shadowing effects are quite dramatic and sometimes complimented by mini-rainbows playing in the spray of the numerous waterfalls.

The going is easy and there are numerous secret spots simply to sit and breathe. On a warm summer day, this is a very special place indeed and although it is not a long ride it certainly earns its right to inclusion in this guide based on quality not quantity. Perhaps Paradise only comes in small helpings. The surface is on well-maintained forest roads and the gradients are slight.

Main Access Points

The Inverlael Forest Enterprise Car Park just north of Inverlael hamlet off the A835.

The Route

The Riverside Ride is waymarked from the Northern Inverlael Car Park, just off the A835, north of the hamlet of Inverlael. The route is off to the east and is clearly waymarked with purple markers. Another ride, waymarked red, starts at the car park but this is quite demanding and also includes a section on the main A835.

Inverlael Forest is well into its second forestry rotation so there are a wide variety of species and states of maturity. There are also some colourful heathers and mosses on the river banks which are well worth your closer inspection. On a clear day you will be able to see the Summer Isles at the outlet of Loch Broom.

Nearby

If you do not know the town, Ullapool will very quickly charm its way into your mental list of favourite places. In 1788 Ullapool was a new town, in much the same sense of our modern new towns, set up by the British Fisheries Society to capitalise on the great shoals of herring that were available in the unusual Atlantic conditions.

The herring are now long gone, but the tourists are not. Ullapool has the makings of a truly cosmopolitan resort, almost in the same sense as Monte Carlo or Stratford-upon-Avon. The harbour front walk in the summer is a genuinely international experience.

A couple of interesting and slightly diverse exhibits in the small museum in

Ullapool are Lord Nelson's razor and a scented pastille reputed to have come from Charles I's pocket after his execution.

Corrieshalloch Gorge is situated near Braemore Junction (the A835 and the A832). Corrieshalloch Gorge is an extraordinary box gorge, 200 feet (61 metres) deep and one mile (1½km) long. It boasts the 150 foot (46 metre) Falls at Measach where the River plunges into the Gorge. The site is in the ownership of the National Trust for Scotland and is well worth a visit.

Waterfall, Inverlael Forest

Ride 49
The Isle of Arran

A ride around the magnificent coast of the Isle of Arran.

Map: Landranger 1:50,000, Sheet number 69.

Distance: 67 miles (108km) around the coast.

Waymarked: Follow the A841.

Gradients: The coast road is undulating but quite manageable for family cyclists or beginners. The forests and inland roads are fairly hard going. Generally, the south of the island is flatter, softer and easier for cyclists than the north.

Surface: The coast road is tarmac.

Future proposals: N/A.

Other cycle routes linking: Take a diversion into the forests of the south. Here, there are plenty of rides, easy or challenging.

Bicycle hire: Enquire locally.

Shops and Refreshments: Plenty of opportunities in the towns and villages. It is always advisable, however, to carry some food and drink along with you.

Introduction

Arran is situated between the Kintyre peninsula and the Mainland in the Firth of Clyde. It is a big island, some 20 miles long from north to south and eight to ten miles from east to west. The access to the mainland is via ferries, sailing from Androssan or from the Kintyre peninsula, and taking roughly an hour or half an hour respectively. To simplify Arran would be to describe it as Scotland in microcosm. Wild high mountains in the north and soft fertile plains and forests to the south.

Although this is suggested as a coastal trip around the island, anyone preferring a really very easy and pleasant day trip should stay in the south of the Island, perhaps venturing into the forest as a diversion from the main road. Whatever you decide, the main road is quiet, the views are superb, both inland and out over the water, the hospitality is exceptional and the pace of life is far removed from that of the mainland.

If Arran had a capital, it would be Brodick, a jewel of beauty even amongst the exceptional attractiveness of Arran's coast. It has the imposing bulk of the 2,866 foot Goat Fell at its back, and overlooks the lovely sheltered sandy bay, the old harbour and the pier which somehow conjure up images of Neil Munro's "Para Handy" tales with the occasional old Puffer steaming in and out to serve the isolated highlands and islands in the area. The ferry from Androssan arrives at Brodick and it is from here that the coastal ride starts.

Main Access Points

Daily ferries sail to Arran all year round, taking just under an hour from Ardrossan, landing at Brodick on the eastern side of the island. During summer months, a ferry sails the half hour trip from Claonaig on the Kintyre peninsula to Lochranza, in the north of the island.

Views over the Clyde estuary

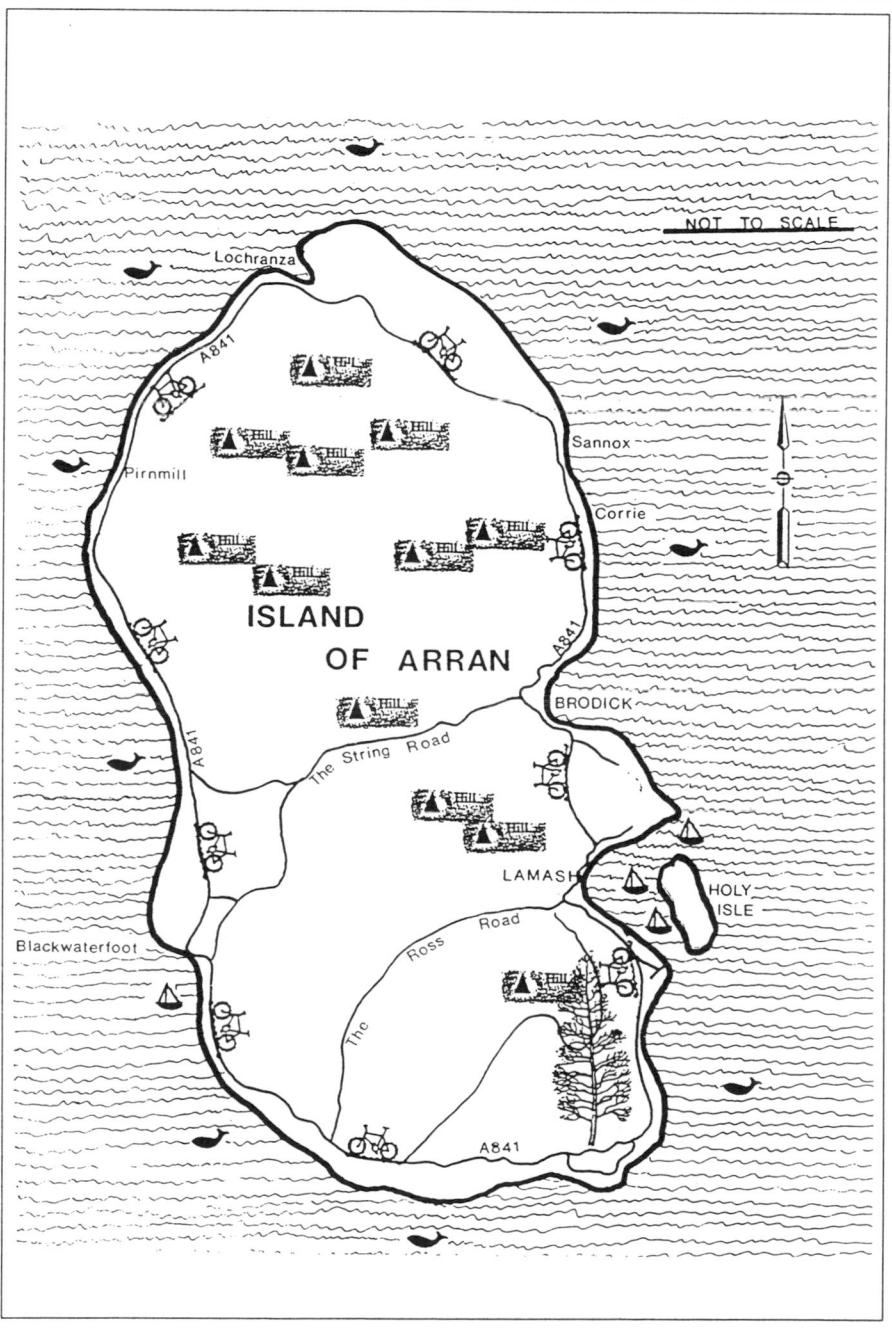

NOT TO SCALE

Lochranza

A841

Sannox

Pirnmill

Corrie

ISLAND

OF ARRAN

A841

BRODICK

The String Road

LAMASH

HOLY
ISLE

Blackwaterfoot

The Ross Road

The

A841

The Route

This requires little explanation. Turn left out of Brodick towards the more gentle south of the island with its forests and green fields. Turn right out of Brodick for the north of the island with its more rugged mountainous scenery. The road goes around the whole island with the sea always close at hand. If you venture inland, be prepared for a steep climb, especially in the north.

The main centres of population outside Brodick are Lamash, Blackwatersfoot and Lochranza. Lamash, just to south of Brodick, overlooks the massive rocky sentinel of Holy Island which rises 1000 feet out of the sea. It has a delightful sheltered bay and is a water sports centre. Blackwatersfoot is situated in the south-west of the island and Lochranza is in the north. Both have lovely scattered cottages and gems of history dating back beyond the time of the earliest Christian settlers, to ancient Bronze Age remains.

Nearby

A couple of particular points of interest on Arran are the Bronze Age Monument which is situated at Auchagallon some five miles north of Blackwatersfoot, on the west coast. In Brodick, pay a visit to the Rosaburn Heritage Museum which describes, in a most interesting way, the modern and ancient heritage of Arran.

Ride 50

North Uist, South Uist and Benbecula, Western Isles (Outer Hebrides)

An unusually beautiful ride around the Western Isles

Maps: Landranger 1:50,000, Sheet numbers 18, 22 and 31.

Distance: 80 miles (130km).

Waymarked: A865 and A867. (Not as busy as mainland "A" Roads.)

Gradients: Nothing to worry about as long as you keep to the road. These relatively flat roads make for easy cycling.

Surface: Tarmac.

Future proposals: N/A.

Other cycle routes linking: Visit Barra, the small island to the south.

Bicycle hire: Mainland.

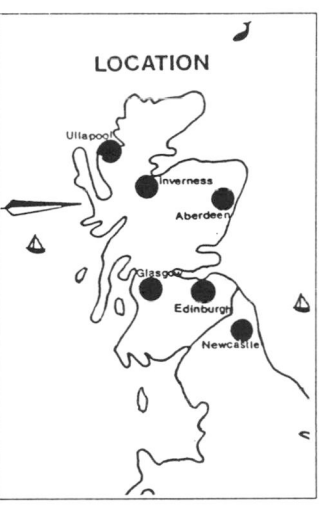

Shops and Refreshments: Plenty of facilities throughout the towns and villages.

Winds: Try to plan your trip when forecast winds are light. The route is very exposed to the full force of the Atlantic's best gales.

Introduction

While this guide does not emphasise on-road cycling, since most of the routes are over 90% traffic-free an exception must be made for the sheer beauty of the Isles of South and North Uist and Benbecula. The narrow roads pass through some of the most dramatic scenery in the western world while enjoying remarkably low traffic density. Assuming that you are a visitor to the Islands, this is a bicycle ride that you will remember and cherish for years to come. Take a camera for the memories; it is more than just a bicycle ride, it is a trip into another world, a toe in the water of life in the Islands, sometimes almost literally.

All along the Atlantic Coast, the powerful waves constantly try to pound the staunch shorelines into submission with a relentless attack of spectacular waves. There are many points of interest apart from the dramatic scenery. These include a veritable feast of prehistoric standing stones, chambered cairns and brochs (cylindrical dry stone defensive towers dating back to Iron Age). At Milton is the birthplace of Flora MacDonald, the gentlewoman famed for smuggling the "Young Pretender" to Skye in 1746, disguised as her maid.

In all, the ride is a little over 80 miles, and to enjoy the route without too much exertion, plan for eight to ten hours solid cycling. Spread it over a couple of days or more. There is so much that can be enjoyed do not rush it too much. A great deal can be appreciated by just stopping and looking and listening. I wonder if you will make these observations. "Where are all the trees?" ... "Is that what Gaelic sounds like spoken as a first language?" ... "These people are so friendly!" ... "The sea is so clear, I can see the bottom at a depth of thirty or forty feet!"...

Main Access Points
Base yourself in Lochboisdale or Milton. Everywhere is a beauty spot.

The Route
From the mainland take the ferry from Oban to Lochboisdale in South Uist. From here, take the road across to Daliburgh and turn right towards the north. The road runs down the spine of the island, occasional side roads leading down to the coast as it runs north. The Atlantic is always on your left, in the west, pounding the shores in a never ending battle of nature. To your right, in the east, are the towering dark hills rising to nearly 2000 feet on the peaks of Beinn Mhor and Hecla. Just keep to the road and the riding is relatively flat and easy. Do not miss the 30 foot high, "Our Lady of The Isles", a Madonna and Child statue looking ominously down over the Rocket Ranges that point out over the Atlantic Ocean.

The road will take you over Loch Bee, onto the wild straits of Bagh nam Faoilean and thence to Benbecula. Keep left to the Atlantic coast and the road will lead over the sound via Grimsby to North Uist. Here, go east or west, as you please, it makes no difference. The road circles the Island, crossing or passing more water than dry land before bringing you back to retrace your route south and back to your starting place.

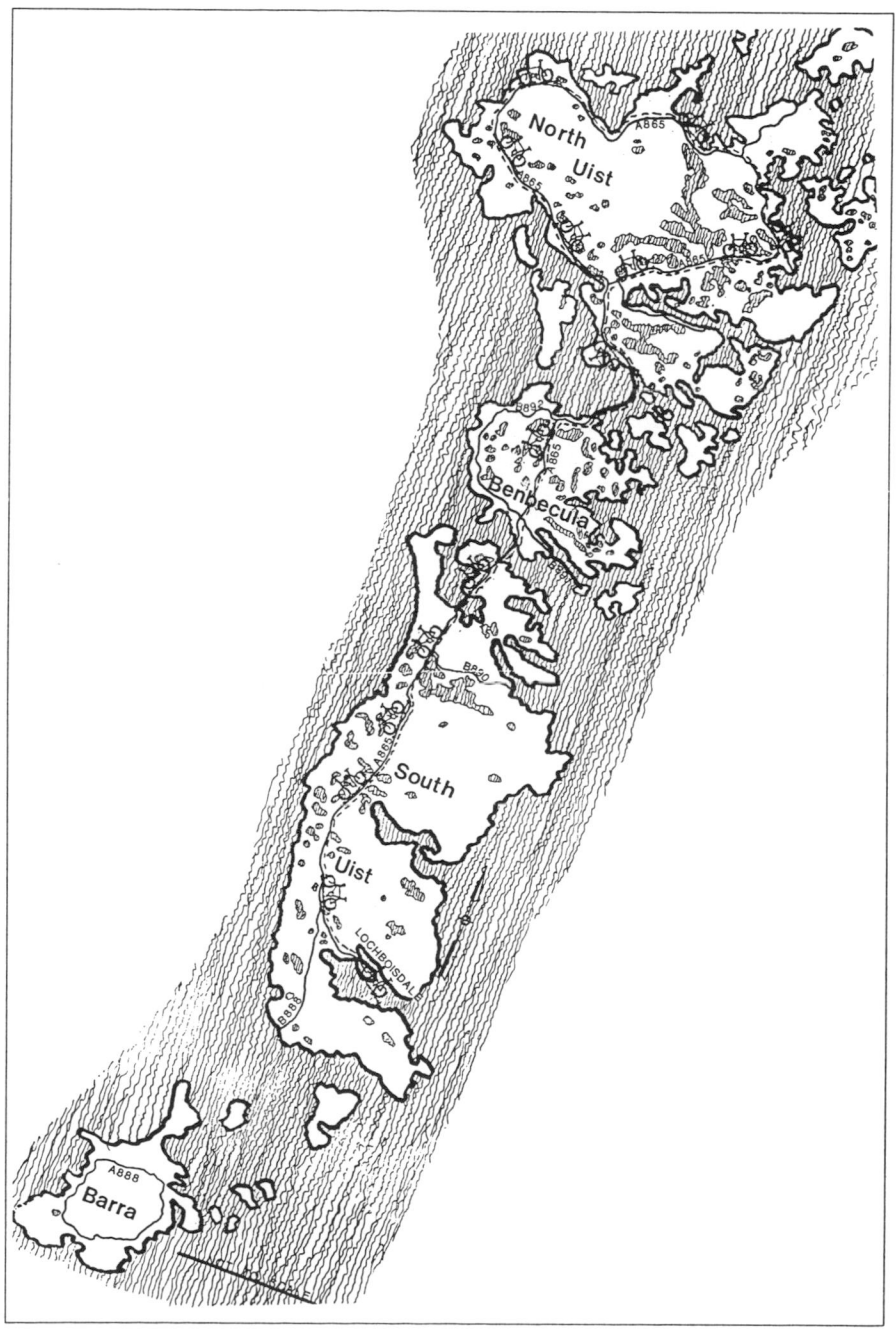

Nearby

The ferry trip from Oban is an experience in itself. The boat steams a north-westerly course out of Oban Bay and after crossing the Firth of Lorn continues up the Sound of Mull, never far from land on either beam. Eventually it breaks out into open sea with almost half the journey completed. If your schedule allows, drop off at Barra, to the south of South Uist. Here you will land at Castlebay, a lovely little community. From here, visit Kiessimul Castle; the views are stunning and the water is clear and clean. If by any chance you decide to visit Barra by air, make sure that the aircraft's captain has his tide tables handy because the airstrip is covered by the tide twice each day.

Beach airfield at Barra (photo courtesy of Western Isles Tourist Board)

APPENDICES

The Cyclist's Touring Club
Cotterell House
69 Meadrow
Godalming
Surrey GU7 3HS
Tel: 01483 417217

Forestry Enterprise
Forestry Commission
231 Corstorphine Road
Edinburgh
Tel: 0131 334 0303

The Scottish Cycling Council
Monksmill
Castle Douglas
Kirkcudbrightshire
DG7 2NY
Tel: 01556 67395

The British Medical Association.
BMA House
Tavistock Square
London
WC1H 9JP
Tel: 0171 387 4499

The Scottish Tourist Board
23 Ravelston Terrace
Edinburgh
EH4 3EU
Tel: 0131 332 2433

The Northumbria Tourist Board
Aykley Heads
Durham
DH1 5UX
Tel: 0191 384 6905

Sustrans Ltd
53 Cochrane Street
Glasgow
G1 1HL
Tel: 0141 552 8241

Friends of The Earth
26-28 Underwood Street
London
N1 7JQ
Tel: 0171 490 1555

British Waterways Board
Countryside Ranger
Union Canal
Canal House
Applecross Street
Glasgow G4 9SP
Tel: 0141 332 6936

British Waterways Board
Pier Square
Ardrishaig
Lochgilphead
Argyll   PA30 8DZ
Tel: 011546 603210

The Post Bus (Remote Areas Service)
Royal Mail PR Unit
West Port House
102 West Port
Edinburgh EH3 9HS
Tel: 0131 228 2281

Scotrail Network
Edinburgh: Tel. 0131 556 2451
Glasgow: Tel. 0141 204 2844
Aberdeen: Tel. 01224 594222
Inverness: Tel. 01463 238924

Caledonian MacBrayne Ferries
The Ferry Terminal
Gourock
Renfrewshire
PA19 1QP
Tel: 01475 650100

Orkney Islands Shipping Co
Head Office
4 Ayre Road
Kirkwall
KW15 1QX
Tel: 01856 872044

P & O Scottish Ferries
PO Box 5
Jamieson's Quay
Aberdeen
AB9 8DL
Tel: 01224 572615

Western Ferries (Clyde) Ltd
16 Woodside Cresent
Glasgow
G3 7UT
Tel: 0141 332 9766

Avis Car Rental
100 Dairy Road
Edinburgh
EH11 2DW
Tel: 0131 337 6363

Hertz Car Rental
10 Picardy Place
Edinburgh
EH1 3JT
Tel: 0131 556 8311

Glasgow Airport
Tel: 0141 887 1111
Edinburgh Airport;
Tel: 0131 333 1000
Inverness Airport
Tel: 01463 232471
Aberdeen Airport
Tel: 01224 722331

Scottish Youth Hostel Association
161 Warrender Park Road
Edinburgh
EH9 1EQ
Tel: 0131 229 8660

Scottish City Link Coaches
St Andrews Square Bus Station
Edinburgh
Tel: 0131 557 5717

Caledonian Express Coaches
Buchanan Bus Station
Glasgow
Tel: 0141 332 9191

A Selection of Bicycle Hire Centres

(This is not meant to be a full list.)

DURHAM AND SUNDERLAND AREA

Derwent Valley Bikes
38 Front Street
Whickham
Tel: 0191 496 0266

Darke Cycles
3 St Thomas Street
Sunderland
Tel: 0191 510 8155

Derwent Valley Bikes
Station Road
Rowlands Gill
Tel: 01207 545005

NEWCASTLE UPON TYNE AND NORTHUMBERLAND

Weardale Mountain Bikes
39 Front Street
Frosterley
Weardale (Off A689 near Stanhope)
Tel: 01388 528129

Tyne Valley Cycles
1 Tyne View Road
Haltwhistle
Northumberland
Tel: 01434 322793

Newcastle Cycle Centre
165 Westgate Road
Newcastle upon Tyne
Tel: 0191 222 1695

Kielder Bikes
Hawkhope Car Park
Kielder Water
Tel: 01434 220392

SOUTH WEST SCOTLAND

K L R Cycles
17 Catherine Street
Gatehouse of Fleet
Dumfries and Galloway
Tel: 01556 504542

Ace Cycles
11 Church Street
Castle Douglas
Dumfries and Galloway
Tel: 01557 814392

Belgrano
81 Main Street
Glenluce, Dumfries and Galloway
Tel:0581 3554

Woodlea Hotel
Moniaive
Dumfries and Galloway
Tel: 0184 82209

McWilliam Garage
New Galloway
Dumfries and Galloway
Tel:0581 06442 233

Creebridge Caravan Park
Minnigaff, Newton Stewart
Dumfries and Galloway
Tel:0671 2324

K Gunn
Loncastle School House
Whauphill
Newton Stewart
Dumfries and Galloway
Tel: 0198 884 276

Drumlanrig Castle
Thornhill
Dumfries
Dumfries and Galloway
Tel: 01848 31555

Loch Ken Holiday Centre
Parton
Castle Douglas
Dumfries and Galloway

Tel: 016447 282

Grierson and Graham Ltd
10 Academy Street
Dumfries
Dumfries and Galloway
Tel: 01387 59483

HIGHLANDS
Alex Dan Cycle Centre
67 Kenneth Street
Stornaway
Tel: 01851 704025

Aviemore Mountain Bikes
The Mountain Bike Centre
Aviemore Mountain Resort

Tel: Aviemore 811007

Bicycle Bothy
Ar-Dachaidh
Badnellan
Brora
Tel: 01408 621658

Oban Cycles
9 Craigard Road
Oban. Tel: 01631 66996

Kyle Cycles
Old Plock Road
Kyle of Lochalsh
Tel: Kyle 4842

Crinan Cycles
The Pier Workshop
Unit 6, Pier Square
Ardrishaig
Tel: 01506 632727

Gunn Bike Shed
Forestry Buildings
Glen Nevis
Fort William
Tel: Fort William 703601

EDINBURGH
Corstorphine Cycles
9 Featherhall Avenue
Edinburgh
Tel 031 334 2748

Dalkeith Bike Shop
68 Chambers Street
Dunfermline
Tel: 01383 620708

Dalkeith Bike Shed
1d Talt Street
Dalkeith
Tel 0131 654 1170

New Heights
134 Lothian Road
Edinburgh
Tel: 0131 229 2233

The New Bike Shop
14 Lochrin Place
Edinburgh
Tel: 0131 228 6363

Sandy Gilchrist Cycles
1 Cadzow Place
Abbeyhill, Edinburgh
Tel: 0131 652 1760

Roving Cyclepaths
13 Greendykes Road
Broxburn
Tel: 01506 852 330

GLASGOW NORTH

Discount Bike Hire
5/11 Auchinairn Road
Bishopbriggs
Tel: 0141 762 1616

On Track Bikes
The Visitor Centre
Queen Elizabeth II Forest Park
Aberfoyle
Tel: 01877 382858

New Heights
26 Barnton Street
Stirling
Tel: 01786 450809

Forest Cycle Centre
Main Street
Aberfoyle
Tel: 01877 382802

Trossach Cycles
Trossachs Holiday Park
Aberfoyle

Tel: 01877 382614

West End Cycles
16/18 Chancellor Street
Partick
Tel: 0141 357 1344

GLASGOW SOUTH

Discount Bike Hire
Unit 16, Phoenix Retail Park
Linwood
Tel: 0141 889 9111

MGB Ralton Cycles
6 Avon Street
Hamilton
Tel Hamilton 284926

AMG Cycles
55 Dalblair Road
Ayr
Tel: Ayr 287580

Mapes
4 Guilford Street
Millport, Cumbrae
Tel: Millport 530444

Bike Box
5 The Cross
Prestwick
Tel: 01292 77360

Kilmarnock Cycle Centre
33 High Glencairn Street
Kilmarnock
Tel: 01563 38938

Irvine Cycles
23 Eglington Street
Irvine
Tel: 01294 272712

ABERDEEN
Reid's Cycles
44 Broom Hill Road
Aberdeen
Tel: 01224 586974

BG Cycles
The Barn
Aboyne Mart, Aboyne
Tel: 013398 85355

Aberdeen Cycle Centre
188 King Street
Aberdeen
Tel: 01224 644542

Cycling World
45/47 Cross Street
Fraserburgh
Tel: 01346 513355

DUNDEE
Dunkeld Mountain Bikes
The Chalet
Tay Terrace
Dunkeld
Tel: Dunkeld 728744

Clan Green Ltd
33 Ferry Street
Montrose

Tel: 01674 77199

Crieff Cycle Centre
Leadenflower Road
Crieff
Tel: 01764 652599

All Areas

Some Forest Enterprise Centres, Sustran's Centres and Groundwork Enterprise Trust Centres, offer bicycle hire. Check with local offices and if all else fails, try the yellow pages telephone directory.

This list of hirers is included as a supplement and not as recommendation. I do not know anything about most of these hirers, except these addresses and phone numbers, which are subject to constant change.

We publish guides to individual towns, plus books on walking and cycling in the great outdoors throughout England and Wales. This is a recent selection:

Cycling . . .

CYCLE UK! The essential guide to leisure cycling – Les Lumsdon *(£9.95)*

OFF-BEAT CYCLING IN THE PEAK DISTRICT – Clive Smith *(£6.95)*

MORE OFF-BEAT CYCLING IN THE PEAK DISTRICT – Clive Smith *(£6.95)*

50 BEST CYCLE RIDES IN CHESHIRE – edited by Graham Beech *(£7.95)*

CYCLING IN THE COTSWOLDS – Stephen Hill *(£6.95)*

CYCLING IN THE CHILTERNS – Henry Tindell *(£7.95)*

CYCLING IN THE LAKE DISTRICT – John Wood *(£7.95)*

CYCLING IN LINCOLNSHIRE – Penny & Bill Howe *(£7.95)*

CYCLING IN NOTTINGHAMSHIRE – Penny & Bill Howe *(£7.95)*

CYCLING IN STAFFORDSHIRE – Linda Wain *(£7.95)*

CYCLING IN THE WEST COUNTRY – Helen Stephenson *(£7.95)*

CYCLING IN SOUTH WALES – Rosemary Evans *(£7.95)*

CYCLING IN NORTH WALES – Philip Routledge *(£7.95) ... available 1996*

Country Walking

FIFTY CLASSIC WALKS IN THE PENNINES – Terry Marsh *(£8.95)*

HILL WALKS IN MID WALES – Dave Ing *(£8.95)*

WEST PENNINE WALKS – Mike Cresswell *(£5.95)*

YORKSHIRE DALES WALKING: On The Level – Norman Buckley *(£6.95)*

WELSH WALKS: Dolgellau /Cambrian Coast – L. Main & M. Perrott *(£5.95)*

WELSH WALKS: Aberystwyth & District – L. Main & M. Perrott *(£5.95)*

WALKS IN MYSTERIOUS WALES – Laurence Main *(£7.95)*

RAMBLES IN NORTH WALES – Roger Redfern *(£6.95)*

RAMBLES AROUND MANCHESTER – Mike Cresswell *(£5.95)*

EAST CHESHIRE WALKS – Graham Beech *(£5.95)*

CHALLENGING WALKS: NW England & N Wales – Ron Astley *(£7.95)*

LONDON BUS-TOP TOURIST – John Wittich*(£6.95)*

TEA SHOP WALKS IN THE CHILTERNS – Jean Patefield *(£6.95)*
BY-WAY TRAVELS SOUTH OF LONDON – Geoff Marshall *(£6.95)*
BY-WAY BIKING IN THE CHILTERNS – Henry Tindell*(£7.95)*
PUB WALKS IN SNOWDONIA – Laurence Main *(£6.95)*
BEST PUB WALKS AROUND CHESTER & THE DEE VALLEY – John Haywood *(£6.95)*
BEST PUB WALKS IN GWENT – Les Lumsdon *(£6.95)*
PUB WALKS IN POWYS – Les Lumsdon & Chris Rushton *(£6.95)*
BEST PUB WALKS IN PEMBROKESHIRE – Laurence Main *(£6.95)*
BEST PUB WALKS AROUND CENTRAL LONDON – Ruth Herman *(£6.95)*
BEST PUB WALKS IN ESSEX – Derek Keeble *(£6.95)*

More Pub Walks . . .

There are many more titles in our fabulous series of 'Pub Walks' books for just about every popular walking area in the UK, all featuring access by public transport. We label our more recent ones as 'best' to differentiate them from inferior competitors!

Explore the Lake District:

THE LAKELAND SUMMITS – Tim Synge *(£7.95)*
100 LAKE DISTRICT HILL WALKS – Gordon Brown *(£7.95)*
LAKELAND ROCKY RAMBLES: Geology beneath your feet – Brian Lynas *(£7.95)*
FULL DAYS ON THE FELLS: Challenging Walks – Adrian Dixon *(£7.95)*
PUB WALKS IN THE LAKE DISTRICT – Neil Coates *(£6.95)*
LAKELAND WALKING, ON THE LEVEL – Norman Buckley *(£6.95)*
MOSTLY DOWNHILL: LEISURELY WALKS, LAKE DISTRICT – Alan Pears *(£6.95)*

Sport . . .

RED FEVER: from Rochdale to Rio as 'United' supporters – Steve Donoghue *(£7.95)*
UNITED WE STOOD: unofficial history of the Ferguson years – Richard Kurt *(£6.95)*
MANCHESTER CITY: Moments to Remember – John Creighton *(£9.95)*

- plus many more entertaining and educational books being regularly added to our list. All of our books are available from your local bookshop. In case of difficulty, or to obtain our complete catalogue, please contact:

**Sigma Leisure, 1 South Oak Lane, Wilmslow, Cheshire SK9 6AR
Phone: 01625 – 531035   Fax: 01625 – 536800**

ACCESS and VISA orders welcome – call our friendly sales staff or use our 24 hour Answer-phone service! Most orders are despatched on the day we receive your order – you could be enjoying our books in just a couple of days. Please add £2 p&p to all orders.